SHE]

An Appalachian Trail Story

EMILY HARPER

CONTENTS

ONE

Test Run • 7

TWO

Georgia • 13

THREE

North Carolina • 26

FOUR

Great Smoky Mountains • 39

FIVE

The Last Straw • 52

SIX

Solo Female Hiker • 63

SEVEN

Count and Smurf • 79

EIGHT

Humored • 100

NINE

Rain Fly • 112

TEN

Scavenger • 121

ELEVEN

The Other Germans • 135

TWELVE

A Bit of Home • 146

THIRTEEN

Many Visits • 157

FOURTEEN

Playing Catch-up •165

FIFTEEN

Familiarity Breeds Contempt • 178

SIXTEEN

Back with the Crew • 191

SEVENTEEN

Keeping It Pure • 204

EIGHTEEN

Sticking to the Schedule • 215

NINETEEN

The Whites • 234

TWENTY

Bears and Swamp Donkeys ▪252

TWENTY-ONE

Pickles, Crumbs, and Florida Girls ▪262

TWENTY-TWO

Katahdin ▪ 271

HIKER GLOSSERY

DEDICATED

TO MY CONCERNED MOTHER

TO MY LIGHTHEARTED JESSICA

TO MY HELPFUL AMY BABY

AND

TO MY FELLOW HIKERS

ONE

Test Run

My father clapped the Bible shut. "Anyone have a prayer request?"

"I have a prayer request," I said. "Pray that I have a safe hike on the Appalachian Trail next year."

My mother and father exchanged looks. This wasn't new. My mother and I had been arguing over my plans to hike the Appalachian Trail.

"We don't have faith for that right now," my mother said.

"Then pray that you will have faith."

After we all took turns praying, I sat on the floor near my mother.

"Emily," she paused. I knew it was coming. "I don't think you are ready to hike."

"Mom, I'm eighteen. You don't need to allow me to go. I can go if you want me to or not."

"I don't want you to go until you are more experienced."

"You want me to be experienced? Great, I'll get experienced as I go."

"I'm not much of a hiker, but I don't approve your choice in gear. And you need a hiking partner."

I rolled my eyes and sighed at the same time. "Mom, I'll find a hiking partner on the trail. Many people will be going the same time as me, and I'll have my pickings from there."

"Who will look after you if you don't have a hiking partner?"

"I'll be one of two thousand others starting out. It's not like I'll be alone."

"But, they won't be responsible for you."

"I don't want anyone responsible for me. I can take care of myself."

"That's just the attitude I fear. What if you're alone and you get hypothermia, like the guy who was found with all his clothes off outside his sleeping bag?"

"Come on. Is that what has you worried? That book I got you was to help you be on my side."

I was so frustrated. I didn't want to be rebellious, and I knew hiking on the trail without my parents consent, wouldn't be worth it. This wasn't some walk in the park. I wanted to thru-hike the two thousand miles of the Appalachian Mountains, which takes six months to complete. I needed support for such a big undertaking. *Don't they know how hard it's going to be when I'm actually on the trail? Aren't parents supposed to help their children?*

"Mom, it's not like I'm asking for money. Any other kid on the trail has their parent's paying for their trip and they're probably proud of their children. I'm working my butt off. Why can't you just be happy for me? It's not like it's my first time away from home. Remember, I lived in Denmark for a year. And remember you acted the same way when I first mentioned being an exchange student, but everything was okay."

She started ranting about the problems I did have, as if to validate her previous concern. I couldn't take it anymore, and bid her a good night.

I waited for a rainy day to show I could last in any kind of weather. One afternoon I heard the rumbling of thunder and knew it was time to test my gear in my backyard. *Living on the Appalachian Trail can't be that hard.*

The less weight a hiker has to carry, the better. Tarps are the lightest shelter. I had never set up a tarp before, but the cold rain had me setting up fast. I followed some directions by, finding a tree and licking a finger to pinpoint the wind. The direction I chose was sloping downhill.

After dark, I went out with my arms full of sleeping gear to settle in. I was too excited to sleep, but forced my brain into submission.

I woke up with the bottom of my sleeping bag hanging out in the rain. I had to army crawl back up the slippery slope, but kept inching down.

My head was filled with thoughts as I tried to sleep. *This is stupid. I can't sleep on this sliding board. Can't I just go to bed? No you don't. You heard your mother, you need experience. This is how you get experience, even if you stay up all night. You don't want to hear what your family has to say. But, I have work. I need sleep. What's more important work, or hiking? Hiking, but this is suffering.*

When the pegs failed and the tarp started to flap in the wind, I was exposed to the cold, rainy wind. The stakes were lost in the soft dirt, so I resorted to breaking off branches from the dogwood to use as stakes.

With the continual inching of my sleeping bag and the finicky stakes, I was fed up by eleven o'clock. I grabbed everything and ran to the porch. I struggled with the locked door. Inside, I saw Serena on the phone with her boyfriend. She came to the door and said, "What are you doing outside?"

I told her the story, but she was listening to her phone. And she scoffed, "Yeah. My sister got wet in the rain."

The next morning, my mom asked if I heard the thunderstorm. I gave out a feeble "no" as I ran upstairs.

At the top, my dad teased me, "So when you're on the trail and get wet, are you going to run to your bed?"

I headed to my room and shut the door without a word. *Why did this have to be so difficult? Hiking the trail is the perfect opportunity to get in shape and lose weight. Though, I can't tell them that, they'll think I'm insecure with myself. And why do I have to prove my capability? I'm eighteen. I can do what I want.*

Failing to make it through the night was a hard blow. And my success rate on following test runs were making me look bad. My mother made it clear I wouldn't be going without a hiking partner. It wasn't like I hadn't looked for a hiking partner. Several people showed an interest, but they fell through.

I thought by my nineteenth birthday my mother would accept that I was old enough. I addressed the situation while she was blow drying her hair.

"You need a hiking partner," she said for the millionth time.

I had an online journal of my progression. I wrote, "I'm not allowed to hike, because I don't have a hiking partner. My mom thinks I'll die from hypothermia."

The next day I had pages of responses. People reassured me about the safety of the trail and others offered to hike with me. I printed out the pages and shoved them under my mother's nose.

"Mom, look all these people think hiking the trail is safe. This lady says the trail is safer than a mall parking lot."

"I need my reading glasses."

"Mom, just listen," I said and began to read the entries to her. My mother narrowed down the list of volunteer hiking partners, until she only had two women. "I think you should go with Katherine. She just graduated high school."

"When is her departure date?"

"March fifth."

My departure date, or the date I had chosen to leave was March twelfth. That date had been seared in my mind. I had told my friends and family I was leaving then. How could I just give it up? But what was the point of having a departure date, and not being allowed to depart?

"So I can go with her?" I asked warily.

"Emily, you can't ask me anything about your hike for the next twenty four hours."

I wanted to complain, but that would jeopardize my hike. I was officially on the chopping block, and all I could do was lie still.

All of a sudden, I was concerned. What if they said no? Would I run away and hike anyway? I wondered if all the research, all the packing, and all the dreaming were to be wasted. I didn't like that the decision was out of my control, but it seemed to be my best strategy. I waited silently, slipping depressed sighs wherever I went. If I made it to the trail; the hardest part of my hike would be over.

My mind was full of thoughts. *My mother is ridiculous. My parents don't care if they leave me hanging like this. They don't love me. What's the point of even hiking? If I killed myself, I bet they'd feel guilty.* I snapped out of my misery. Wait just a minute. Little devil man was sitting on my shoulder whispering disparaging thoughts. This wasn't the end, *who knows maybe it will all work out.*

I couldn't wait for the twenty-four hour period to be over. I didn't want to ruin my chances by asking too early, so I waited past the twenty-four hour mark to ask, "So Mom, is it okay if I hike with Katherine?"

"Well, we figure she'll keep you safe."

"So I can?"

"Since, we are leaving to go on vacation to Florida the second of March; we've been looking at maps to figure out the best way to drop you off."

"So you'll take me?"

"You'll have to pay," my father poked in.

"What? You're going down that way anyway."

"No, were going to Florida, not Georgia. It'll take longer, and use more gas. Do you want us to take you or not?" he continued.

I scowled. "I want you to take me."

"You'll need a place to stay. Maybe your cousin Rodney can take you in if Katherine doesn't," said my mother.

Suddenly, I was going, and only in a couple weeks. I was frantic getting everything together. After a couple new test runs I realized I needed to order a new sleeping bag, a Z-rest, and a liner. The backpack I bought was small. The idea was, the smaller the backpack the less I could bring. I purchased a bivy, which is similar to a tent. And I didn't get a stove.

The day before I left, I had my friend cut my hair; I wanted it to be manageable. It got cut so short, I only had a couple inches left.

All I could do was smile as we drove to Georgia. Before I knew it, I was in sunny Atlanta with a day-pack weighing thirty pounds.

We drove to Chick-fill-a to meet Katherine and her parents. I was jittery with nerves as I walked in. There she was a tall blond. Katherine invited me and my parents over to the table to shake hands with her parents. I sat at the table, nibbling my sandwich, and listening to the parents talk. It felt to me like an arranged marriage.

Katherine had a schedule she wrote for herself, since she needed to finish her hike before collage. I flipped through the pages and saw one of the zero days, "What if I don't want to take off then?"

"Then don't," she said, annoyed.

I was happy when it was over, because I felt inexperienced near Katherine. And I panicked every time they stopped to ask me a question.

My mother made me promise to stay with Katherine until I got past the Smoky Mountains. "The weather can be really bad. Sometimes it snows. I just want you to be with her, in case anything goes wrong."

At my cousin's house, I played with his two little boys. The morning my parents departed for Florida, my mother woke me up to say goodbye, "Emily. Hey. I was thinking you should take your winter coat with you. Just in case it gets really cold. Would you do that for me?"

"Fine," I mumbled, "if it makes you happy." I said, knowing this was the last thing she could ask of me.

TWO

Georgia

March 5th – 12th

Day 1

The taste of freedom was so sweet. Nothing could wipe the smile off my face. "Look a green bush, it looks so pretty!" I exclaimed. I finally had a hiking partner, I didn't have to argue with my mother, and I was finally on my way to what I dreamed and planned for months. Hiking the Appalachian Trail was actually happening.

I breathed hard, climbing up the wet stones of Springer Mountain. Katherine had not waited for me. All I had for comfort were the white blazes leading me up the foggy trail. Katherine was still at the summit when I arrived. We stood there for a moment; we were officially at the start of the trail.

I didn't like hiking alone, so I joined Katherine down the mountain. She had long strides and I strained to keep up. "This is my slow pace," she said.

It might have been slow for her, but I was practically running.

"I've hiked the entire Georgia section before," she said. "My dad has done most of it. He'll be with us for the first week."

I couldn't wait to get to the shelter. Keeping up with Katherine was wearing, but I dealt with it for fear I'd miss the shelter without her. Finally we got to the sign.

At Hawk Mountain shelter, two pit bulls welcomed us with vicious barks. The creatures were shivering in cotton tee shirts. The owner, Richard said, "If my dogs start barking, just kick them. I'm training them to like people."

When Richard was out of earshot, people complained. "Why is there a homeless guy staying here?"

Since I didn't have a stove and Richard mentioned making a fire, I went out looking for him. I didn't care if he was homeless.

I found Richard outside trying to light a fire. "I'll get wood," I said, and I went around sawing up wood. I came back with a nice stash, ready to throw onto a ripping fire, but the only hint of a fire was a feeble ribbon of smoke. I assisted him and before long my supper was cooking.

"I expected you to have a nice fire, aren't you out here often?" I asked.

"No, not really. I'm just out a couple days. I've been staying here for the past two days, because I can't risk getting the dog food wet."

"Hey, do we need to purify water?" I asked.

"Oh no, the water around here is the best you'll ever come by. Don't spoil it with chemicals."

I agreed with him. The Aqua Mira purification drops my mother persuaded me to buy didn't seem healthy, and I didn't appreciate the bitter taste it left in the water.

Back inside the shelter, I was so happy, I couldn't help giggling constantly.

Katherine and I played cards using our headlamps. Everyone had their lights off when I realized I was supposed to hang my food, which was called bear bagging. I had no clue what I was doing. I found a limb and hung it up. I didn't see the point of hanging my food in the rain.

Day 2

Day light came, but no one left, because the rain was coming down hard. I was antsy and left as soon as the rain stopped. I wanted to get ahead. I knew Katherine and her dad would catch up. Down the trail from the shelter, I came to the AT. I took a couple steps before I psyched myself out, "Where are the blazes?" I turned around and tried walking up another path, but that turned into a stream.

I considered going back to the shelter to ask Katherine, but that would only make me look more like a moron. I went over to a man to ask where the trail was, before realizing he was urinating. I turned the other way until he was finished. The man,

Paul excused himself and confidently pointed towards what I believed was south.

"I'm pretty sure this is the way we came," I said, knowing he had just started yesterday from Springer.

"Oh no, I made myself a mental note last night. This is the correct way," he insisted.

My mind spun. I wondered if in some way or another, I was so confused that I thought I had come from that way. *It could be possible.* Since Katherine was out of the question to hike with, I figured maybe this man could be interesting hiking company for the day.

Following Paul with no further questions, I was happily surprised he was talkative. I found Paul helpful, like when the wind blew my trash bag above my head, he helped to tuck it around my pack.

I was quite sure we were going the wrong way, but I told myself I'd let him figure it out himself. At a familiar overlook, Paul was having second thoughts. Spotting a man coming towards us, we agreed to ask him which direction he was headed. "North," he answered.

"Oh really," I said. "So are we. We just had a hiccup and went the wrong way this morning."

Paul could not believe it. He kept saying sorry and tried to figure out his mistake. Turning around, we hiked several miles together passing Hawk Mountain shelter and continuing on to Gooch Gap shelter.

Paul was a slower hiker than me, but I waited for him. He decided to stay at Gooch Gap. I couldn't blame him for wanting to stay. The hikers there were friendly and a fire was being built.

I looked at the hikers in the shelter all snuggled in their sleeping bags, "Are you *Feisty*?" asked the one girl.

"Yeah," I answered to the name I had given myself.

"Some hikers were asking about you."

"Do they know I went the wrong way?"

"Yes, I believe they do."

I had to catch up to Katherine and her dad. They were at Woody Gap, five mile away. Through the long miles, I wondered what Katherine would think of my blunder.

When I got to the Gap, it was an air tunnel. The trees bent and waved. It was luck that I spotted Katherine. She led me to the campsite, where several tents were set up. Joe seemed relieved to see me and Katherine chatted while I set up my bivy. I asked where she planned on us staying for tomorrow. I didn't have a guidebook so I made a mental note of the miles and place.

"Make sure to put your water bottles in your sleeping bag or they might freeze," said Katherine, before she vanished into her tent. There were two other people in tents who didn't show their faces. It was too cold to eat outside, so I crawled inside my bivy.

I ate a pouch of tuna, as I heard ice hitting the thin material protecting me.

I felt so discouraged. I wasn't sure if I could keep up with my group. I could tell Katherine was less than impressed and if there was one thing I hated it was being unimpressive. Hiking an extra four miles was a silly thing to do. Paul, whom I tried to befriend, was behind. I had to focus on keeping up with the group I was with. *Katherine may be faster, but I can get up earlier,* I thought, setting stage to my strategy.

Day 3

I felt sick, I didn't sleep well, and I really didn't want to get up in the middle of the night to go pee in the gusting wind and ice. I felt like my right knee would give out as I shuffled in my frozen sneakers that weren't on right. Then I crawled back into my tent and tried to recover the warmth I had before.

I woke up before the others and paced back and forth inhaling thick slices of pepperoni. I loved the frost covered atmosphere. Joe had laid his socks out to dry and overnight curly frost had grown on them.

A kid, I later knew as Andy, peaked his head out, before starting to unpack. My instincts to race kicked in, I quickly fetched water and started hiking, but he caught up and passed me. He was soon out of sight, as I made my way up a switched backed mountain.

At the top of the climb, I stood, surrounded by mountains. With no foliage to block the view, I could see far beyond the nearest surrounding mountains. It was beautiful how the frost covered the plain leafless trees. Hundreds and thousands of trees shimmered white in the crisp morning light.

Past the summit of Blood Mountain, I lost the trail. It seemed that the trail went straight down the mountain. After inching several yards down, I decided there was no possible way I was on a trail. I had to climb back up to find the trail. Later Joe, Katherine's dad, read in his guide book that another hiker got lost at the same spot, except he couldn't make it back up so he bushwhacked down the steep side of Blood Mountain until he ran into another trail.

Then a historic thing happened: I made it to Neels gap! It was a bit of a milestone. A large percentage of hikers quit at Neels Gap, only thirty-two miles from Springer Mountain.

A road goes through Neels Gap, and there is an outfitter with a hostel to stay at, which is a cheap place to stay. People were abundant. Many were resupplying and shipping unneeded supplies home.

The workers at the store of Neels Gap see hikers in all kinds of conditions. One year, a hiker came trudging into the store with a twenty pound propane tank strapped to his pack. He intended it to be his stove fuel for the next two thousand miles. I'm sure people must have nagged him to get rid of the unnecessary weight, but it was those at Neels gap that actually got him to drop it.

Neels Gap is famous for shakedowns. Past thru-hikers come out to go through backpacks to lighten loads. I watched two hikers get shake downs.

"Today I helped a hiker get rid of twenty pounds of cotton. He had shirts, pants, socks, underwear…wet cotton won't do you any good out here."

Lumpy did my shakedown. All I needed was a waterproof food bag that could be hung as a bear bag.

"Where's the hiker box?" I asked.

"Let me show you." He led me to the hiker box which was full of items other hikers had left. I picked out a spork. As I left, he lowered his voice, "You'll find that many guys will be throwing themselves at girls like you on the upcoming miles." I imagined a version of The Bachelors. I laughed at the thought until I pictured creepy hairy men.

At a campsite, I hung a bear bag for the first time. Katherine stopped me from throwing my food bag over the tree limb. "You have to tie a rock to the end of the rope." Again, she was less than impressed. I was surprised that, in all my research about the trail, I had never heard about bear bagging.

Again, Andy was there at the campsite, but wordlessly stayed in his tent.

Day 4

The moment the skies brighten, I packed up. The hike was easy except for one sharp climb. While I was eating lunch, Andy came by. I tried talking to him before, but he hadn't said much. "You just missed it. People were handing out food," he said handing me an oatmeal cream pie.

I found it intriguing that even though I missed the trail magic it still found its way to me. The best part of the trail magic was the opportunity to finally be acquainted with Andy.

"What brings you to the trail," I asked.

"My first idea was to walk along the shore, but at the last moment I decide to hike the trail."

Andy was annoyed that his coworkers taped up a map of the Appalachian Trail in their lunch room to track his progression. I didn't understand why he took it as a bad thing. To be honest, I was a bit jealous that he had a group of people *that* excited about his trip that they went out and bought a map.

"I just don't want to deal with keeping them updated on where I am all the time," Andy said.

We found the campsite that we thought was the one Katherine told us to get to. I had fun talking to Andy as we set up our tents. I was collecting wood for a fire when Katherine and her dad arrived. "We came just to let you guys know rain is coming and we're staying at Low Gap shelter." I didn't like the sound of backtracking. That meant walking the same section three times in all. The choice seemed made for me; I didn't want to stay and have to pack up a wet tent in the morning. I thought of hiking north to the next shelter without the others, but it was a bit far. So Joe picked up my collection of sticks and we backtracked over a mile.

At the shelter, I made a fire and cooked instant mashed potatoes and couscous. It was a lot of food, but I was running low on cold meals, and thought, *If I eat more for supper, I won't be as hungry for breakfast.*

I joined the others around the picnic table. Katherine said, "I heard you missed the trail magic, they were just setting up when you passed. *Too bad.*" She smiled smugly as she handed me a packet of M&Ms. "Not all early birds get the worm."

"Not all early birds get the worm," was her way of saying she was better than me. I wasn't sure how we got off on the wrong foot, but I didn't know what to do to fix it.

The shelter was packed. We were all squeezed in, shoulder-to-shoulder. I was sandwiched between two guys. The one was ill prepared, without a sleeping pad.

In our sleeping bags, I rallied up a group of hikers to play cards. Andy simply watched. We joked around a bunch and Katherine was calling people stupid left and right. A guy joked that before long she would be calling everyone stupid.

"Hey, he really was stupid. I told him he should stay at the shelter, but no he camped in the rain, and got drenched," Katherine said about a lone kid named David.

Several hikers arrived later and had to set up tents. A hiker in the shelter said to them, "You should sleep under the shelter. I've seen people do it before." I wasn't surprised when no one attempted to sleep under the shelter, it looked like a tight squeeze, and the ground was rocky and sloped.

One particular fellow, who was small in stature, was able to squeeze onto the edge of the shelter. During the night he rolled out and hit the steps on his way down. When I first heard of it, I laughed in astonishment, but later felt bad, because he was hurt. He became a character of trail-lore, and even months later people would mention him. With pride I would say, "By the way I was there."

Day 5

A hotel in Helen Georgia was my group's destination. I sloshed ten miles through the cold rain. About halfway through, the others caught up and we sang songs. I didn't want to go to the hotel, but after stopping at Blue Mountain Shelter (where it was packed) and being sopping wet, I decided to keep with my group. And I was glad I did. Beds never seemed so delightful. There was no unpacking. It was great! The hot shower and warm clothes were heavenly!

I called my dad and he asked me what state I was in. *Was he joking?* "Georgia?" I replied. *What did he expect?* It was as if he thought I should have been farther along. Before long, my father said he had to go; they were heading to the beach.

Day 6

Katherine and Andy both liked eating at McDonald's; they seemed to like the same things. I felt a little left out sometimes; for example, when they talked about their favorite cereals, since it seems irrelevant to me, but they both lit up at the subject.

We ate breakfast at the hotel: eggs, sausages, muffins, milk and biscuits. The news was on, telling us of floods, tornadoes, and such. I was glad to head back to the woods.

The weather looked bleak on our taxi ride to the trail. When we got there it was raining. The rain turned icy and then the freezing rain turned to snow. It was bearable not wearing rain gear. When I took breaks I got really cold and it took forever to warm up again. Katherine got annoyed that I don't appear cold, "Oh that Pennsylvanian," she said. I thought it was funny.

   As I hiked, I made up a rap. I thought of several lines, and then stopped to write them down. It went like this:

□■□

I made a little rhyme for you

I'm hoping you do not boo.

I am really liking,

I'm out here hiking.

On the first day I was giggly and happy

But that didn't stop the weather from being crappy.

We all sheltered at Hawk,

Andy in the corner, he didn't talk.

On the second day Paul and I got lost,

You guys were worried and a little cross.

I owe ya'll an apology

I hope you're not mad at me.

Once we made it to Hog pen,

We all knew Andy was our friend.

Joe, thanks for picking up my krocs

That really rocks.

Katherine's as cute and funny as cupid,

But she likes to call people stupid.

Lastly our good friend Andy,

He likes cheese, M&M's, and candy.

Thank you for all you've done,

It's been a lot of fun.

This may be a little sappy,

But I'm hoping it made you happy.

If it didn't and you thought it was lame,

I still like you all the same.

You are all so dear,

I am extremely happy to be here.

□■□

The hike was a long thirteen miles. Deep Gap shelter was two stories, with a kind of doorway/opening. Katherine made me some hot chocolate. And Joe filled my water bottles. They felt bad for me, because I was shivering. I had my winter coat on and was thankful for once that my mom made me take it.

I shared my rap with my group, and then they decided to write their own. They later shared them, but Andy was too shy to read his aloud. So Katherine read it for him.

□■□

Now this is our story, our theme song,

The one we've been singing all along.

We may not have known it then, but we'll know it by the time this rhyme is gone.

Here we go! One... two... three perfect strangers and the father of a girl I never knew.

That's what makes up this gang, this posse, this crew.

One of us got lost, but we stuck together like duct tape.

And the fastest one of us is the one that wakes up late.

Some rappers make it rain, but we're so "G" we made it snow.

When we got off the trail, it rained four inches. We're so sorry. We didn't know.

We're so cool; we get applause everyday at noon.

The word "applause" looks like the word "applesauce" and now I'm craving food.

Katherine doesn't think her name is gangster and I'm starting to think she's right.

I can't think of a way to make it gangster, so I guess I'll continue to write.

Feisty runs down hills and jumps in puddles.

I don't know what rhymes with

"Puddle" except for "huddles."

And Joe knows something about those because he used to coach soccer.

Although, now that I think about it, maybe you don't huddle in soccer.

Admittedly, I don't know anything about soccer.

So I guess I'll wrap this thing up like a beef stick in a tortilla.

Oh yeah, I forgot to mention Crazy Laundromat Guy.

That dude was on crack and that's no lie.

□■□

I asked each person who came in the shelter to cover the opening. Someone eventually tied up a tarp and put boots on the bottom so it wouldn't blow inwards. The only problem was that there was still an opening! People used my side of the tarp during the night and didn't bother to close it. I was glad morning came as soon as it did, because my sleeping bag was soaked from blown-in snow.

Day 7

At a road crossing we were met by Katherine's mother and brother. They gave us a lift to town. Katherine's mom brought us a bunch of amazing snacks.

Katherine and I stocked up on food. I got too much; mine weighed a ton. See, I went crazy at the grocery store. There were too many options. I spent like fifty dollars on cheese, trail mix, tuna, rye bread, muffins, and chocolate milk. We also had a pit stop at the library, where I need an ID to use the computers. I had thought that in the woods, one wouldn't need an ID.

Katherine's dad finished his hike with us. I could tell Katherine's parents knew she was ready – at least more ready than I was.

Sitting on the Blueberry Patch hiker hostel's floor we were surrounded by food. Andy picked up a packet of tuna in his drop box and smelled it thoughtfully. "Does this smell funny?" he asked Katherine.

Katherine had her food separated by day. There were rows of gushers, applesauce, snickers, pop tarts, and Mac n' cheese. "Katherine, all your food has sugar in it," I said.

Her mother perked up, "Yeah you're right. Katherine, perhaps, you should get a few pointers from *Feisty*. She looks like she has more of a balanced diet."

Katherine did not seem please with the criticism and I knew she wouldn't ask *me* for food advice in a million years.

After Katherine's parents left, we had the place virtually to ourselves. Outside were donkeys and goats. I showed Andy and Katherine how to feed the goats in order to get them to come close. They said I punched the goat – I tapped it – But after that, every time we met someone new they say, "She punched a goat." How embarrassing.

Day 8

The hostel owners made breakfast for us. Pancakes with blueberry sauce, eggs, and sausage: what a great breakfast. They were Christians, so that was how they ministered to people. I loved everything they did, except one thing. When he blessed the food, the man turned his prayer into a sermon. Perhaps he was trying to make some converts; instead he made us feel uncomfortable.

The fee was by donation. "I have no idea how much to donate," said Andy.

"Between five and ten should be good," I said.

He fingered the money in his hands, "I still don't know."

"Try the middle, seven should work," I said.

The Blueberry Patch man drove us back to the trail. I led, but then Katherine and Andy got bored of going slow so we did Indian rows, were one person leads for a short while. I couldn't handle walking so fast. I was gasping for air, but tried my best. Soon they went on without me. "We should all be together when we pass the border," were the last words Katherine said.

The whole way was a climb, and my pack was so heavy, but I hurried more than usual, because I knew they were waiting for me at the border. Turns out they kept going. I passed the border all alone. I was half relieved they hadn't waited, because I didn't want to be a nuisance. But then again where was the little effort in caring for a friend and keeping their word? For me it was a big deal to be passing from Georgia to North Carolina, however it saddened me that there was no one to share it with.

I had one state down, and thirteen more to go. I passed the famous gnarly tree a bit further in Bly Gap. The mountain sure did climb. I beasted it. I conquered it. I was victorious. I kept telling myself, "Until I reach the top, I will not stop." Singing always helped.

I sang, "Hey now you're a rock star," as I marched into Muskrat Creek Shelter. I was pooped, and wanted to hear a congratulations on my long uphill miles, but everyone was buzzing around, busily cooking early suppers. Many of the hikers there were young guys who appeared unscathed from the mountains as if they had a chopper ride to the top. Andy was reading in the corner. A fire was built and someone used my saw for firewood. It was fun carrying the saw, because I got a huge reaction. David used my saw to cut out and carve a spoon.

The one guy was introducing himself with his real name when his friend said, "I thought you were going to keep the name that *Hickory* named you."

"Oh yeah, *Hickory* was strange. He looked and talked in a grim but serious way. *Hickory* gave me the name *Llama Legs.* When I asked him why he thought llama legs would be a good name, he said that he always wanted to name someone llama legs and then started rambling about how strong llamas were and how they could carry heavy loads."

When I went to hang up my bear bag, two other kids took advantage of the fact that I had rope. "Can't we just tie our food bag to yours?" they said. The branch holding up the bear bags started to bend towards the ground.

"Um, guys? If a bear comes... our food is done for," I said.

"No bear will come. There are too many people around," reassured the one kid.

THREE

North Carolina

March 13th – 20th

Day 9

Halfway through the day Katherine and Andy caught up. We hiked over Standing Indian Mountain and paraded through the forest, laughing and chatting as we went. We whistled theme songs and talked about school. I learned about Andy's family. He went back and forth between his parents' houses. We were pretty rough on Andy, calling him anti-social and what-not. He said he won't talk to people until he figures out if he likes them, has something in common, or has something to gain. So I called him shallow.

I was worried Katherine didn't like having me around, but after we talked I felt better.

On one of our breaks, I had the curious feeling that I might just hurl. I sat there, uncomfortable. It was nice to loosen my hip-belt from squeezing my waist and just stare into nothing. The others broke out a snack. They weren't too helpful when I told them my predicament. "Make sure to puke away from me!" Andy said as he got up to move.

"You're probably sick from drinking *unpurified* water," Katherine said in the same way Lucy would critique Charlie Brown.

They found some beef jerky on the ground. There's a saying that if there is an M&M on the ground a day hiker would notice it. A section hiker would stop and look around to see if anyone was watching before they ate it. Lastly, a thru-hiker would pounce upon the chocolate morsel, and then start digging for more. I guess we weren't at that point yet.

Soon we were at the shelter. It wasn't often that the shelters felt like a private place. More often than not, shelters were used much like public restrooms. They were noisy, crowded, and mutilated.

At this particular shelter there was profanity written in huge arm strokes. Instantly, I had my fill of venomous language from the wall. I felt compelled to save others from such slander by creating a more positive welcome. By changing one letter I made it say, "You are a duck," and I drew a duck, with a green color pencil I found lying on the ground. I got some strange looks from Katherine and Andy, but I felt like I did a service to humankind.

Andy had been reading a book religiously. I tried to make him be more social. So I hopped beside him and said, "How about you read aloud to us?"

"No."

"May I?" I then proceeded to read his book, but I only finished the first page when I said, "What kind of book is this?" It had something to do with aliens and malicious murder. I think he was insulted, since he took the book from my grasp. I tried reading over his shoulder, but he slammed the book shut. Katherine joined in and tried to find the page.

Andy seemed a bit distraught. "Can someone make me food?"

"Sure." I then proceeded to make a fire and cook rice. I gave it to him and cooked up my own. He didn't touch it. "Aren't you going to eat it?"

"I didn't think you'd *actually* make me food," Andy protested.

"So you're not going to eat it?" I asked in disbelief, as he started up his stove to cook his own meal.

Later an older man came along. He was very talkative. So talkative that he eventually became an annoyance. By bedtime, he informed us of the sad truth that many men his age and size chronically had, the curse of giving everyone else a sleepless night. A snorer. Jokingly, I suggested that he could sleep behind the shelter on a tiny platform. Katherine and Andy looked at me shocked and muffled their laughs. The man just nonchalantly offered us earplugs.

Once it was dark, we all tucked ourselves in bed. Everything was quiet. Until the older man started talking about how insane it was for us *young* kids to be hiking out in the *wild*.

I said, "Yeah, we could get killed out here," which shut him up. He couldn't have been too hurt since moments later the snoring started. After a few minutes of his snoring, I cracked up laughing.

In the pitch dark, Katherine nudged me, "Are *you* awake?" I laughed even harder. To clue them in, I imitated the man's snore and said, "Luke, I am your father." They laughed. We dubbed him Darth Vader.

As if his snoring wasn't loud enough, whenever he shifted around, his raft of an air mattress made a racket. For hours we told stories in the pitch black, and laughed at Darth Vader.

Day 10

As I tiptoed across a log that spanned a stream, I started to whistle. Andy was excited when he recognized the tune. "It's the Indiana Jones theme song!" After that he joined in the whistling whenever we crossed a stream. I was happy to finally have something in common. Katherine couldn't whistle.

It was a chill day. Except for Mt Albert, which was a beast! Andy and Katherine would say "a bitch". We all paraded up, following Katherine. Andy and I tried our best to keep up. I was the last to summit mount Albert, which was a .3mile straight up climb.

We had the shelter to ourselves. We made a human pyramid and took a picture to celebrate the first hundred miles completed.

I felt happy. "When we make it to Pennsylvanian I can cook for you at my house."

Day 11

The rain had me waiting for the others. I led the group trying to go as fast as I could without hurting myself. About two miles in, my throat went dry. "Do you guys mind taking a break?" I asked.

"Nah," they said.

"I just need a drink of water." I was suffering. I stopped, and they marched right past. I had never been treated so badly and I couldn't believe how heartless they were. Couldn't they see I wanted to hike with them?

I chugged my water as quickly as I could and flew down the trail. The terrain was flat so I ran, pack bouncing and all. Part way through I tripped and fell, tearing my pants. After several minutes of running, I could see them ahead. I moved like a shadow behind them and followed instep. They had no idea I caught up, until I said, "Hi guys." Katherine freaked. I gave out a laugh rooted in revenge. I later apologized, but that didn't mean I wasn't upset. We hiked together until lunch break. After lunch, it got steep and I gave up all together.

I wasn't sure where the shelter was, but I sure couldn't wait to be warm and dry. At the top of the mountain there were vacant Man/Woman sided bathrooms – best thing I had seen all day.

Before the descent, there stood a stone tower. I imagined every hiker before me had probably climbed it, but the fog was too thick for any view. Instead, I went forth to seek out the shelter. I heard an ax in action and told myself I had to be close.

I hiked on and on, frustrated by the taunting crack of the ax. I imagined huddling by the flames, eating a hot meal.

Finally, I saw guys gathered around the fire. I didn't see a shelter, so I moved on. As I passed, a sinking feeling hit my gut. *What if that was the shelter?* I doubled back to join the guys around the fire. They told me that there was no shelter at the camp spot. They said they were hiking a different trail than the AT. I was answering some questions, when I realized all of the guys were listening to me. I felt honored and wished I had friends like them.

At the shelter with Katherine and Andy, there was a couple reading in their sleeping bags. They introduced themselves as *Thin-mint* and *Lizard*. After hearing that they had started in

February, I wasn't surprised that they sat in the shelter all day, reading. "Why hike when it's raining?" was *Thin-mints* motto.

"Have you guys talked to *Three Bags?*" asked *Thin-mint*. "He started the trail with three bags. Like all strapped around him and each weighing a considerable amount. He got lucky though; some guy re-outfitted him with top of the line gear. He is hilarious to listen to. He is the most southern guy I've met. It takes a while to understand him, since he has such a strong accent."

"Have you heard of *U-Haul?*"Continued *Thin-Mint*. "He's the only black guy I've seen on the trail. He's carrying literately a hundred pounds. Most of it is food. He was cooking the other night, and man that guy goes all out. Apparently he's carrying two laptops, but you know what he doesn't have? A guide book. So he only hikes from one shelter to the next. Be it five miles or ten.

"Did you meet the homeless guy with two pit bulls? People say he milked them, and drank the milk!"

"Did he really?" I said.

"There's this one guy named *Green Light*. He fell out of a shelter."

"We were there," I answered.

There was delight in *Thin-mint's* expression when a group arrived. He called them the Minstrels: for they all carried string instruments. The loudest of the three proclaimed in a friendly, deep voice, "Today was such a beautiful day." He was later named *Blue Sky* for his sunny outlook on life. It was *Blue Sky* that asked, "Anyone lose a leopard print hat?" It was my third lost and found.

Katherine complained, "This cannot be happening! Whenever you lose something it always comes back."

I told Andy and Katherine about how I had lived in Denmark for a year. They had me speak Danish for them, but they said it sounded like I was making up gibberish. In the end, Katherine and Andy decided that I was uniquely sheltered.

Andy said he had no clue why I was hiking the AT. "Perhaps to crash and burn."

"What do you mean *crash* and *burn*?" I asked.

They both raised their eyebrows and looked at each other, "You really are sheltered."

Day 12

I got up before light. I made sure not to wake anyone up, until I found Andy lying on my sleeping pad, I had to wake him to get it. Then, as I was on my way out, Katherine awoke and asked for her food bag, so that she could eat breakfast in her sleeping bag.

They caught up about the time I was suffering from cramps. I was in so much pain that I just lay on the side of the trail. At the top was a metal lookout tower. Andy didn't take a look, but I joined Katherine for the clear panoramic view.

The next six miles were all downhill, but I was suffering. I took an ibuprofen, which helped. We were going to stay at a shelter a mile before the Nantahala Outdoor Center (NOC), as agreed the night before, but they weren't there. A hiker was relaxing by a tree. I asked him if he'd seen my buddies, a tall blond and a quiet guy.

"Oh, they ditched you," he replied. "I think they left you a note at the shelter."

I left my pack and hiked up the small hill to retrieve the note. It read, "Sorry for the inconvenience, but we are hungry for town food. You are welcome to join us."

The guy at the tree told me I should forget *them* and hike with better people. I thought about staying at the shelter, but I was a bit scared of staying the night with some random scruffy hikers. So I went the extra mile to the Nantahala Outdoor Center, a bit confused and hurt for being left behind.

I felt so out of place. There were cars and bikes flying by and people were everywhere. I had no idea where to find Katherine and Andy. Out of the generosity of others, I was pointed in the correct direction. I must have looked bad since I didn't even have to ask for the help. I found the place we were staying at, got a key, a towel, and an undesired lecture. The bunkrooms were separated by gender, so I got a bunk in Katherine's room.

Then I picked up my first mail drop for the next twenty-eight miles. It was huge. Right off the bat, I dumped the rice into a hiker box. I wept for joy when I found a mango, which my mom had put there, plus notes from several family members.

Katherine and I split a mail-drop from someone who had read our trail journals. There were all sorts of goodies. Katherine and Andy invited me to get something to eat, but I took a hot shower instead.

Later, I took a stroll while indulging on cotton candy, and found *Mile High*, *Llama Legs* and *Data*. I offered them some cotton candy before they headed into a restaurant.

Day 13

Katherine and Andy went to a restaurant for breakfast. I'm not the eating out type, so I took my last look at the NOC.

The hike out of the NOC was insane. The mountain could easily be described with profanity. It was eight miles of steep grade. There were no downhill sections whatsoever. Flatness was rare. This was no trail. This was an obstacle course. There were a dozen fallen logs and I had the option of either straddling them or squeezing beneath. Because of my shortness, I chose the lesser of the two evils by going underneath. It was scary to wedge myself between rocky ground and an unmoving chunk of tree.

The trail kept at a painful yet steady climb. There were different forms of up: the lunge-up, the tiptoe-up, and my-bundles-of-muscle-are-killing-up. All with a refilled burden drooped downward. Sweat burned my eyes. Many times I was convinced I was at the top, only to discover more mountain to endure. At one point the blazes stopped. All of that uphill and I didn't know if I was on the correct trail! I thought the terrible, haunting thought of turning back, but instead soldiered on, praying I wasn't lost.

I was relieved when I finally got to a shelter, where *Llama Legs*, *Mile High*, and *Data* (David) were eating lunch. They had a tent hung up which they were drying out from the rain that came overnight. I traded chocolates for hot cocoa. I devoured a family size tuna pouch, while getting bits of acknowledgment considering the frustration I had just endured.

Andy showed up at the shelter, but didn't talk to the guys. They guys whispered, "Why doesn't he talk to us. Is it something we did?"

"No, it's just the way he is."

I made sure to leave when Andy did. When I saw the far-off top I challenged Andy to race me. He declined so I headed off myself. I ended with a sweat-drenched face, but wore an enormous grin.

At the top of Cheoaha Bald were the Minstrels. They brought nail polish to paint their ukuleles, but seemed unfamiliar with the toxic fumes.

"We're going to have a safety meeting if any of you want to join us," said *Blue Sky*.

"Why do you say safety meeting? Why can't you just say what you're doing?" The minstrels had invited us to safety meetings before, and Katherine just recently clued me in on what they were actually doing.

"Uh," *Blue Sky* seemed unsure what to say. "We don't want to offend anyone." He flashed one of his brilliant smiles.

I made some badges influenced by Andy, to show off how tough we were. I created them from things I carried. Safety pins from my first aid kit, hard plastic from my New Testament cover, and rope used for tying on my krocs. I even had superglue in case I needed gear repair and tried my best not to superglue my fingers together.

While the others rested in their tents, I got sun burnt, sawing wood all afternoon in preparation of a St. Patrick's Day bonfire. I got the Minstrels to carry up armfuls of firewood.

The night was a success. As we watched the sunset, we gathered around the fire and chatted. It was how I had pictured the trail to be. I was glad that it finally came to life.

Day 14

I had a steep climb up Jacob's ladder, and I had to take multiple rests. I kept thinking, *Okay, take ten breaths. Okay now you see that tree. Get there then take ten more breaths.*

I couldn't shake the three dudes that were on my tail, all day long. At first I was scared of them, but realized later how friendly they were. The French guy handed me my kroc, "I think you dropped something." The French guy named himself *Corsican,* but he later became known as the *Snickers Guy,* after he bought all the forty cent Snickers from Uncle Johnny's in Erwin. By the time I got to Erwin, there was a limit to the amount of snickers one could purchase, because of him. He also became known for his high mileage, some challenged themselves in trying to catch up to him. It was said he hiked in his underwear to travel lighter.

We all took a moment to jot down our raps. Andy's went like this:

☐■☐

It's Friday, our rap day,

Our "these were the haps" day.

This week saw lots of laughs, lots of snores, and one dead rat.

We stayed at the Blueberry patch where Katherine read what I wrote.

I accidentally grabbed a wasp and Feisty punched a goat.

Climbed Albert Mountain, otherwise known as Albert the Fucking Wall.

Georgia started it, but North Carolina took it too far.

Hurdling downed trees on an overgrown trail,

Vertical hills and dirt under my nails.

Slept out on a bald and Katherine slept in.

While Feisty and I hiked, the sun plotted to burn Katherine's skin.

This trail doesn't know what to do with itself.

We're too good at this. We dealt with rain-snow-fog-wind and everything else.

We're holding on until we can't let go.

We're spitting out these rhymes so everybody get low.

That's just our style, like our Bad Ass Badges.

Thru-hiking is more fun than I ever imagined.

□■□

We were at a little, old, mice-infested shelter. My buddies were having the creeps. I found it entertaining. We could see the mice running on the rafters. Andy and Katherine didn't want to sleep on the edges, where the mice had their own highway; instead they slept with their heads towards the entrance. First I made fun of them, but after a mouse brushed past me, I reoriented my position as well.

All night I could hear the mice running about and squeaking. I wanted to smash one with my boot, like I read in a book once, but I just never did. In the morning, I found a mousetrap and put some of my cheese on it, and guess what? I got one! I ran out with it to bury it. When I came back for my shoes, I held it dangling over Katherine's area. She freaked, "Get that thing away!"

□■□

I told Darth Vader he could snore down there,

Instead his air mattress was hard to bear.

I busted out in laughter

Got tears from giggles a little after.

The climb out of NOC was foul but

How does it measure from one to Albert?

We got traditions now you see,

They will be with us as long as can be.

We sing Indiana Jones

When crossing streams and hopping stones.

We document this quest, by the way,

Of telling raps every Friday.

At noon they like to clap

At blueberry hostel, donkeys do I slap.

You can never go wrong with Andy;

He likes all different kinds of candy.

I made Andy rice and a chair.

He said yes, but he doesn't care.

When I finish hiking, I completely crash.

For Katherine it's a breeze and she picks up my trash.

She has Mac & Cheese for dinner,

For me anything I choose is a winner.

I'm trying not to whine,

I've had a fun time,

I just don't like being left behind.

□■□

Day 15

We had a short hike to Fontana Dam. Katherine's plan was to stay at the Fontana Dam Resort, but we needed a ride. There was a couple hitching up a boat. The other two were nervous to ask for a ride, so I volunteered. Soon we were flying by, with wind whipping through our hair. After we were dropped off, it was still a hike to the resort.

We then booked a room with two double beds. I picked up yet another mail drop; it was heavy, but I was glad it would be a while until I had to lift my pack again.

We explored the place, sitting on the couches and looking at the pool. Andy and Katherine were surprised that I joined them for lunch at the resort, but they looked disgusted at the sandwich I ordered, "I hate honey mustard," they both said.

Andy and Katherine said they tried to keep their arms down, since they could smell themselves. I couldn't smell anything under my arms. When I told them that I had deodorant, they freaked, "You don't carry a real tent because it's *too* heavy, but you'll carry deodorant!" After lunch, I took a shower and applied my deodorant one last time before tossing it away.

Gingersnap, a girl Andy and Katherine met on day two, shared our room. She had some funny quirks. She got insulted when people called her a redhead. She insisted that she was a ginger. About every conversation she had, she explained, "Normally I don't zero, but I need to rest my IT band. I'm afraid it might end my hike."

Some middle-aged men teased *Gingersnap* for not knowing what special lunar activity was happening that night. They said, "You seem like a smart girl, but you don't know the moon is the largest it has been in twenty years?" She tried to explain that she had been in the woods for weeks, but they were unrelenting.

Day 16

Katherine's family came, which was neat; we were so spoiled, getting our tummies full of Chinese and wearing clean garments. We ran around town to find odds and ends, such as power bars for Katherine and marshmallow fluff for Andy. I got apples and a flower hairpiece to celebrate the first day of spring.

The Hilton shelter was nice, I guess. There was a bit of over exaggerated excitement from people praising the shelter. They made it sound like a mansion. It had showers, but they were a three minute walk, and I had already taken a shower. I guess after staying at a resort I got soft.

Andy and I got a ride with Katherine's parents to the dam to pick up registration papers for the Great Smoky Mountains. I was really excited to be getting into the Smokies the next day, but was also nervous about all the elevation gain.

Later in the evening, as I was helping a guy make a fire, he told me twice, "I heard you're an excellent fire maker." *I guess I'm getting famous.*

There was a buffet of food because everyone wanted to lighten up before the Smokies. I didn't even touch my own mountain of food. I warmed up a slice of pizza on the fire as the Minstrels played.

FOUR

Great Smoky Mountains

March 21st – 27th

Day 17

In the moonlight, I ate an apple while waiting for Andy since he insisted on coming with me. He asked if I wanted to drink his extra water before he dumped it out. As I brought the water to my lips the container doubled over and cold water poured down my shirt. "The same thing happened to me before," Andy commented.

I looked at him, annoyed. "Then why didn't you warn me?"

He went on about a time he had to take a leak, but it was too cold to leave his sleeping bag. Once he finally got up, he took a swig of water, and his platypus dumped on him. He was so shocked that he went directly back to bed with wet shorts and a full bladder.

Andy's fast pace across Fontana Dam made my calves cramp up. I persuaded him to stop for me to stretch out a bit, but my calves were tight as rubber bands. Then my shins started to shriek in pain. Next my feet began to tingle and fall asleep. By the time we had stepped off the pavement and were following a trail uphill, my face was dripping in sweat. I couldn't see straight because my glasses had fogged over.

I was fighting a losing battle and finally gave up. Andy went on. I stretched a bit, and then went on at my own pace. My legs stopped rebelling and I was back on track.

Day 18

I found out that I could catch up to people when I ran down hills. There was a group that I kept passing when we got to a downhill, and they eventually stopped before every downhill to let me pass. My pace was good. I was proud of myself and half surprised.

We meet a guy named *Found*. I heard he started out with a buddy named *Lost*. *Found* and Katherine had been hiking together some. *Found* hikes too fast for me. He was like the pro out here, since he thru-hiked the Pacific Crest Trail.

Found came up with a trail name for Katherine. It was *Caustic*, which meant a burning sensation. It was cruel to name someone caustic and Katherine did not approve. She had never liked any of the names I gave her, but at least I didn't suggest caustic. Katherine probably offended him, by calling him stupid. Overall, he was nice, like the time he saved me right as I was taking a wrong turn. It was embarrassing of course to be corrected like that from a pro, but I was grateful.

As I put together a fire, hikers rolled up logs. They were laughing and chatting. I cooked up something on the fire, but I was more interested in the hotdogs *Found* was grilling. They smelled so good. I realized that I was not limited to only hiker related food, but that I could pack out any kind of food I wanted.

I watched *Found* toss a page of his guidebook into the fire. "Why are you doing that?" I said, cringing at the valuable information burning. It wasn't just any guidebook; it was the AT Guide, by Awol. It was the best guide book on the trail. I wished I had that guide book.

"It's no use for me any longer," he responded as he snapped a couple of pictures of the hikers around the fire. For *Found* the day wasn't over. He hiked on, passing Clingman's Dome to the next shelter.

Much of the conversation was about how wonderful it was to have a privy again, after not having one the night before. One guy missed the privies so much; he said he wished he had brought a toilet seat with him. We were also walking the border of our third state. We could get water in North Carolina and use the privy in Tennessee!

"Do you guys wanna get up early to see the sunrise on Clingman's Dome?" I asked, addressing Katherine and Andy. "I sure will be upset," I went on, "if there isn't good weather atop Clingman's Dome, this could make or break the way I feel about this hike."

Day 19

Mouse was the only person who passed me on my way up to Clingmans Dome. He said it was only two hundred paces to the top. I needed to stop thinking about the uphill, so I started counting.

At the summit I went up the wheelchair accessible tower where the view was fantastic, but the wind chill was dramatic. The tower had a platform the shape of a ring. Around the tower were the tops of dead pine trees. The sky was so clear, that I could see farther than the pictures on the information boards. I walked in circles looking out at the faded blue mountains, and felt invigorated.

Clingmans Dome was the highest elevation point on the AT. There was virtually no one there, but during the summer the summit would have been hopping with tourists.

The second highest mountain on the AT was Mount Washington, residing in the White Mountain Range located in New Hampshire – the 13th state on the AT. Both these mountains had a road for tourists to drive up to the summit.

The hike downhill wasn't as continually downhill as I was anticipating. The forest seemed much different on the other side of Clingman's Dome. The woods were shaded with evergreens and there were massive downed trees, with the roots all pulled up. Once in a while there were piles of snow lurking in the deepest of shadows.

After I got tired of trying to keep up with Andy, I met Travis a grad student. We hiked through Newfound Gap. The Gap had a parking lot filled with car loads of people. The tourists were snapping pictures and being noisy, but I liked it. They would come over and ask, "So where did you start from?" Some didn't know much about the trail. They thought it started in Texas or something. I saw shy Andy being ambushed and called him over.

I found it exhilarating to be passing Newfound Gap. I didn't want to mention Bill Bryson, but he gave up on his thru-hike at Newfound Gap, and skipped hundreds of miles. I like many hikers have a love/hate relationship with Bill Bryson. First off we all have read his book and loved it, but after we've been on the trail we realize inconsistencies. Not all people are lunatics. Littering is not acceptable. Thru-hiking is difficult, but skipping ahead is looked down upon, so when nonhikers compare us to Bill Bryson we get annoyed, because they have a skewed idea of what we are doing. On the other hand, Bill Bryson has made many people open to hikers and it makes all the difference.

As I passed, I thought, Bill Bryson made hiking sound impossible, and here I am passing him up!

Travis traveled from far away to hike a loop in the Smokies. He was a runner at heart, but he injured his IT Band, causing his knee to hurt. He hoped hiking would help it heal faster.

Around the two hundred mile mark, a ranger told us to find shelter as soon as possible because it was predicted to thunderstorm with a chance of tornadoes. This damaging type of weather was much more typical in the Smokies. I was glad to have sunny weather up to this point.

The Minstrels have this game they play. If I got someone to tell them, "Your beards are coming along nicely," I got a point. But if they caught the person before they said it, the Minstrels got a point. I got Travis to tell the Minstrels: "Your beards are coming along nicely," before they could catch him. I was very excited for my first point. (By the way, they have pretty patchy beards.)

Travis wanted to make a fire in the fireplace inside our shelter that looked like a little cottage home. They all helped me by gathering wood: Andy, Travis, and the Minstrels. I was pleasantly surprised, since I wasn't used to all that help.

Travis had a brochure about the Smokies. He said there was only one fatal bear attack in the park. He remarked, "The bear was only one hundred and twelve pounds! Why couldn't she just defend herself?"

A guy piped up, saying he wrestled a de-clawed Canadian Bear in a bar at nineteen years of age. He said that the bear effortlessly took power over him, and easily knocked him over.

Katherine sent us a text saying that she was staying in Gatlinburg, a town known for its tackiness. She decided to hitch there with a group after she heard about the nasty weather approaching. It fit since she always says, "Don't rain on my parade."

Day 20

I was nervous for my first twenty mile day. It was beautiful. I walked in the dark and I saw the sunrise through the trees. On a ridge; the wind was ice-biting cold. The views of far off mountains were breathtaking.

In some areas the trees were covered in thick frost and I ran where the wind blew the warmth out of me in seconds.

Andy passed me early on. I didn't see him again 'till I got to the shelter. The Minstrels (*Blue Sky*, *Disco*, and *Six String*) took about five breaks. I only took one, so I kept seeing them throughout the day.

It was a long day, and my feet hurt. When I finished for the day, I just sprawled out on my sleeping pad, exhausted. *Blue Sky* thought I was sleeping. "She's sleeping already?" he exclaimed, when he walked in. I didn't respond, but I felt confident with my twenty.

Katherine came, saying, "I knew I wasn't far behind. I kept seeing your boot print."

In the night, when I finally decided to brave the cold to the privy, the privy seat was frosty. Andy said, "That brings a whole new side to the issue of cold toilet seats."

Day 21

That day we had the last part of the Smokies to finish. I started off later than normal, close to 8:00. Andy left with me. We were supposed to be going downhill, but there was definitely some uphill, and my legs put the brakes on, telling me, "Hold up, this isn't what we were expecting." Somehow I stayed up with Andy since he was snapping pictures at the beautiful frosty, scenery and distant mountains clothed in clouds.

After miles of downhill, there were blooming flowers. Katherine passed and we sang a couple songs that she could hear from her iPod.

I met trail repairmen using a chainsaw to remove a fallen tree trunk that was blocking the trail. They had the chainsaw running while I was walking towards them. One man saw me and yelled out, "Stop right there!" in an intense voice, as if I would die if I moved any closer. It was an odd experience, since I've used a chainsaw before, when working with my Dad.

I was stumped at a fork in the road. A lady made her way near me, and asked if I had seen *Mouse*. "I met him on Clingmans Dome," I said. She told me how lucky I was, having summery weather. "This time last year there was waist high snow."

She pointed at where I was to go, along the road across a bridge. I followed her guidance and spotted Andy and Katherine, standing on the bridge. We followed the trail under the freeway, and up a steep staircase built into the mountain. When the uphill hit I was left behind, but I still found Standing Bear Hostel.

The hostel was selling food. There was a bit of a frenzy around the overpriced shop. Although, the prices weren't what you'd call a bargain deal. I got a quart of milk, a chocolate ice cream pop, and two chocolate oatmeal cookies, (the second one I saved for later.)

Andy told me he wanted to share his mail drop. As I sat waiting for him it seemed as if he had all together changed his mind. For whatever reason he decided to give me some hot chocolate mix.

Katherine and Andy stayed at Standing Bear Hostel, and I moved on.

It was a lot of uphill. That oatmeal cookie waiting for me was a real inspiration to finish the day. Once I knew I had to be close, I worried *What if I can't find the shelter? What if there's a scary man?* So I sang some and ran some. Once I got to the shelter, it was empty. The shelter was an old rugged place said to fit six people. The floor was slanted, so I could imagine that if people did manage to squeeze in six, someone would be squashed on the bottom.

After eating my oatmeal cookie, I texted Katherine and Andy telling them I was alright, and reminding them it was Friday-our rap day. Andy later came up with this:

◻◼◻

Consider this our reintroduction

Due to our induction

To the Hall of Fame.

We'll never be the same.

Getting better every day. For everybody watching us,

Get some exercise. You're collecting dust.

I need a bumper sticker for my pack. Yeah, Maine or bust.

This week was all about the Smokies.

I saw a deer and then some turkeys.

Feisty stole my stuff-sack when I wasn't looking.

And yes, I'm skipping scenes. But that's nothing,

Katherine skips entire storms.

While we were cold, she was warm.

Let's all assume it was my company that she mourned.

That or she didn't want to get stuck in a downpour.

Then the fog blew in and the thunder rolled.

400-600 bears. That's what we were told.

But we didn't see a single one. They must have been on Ninja Mode.

I was let down, like when I went to see Avatar.

I want an original story, not just a flashy war.

As for our dynamic, it's shifting like unsteady ground.

Katherine got a name from *Found*

In which she didn't deserve. When I look at Katherine, I don't think "pertaining to being burned."

There goes my turn.

Stay tuned for next week.

Hopefully, my next rap won't sound so very bleak.

☐■☐

Day 22

I took my time packing up. It drizzled some while I was hiking. I came to a road where a tent was set up...*trail magic.*

Apple, a trail angel made me some coffee. I decided not to hike a twenty some mile day to get to Hot Springs, but instead chill with *Apple.* I hung out for two or so hours, waiting for my group to catch up with me.

I helped *Apple* decide to make a fire, and then I roasted some honey buns... delish. They tasted like they just came out of the oven. *Apple* was so delighted with them that he decided to always roast honey buns for his future trail magic. I roasted a honey bun for *Brownie* and then another for Andy.

I left when Andy did, and told southbounders, "Tell a group of three guys, that their beards are coming along nicely. The happy, blond guy has one blue eye and one brown eye if you wanna make sure it's them."

Next up was Max Patch Bald. I hunkered down, peering out at the 360 degree view of mountains. *Brownie* showed up. I had hiked with *Brownie* before. He was a thru-hiker veteran, except he didn't finish. Three fourths of the way through, he got a job offer as a guide for the wetlands in Florida. I asked him why he didn't just finish the last fourth. "I always wanted to do this as a thru-hike," he replied. He was a big, friendly guy, who hikes at a slow speed, even compared to me.

"We should roll down the hill!" I said.

"Alright," he agreed.

We scanned the grassy bald for a safe place. *Brownie* only rolled several yards before getting dizzy. I was determined to roll down to the bottom of the hill, about a half of a mile away. Well, it all was going well, until I hit thorns. I touched my face and saw blood on my hands. Assuming the worst was over, I tucked in, covering my face as I went. Again all was well until I hit some more thorny patches, scratching my legs and piercing me through my rain coat. Defeated, I hobbled back up, weaving in and out of the brambles.

At the top, I asked *Brownie,* "Does that count, since I didn't make it the whole way to the bottom?"

His eye brows rose."You thought you would make it the whole way?"

I smiled. "Yes."

That night at the shelter, while *Blue Sky* described how wonderful hot chocolate with butter tasted, I had a woeful time making a fire. Andy said I could cook on his stove, but I coaxed that damp wood into lighting. I was sad the fire died before I got my hot chocolate on.

All of a sudden, *Blue Sky* announced that he had extra hot water. I was so happy to have hot chocolate after all. When I began stirring it, I realized there was something solid in my hot chocolate! I fished out a cocoa covered lighter. "Yuck!" The hikers roared in laughter. I would have licked the delicious cocoa goodness off, but with them all watching, I just laid the lighter on the table.

I didn't find it all that funny. "Hey, *Blue Sky* did I get all three points?"

"No, two of them came up to me at once. I caught the second one. But, two others got me." He took out his notepad and tallied the points.

"I have three points in all."

"We're only keeping track of "us" and "them." So far we are losing."

"That's because of me," I said, smiling.

Katherine was named *Sky Peach* at Standing Bear Hostel for having a blue shirt and being from Georgia. I tried to name her things like: *Speedy, Lightning, Swift,* or *Mountain Muncher.* I thought *Ninja* was good, even Andy agreed with me, but she didn't feel the Japanese part.

Sky Peach (*Peach* for short) had been having trouble with her water filter. Honestly, it broke. So she asked to use my Aqua Mira. Ironically, she used my Aqua Mira more than I ever had. I would have given it to her, but I liked to be needed, even if it was a tiny thing like this.

I couldn't sleep. An old guy snored in my ear, and it poured during the night. I felt like I was up all night, but apparently I got some sleep, since I missed the thunder that the others were talking about.

Day 23

Trail maintainers had sticks stacked in a pile to warn hikers who missed the blazes not to go that way. But, I stepped over a pile of sticks without realizing it.

Once I was back on track it was easy most of the way. We had two major mountains to climb. Andy was slower because his back hurt, so I walked and talked with him. It could be a chore to get a conversation going with Andy. But people like to talk about what they enjoy.

He started reciting his favorite quotes. He said he could quote anything he'd written in his journals. *Peach* and I teased him about the pink one. He said that the store only had three colors to choose from, and that in order to keep organized, he needed three. I saw his writing; it was similar to a typewriter. He *never* used an eraser, or crossed out *anything*. He never even wrote on the backside of a paper. It was all neat, and well thought-out. It was safe to say that Andy was a very thoughtful person. Not to be mistaken with being nice. Not to say Andy wasn't nice. He just wasn't friendly.

He said that most people, at a first glance, thought he was either stupid or a genius. I asked him what he thought, and he said, "A genius." I remember him saying, "Everything I say is the truth." I thought it was a bit shallow for him to think he was always right, but intriguing nonetheless.

Andy complained about how he missed playing the piano, and how he wished the place where we were staying had a piano. Andy said if there wasn't a piano he would cry. I said if there was, I would dance to his playing.

As we were getting close to Hot Springs, Andy said, "What if Hot Springs is just a joke? What if all this time it's been on the maps and you can Google it, but it's just there to fool people?"

I found this difficult to relate with. "I would be upset," I said. When we got a view of the town, I said, "Look, you don't have to worry. Hot Springs is there alright."

Then he said, "Suppose those buildings are made out of cardboard and it's a joke that people set up just to fool us?"

Then I looked harder. "Looks like real buildings to me," I said.

"Oh but," he responded once more, "what if it's just a whole bunch of empty buildings, and no one actually lives there."

I was just as excited as he was to be almost in town and, it bothered me to think Hot Springs could be a joke, though I tried playing along, saying, "And there are abandoned cars, and fake people scattered all over."

The dirt path turned into a road and the road passed straight through Hot Springs. For a name as widely spoken about, the town was tiny.

Peach wasn't in sight. We needed to know where she decided to stay, since *Peach* planned everything.

We stopped by the Dollar General and saw *Found*. He was the guy that named Katherine: *Caustic*. He pointed out the building that *Peach* was staying at before he left for his second pint of ice cream.

Elmer was the owner of Sunny Bank Inn. He had been cooking for hikers for decades. A young guy named Dan was our tour guide.

Dan said he got a job working for Elmer after he left home and was hitchhiking around as a drifter. He said that Elmer took him in and he has been working at Sunny Bank ever since. Dan showed real enthusiasm for the place. The house was antique, and so was everything in it. There were bookshelves everywhere. There was a music room, a drawing room, a kitchen, and there were ducks, geese, and a dog outside.

Lucky for Andy there was a piano, and I danced a bit.

I met *Skippy*, who got his name because he ate an abundance of peanut butter. "I guess I could have chosen Peter Pan or Jif," said *Skippy*.

"Are you here alone?"

"I'm hiking with a friend, Kelsey. She'd rather tent than stay here. There was a third, but he quit the second day."

"How did that happen?"

"Well, he said he broke a tooth and needed to go to the dentist. But, his family definitely didn't help. No one thought he could make it," said *Skippy*.

"Did you think he could make it?" I asked.

"Not really, but I didn't think he'd quit that early."

"No kidding. The second day? He probably spent more time putting together hiker boxes than he did hiking."

"Yeah," *Skippy* agreed. "It was his idea so I can thank him for that. But yeah all that planning and he's off the trail just like that."

"Do you guys share maildrops?" I asked.

"Yeah, our mail drops will provide us with half the food we eat on the trail. The thing that sucks is that my friend persuaded us pack food both I and Kelsey both hate. And now we are stuck eating it for the next six months."

"What kind of stuff?"

"Velveeta cheese. You know that fake cheese, which happens to be very heavy. I hate it. Absolutely hate it. But, we have it in every mail drop from here to Maine."

"Just call up your mail drop person and ask them to take out the Velveeta cheese," I said.

"I paid for it, so I'm going to eat it," said *Skippy* grimly.

"Do you have a mail drop here in Hot Springs?"

"Not for resupply. I'm waiting for my camera to come in the mail. It was supposed to come today, but hopefully it'll arrive tomorrow."

"How could you forget to bring a camera?"

"Oh, I had a camera, said *Skippy*. "It just rolled into a stream and quit working."

For dinner, I had this feeling that the main dish hadn't shown up after dessert arrived. That was because it was a vegetarian meal. No one had clued me in, later *Peach* mentioned that Elmer had a vegetarian restaurant before he came to own Sunny Bank Inn.

After supper we gathered in the living room, where *Found* wowed us with his vast knowledge of gear. He had a girl named *Butter* laid out all her belongings on the floor, which included a whole pile of unneeded things. There was a full size Bible, an unnecessary large first aid kit, and then most noteworthy, a *glass* jar of fake butter. He persuaded her to buy a new backpack, since hers was too big and she was carrying too much stuff. Overall she got re-outfitted for around eight hundred dollars

FIVE

The Last Straw

March 28th – April 1st

Day 24

For lunch I got vanilla ice cream and mixed in cocoa. As I slurped up a mango, Andy kept reminding me that if I wanted to do laundry, he had something that he missed. I didn't feel like going to the Laundromat. *What's the point anyway? I would be all sweaty the moment I hit the trail anyway,* but looking down at my clothes, which were marinating in mango juice and all dusted in cocoa, I had to admit I was a mess.

As I walked to and from the Laundromat, I waved at Andy and *Peach*, through the glass. It made me concerned that they were eating out with two other hikers without me. So many things were coming between us and I felt helpless to stop it.

I saw *Peach* again inside our room. She had bought her own water purification drops. She proclaimed she was now an ultra-light-weight hiker like me. It was an odd thing to say, I was no ultra-light-weight hiker and neither was she. However I did lighten up my pack, by stuffing my down coat into an envelope and sending it home. It was like magic with all the extra space. It was great; I didn't have to strap half of my pack's contents on the outside of my pack any longer.

I tried to watch Batman with Andy, *Peach*, *Butter* and *Diva*, but instead I talked to a speedy hiker named *Hermes*, who was daily hiking twenties. Afterwards, I went outside to marvel at the spring flowers and chase the ducks.

I made it a point to join the others for dinner. They were talking in code and didn't clue me in.

We walked back to the hostel, where I sat in on a little surprise birthday party for *Diva*. *Peach* and Andy didn't tell me they had gotten him a princess crown and his favorite Ben and Jerry's Ice cream. I joined in singing happy birthday and I smiled as he blew out the candles. They were all laughing like they had been best friends forever. I felt like an intruder. Here I was with my "friends", but I could see they had pushed me aside and replaced me. I didn't know these other people, but Andy and Katherine thought they were fantastic. So much so they threw a party for them. I sat there thinking how I could remedy the situation, but no solution came to mind.

Day 25

My group was planning to hike a twenty. The last time I hiked a twenty I barely took any breaks. I was nervous. I woke up before the sun and soon *Butter* came down to write in her journal. She asked if *Peach* and Andy wanted to go to the diner

"No, I'm sure they want to sleep in," I said, hoping they would so I could get ahead.

She wasn't convinced, so she went to open *Peach's* door. I heard a loud shriek from a startled *Peach*. She laughed. "I almost peed myself." They all ended up going to the restaurant together.

I headed off, walking through town on the sidewalk. For a while the main road made a big deal of imbedded AT symbols in the sidewalks, then all of a sudden they stopped and I had to search for the blazes. At the end of the sidewalk, I found myself peering at a fork in the road. I had no idea where to go, but a man in his car pointed me in the correct way.

In no time, I was sweating. The trail took a steep turn and I got lost again, but caught my error quickly. I hiked a lot of uphill and walked along some roads without seeing anybody.

Five miles down, with five more till lunch. I saw two hikers, digging in a cooler. TRAIL MAGIC! I grabbed two apples and a power bar. I spent the next five miles playing leapfrog with the boys Jack and Isaac – their names made me think of the drink Jack Daniels. I learned that Isaac had part of a sleeping pad across his waist, because he was too skinny for his hip-belt.

I saw *Peach*, Andy, *Diva,* and *Butter,* all trailing behind me. Right as they caught up we arrived at the shelter.

"Feisty, you have to stop littering," Peach accused.

53

"I didn't litter, at least if I did it was an accident. Anyway how do you know it was me?"

"I know it was you because it was a power bar wrapper."

She was right it was mine, but I wondered why she had to be so mean about it. She was all I had and she was dangling me off a cliff with no remorse.

"How's the stream?" *Diva* asked, as *Peach* came back from getting water.

"It's not piped."

I went down to get water and spotted a pipe. I came back saying. "Actually just so you know, there is a pipe." I knew it would rub Katherine the wrong way, but I didn't care.

I took a seat on the picnic table and could see a glow on Andy's face as he took the first bite of his burger.

"Did you get that at a Wendy's?" I asked, making small talk.

Peach interrupted before Andy said a word. "You are so stupid! Did you *see* any Wendy's in Hot springs?"

I was speechless. "No. I guess not." Her words pieced deep. Why? I asked myself. Why was this happening to me? She could call others stupid, in fact she had. I should have known she would insult me, too. But we had gone through so much together. She was the first person I knew on the trail. I had no intention to leave, and hoped this would all go away.

The third five mile section, all five of us hiked in a parade like fashion. The downhills were too slow and the uphills had me out of breath. I didn't complain. It surprised me that *Peach* and Andy didn't mind walking at their slower pace. They had always passed me up when they followed at my pace, what made these new people any different?

At a road we ran into a sign announcing a family dinner just a short walk away. At the steep driveway, I dropped my pack. As I ran up, *Peach* called, "Cheater!"

The man introduced himself as *Hercules*. He said, "Welcome home," with a huge smile on his face. The place was a beautiful cabin with gorgeous, orange wood. *Hercules* asked our names and had us take off our boots. Then he led us to the bathroom to wash our hands.

Sitting at a family table, we were all asked if we would like a waffle. They had a drink menu and I ended up drinking two and half glasses of milk. Then we all got a big bowl of meaty stew, but I couldn't finish it and gave half of it to Jack, who had showed up earlier. Next we had four options for dessert, all including ice cream. We had lots of laughs. I was so full that I was bulging. We were all wondering how we could possibly hike after eating so much.

I didn't want to leave, but I didn't want to get to the shelter after dark either. Like always, I asked *Peach* how many miles we had left. She said, "Five...but it's only three."

I looked at her puzzled. "How could it be five and also only three?"

She looked at me like I was the biggest retard of the century. "You're so stupid! It's three in the afternoon," she said. Her words echoed in my head, but I tried to smother them and smile past the hurtful words.

The fourth five mile section, I lost my group right off the bat. I felt like the fat kid who gorged at Willie Wanka's factory as I waddled along.

At the shelter, I was glad to see a fire was assembled. The guys there were high, but I didn't notice until *Peach* commented about it. The one confessed he smoked when he went out to get firewood. I immediately saw two other guys come in with armfuls of wood. They stacked it beside a monstrous pile of wood.

"I'm pretty sure you have enough wood for tonight," I said.

"We're getting wood for the next people that come." He looked around. "I hear it's supposed to rain. Perhaps we should put the wood under the shelter," he said to his friend nearby.

One hiker was ranting about his idea to mix ramen noodles with hot cocoa. "It would taste sensational."

His friend said, "You've been talking about this since Springer: let's see you do it."

The people around the table began to encourage him. He finally made some, while leaving out the ramen seasoning. Everyone watched him slurp up a spoonful. His face contorted. "This is puke nasty!"

He offered it to his friend, who also agreed it was awful. The concoction was then poured into the privy. "People are gonna think someone had extremely bad diarrhea."

"Anyone up for some privy noodles?" he repeated over and over, roaring in laughter.

As night settled in, the same guys were playing a card game and invited me. They had little candles: one for each player to see their cards. It gave the game a warm feel. We didn't keep score, but if we had, I would have been winning. I played until I was too tired to care.

I then went into my bivy, since there was no room left in the shelter.

Day 26

At midnight I woke up to rain. Condensation drips were wetting my sleeping bag. My mind did summersaults. If all my things were wet, what was I going to do? I wondered if I should just get up and start hiking. I took a deep breath. I needed as much energy as I could get. I had to get to sleep, I told myself to forget the rain. Forget the rain; the words echoed in my head as I tried to think about nothing

When it was about four in the morning, the conditions had become worse and my sleeping bag was saturated. I packed up in the night rain, and then put my backpack under the shelter roof. Everyone inside was sound asleep.

I sat shivering on the dirt floor of the shelter, nibbling on this and that, watching mice run over and under my legs. That was until a man in the shelter invited me up on the platform to keep warm. My feet felt like icicles, but they made me take off my shoes before wedging between two hikers. About an hour later, it was light enough to start hiking.

There was something haunting about the gangly trees swaying and the suffocating fog. The gravestones that were scattered along the trail seemed to fit with the surrounding atmosphere. To keep my feet dry, I had to balance across the ledges of puddles that spanned across the six foot road.

I got to the shelter, the one where I was told we would be staying the night. This was a monumental occasion; I had never been the first one to get to a shelter. I unpacked and got my stuff out to dry.

It was two o'clock when I saw the parade of four approaching. I stood on the picnic table to usher them inside. "Welcome," I said smiling. Instead, they passed by without blinking. I called to them, "Where you going?"

"The next shelter," *Butter* replied, while turning out of view.

I stood still while listening to them talk. It made no sense that they could do something so cruel, so I reasoned with myself that they must have been pulling a prank. I could hear laughing and imagine them hiding along the trail, ready to come back and surprise me. I waited several minutes before calling out, "Hey guys?...guys?" but there was no response.

They had hiked on without me.

I packed everything up in a rush and tried to catch up to them. I thought about home, the only people that cared about me. If I were home I would be at church. I missed worship, and sang some songs that came to mine. I felt bitter. I thought about how Jesus was betrayed by his friends. I sang as loud as I wanted. Singing made me feel a little better.

There were eight more miles to go. The sun peaked out from the cloudy sky only for a moment. I thought I was going quite fast, but I never caught up to the others. I got worried that I missed the shelter as the rain dripped from the sky. I was cold and ran out of water. When it started to darken, I thought about camping along the trail. I gave a sigh of relief when I saw the sign for Hogback Ridge Shelter. Hallelujah!

As I walked into a place that reminded me of a refugee camp, with tents scattered everywhere, I realized I would have yet another night camping in the rain. I looked in the shelter to double check, Andy and *Peach* found room, but at least *Diva* was camping.

On the bright side, there was a fire already lit. The drizzling rain saturated me as I cooked quinoa on the flames. I dumped my food bag on the table. I still had a pepperoni log and there was no way I was going to eat it. I had my share of heartburn and other burning sensations. When I bought it for my mail drops I thought I had struck gold, but now that gold was weighing down my pack and I needed it gone. I had already given a bit to *Blue Sky* and now *Hermes* seemed overly happily to take it. I felt guilty, because I knew what a nasty surprise that pepperoni could punch. I warned, "Make sure to only eat a little at a time."

Because I had such little sleep the night before, my only hope was that it wouldn't pour. I sent my mom a text, saying where I was and hoping it would not rain, before passing out in exhaustion.

Day 27

Ten miles in, we lunched at Big Bald shelter. *Peach* left early after hearing Andy's plan to go to town. He was excited about getting a grease filled hamburger. Then Andy left without a word. *Butter* took her time cooking up beans. I got antsy waiting for her, but got to I hiked with *Diva* and *Butter*.

"Whew, *Butter*. You are flatulent today," said *Diva*, fanning the air ahead of him. "This is unbearable – must be from all the beans you eat. Let me take the lead," he said, as he moved ahead of *Butter*.

"What does flatulent mean?" I asked.

"Sassafras, it's a polite way of saying someone farted." Taking a look at his guide book, he said. "There's an uphill section coming up. If we are going to Erwin tonight we better take it slow so we don't wear ourselves out. *Butter* you have a good pace, but it is too fast uphill."

"I'll lead," I offered.

"You *are* slower," said *Diva*, in thought. "Okay Sassafras, take the lead. Remember, take it slow. And don't sing. I can't stand it when you sing."

It meant a lot that they let me lead. I felt so honored.

"So Sassafras, are you going to town with us?" asked *Diva*.

"Nah, I don't have any reason to push to town."

It was a long hike, our third twenty mile day in a row. *Diva* knew he would have to hike in the dark, and he was planning the logistics. When we got to the shelter at four, Andy and *Peach* were still there. I suppose *Peach* had persuaded Andy not to go to town, but when Andy heard that *Diva* and *Butter* were going, he started packing up at once.

Diva called Uncle Johnny's Hostel while *Peach* kept on saying, "I'm staying." The more she said it, the more I didn't believe her. At the moment she heard *Diva* scheduling a ride to get them to a hotel, she was busy packing up, too. She mentioned that they should find movie theaters to have a movie marathon. They marched off chattering, until I could hear them no more.

I could have ran after them. I could have night-hiked alongside them and split the cost of the taxi and split the hotel bill. I could have zeroed in town with them, watching a movie marathon with *Peach* and enjoying a cheeseburger with Andy. But for the first time in my trip, I was done with them.

I was sick of being treated like dirt. I was sick of hiking high miles. I was sick of them and their cruelty. I didn't know what I was going to do; I was so codependent. Who would be there to tell me how many miles I had to the next shelter? For the entire whole trip I feared being alone, but at that moment it seemed the better option.

I was in a place called No Business Shelter, along with *Fire-Walker* and *Hermes*. *Fire-Walker's* presence gave me the creeps. He lay with a bug net draped over him. He said it kept the mice out. I felt safe with *Hermes*. I got in my sleeping bag, and tried to warm up. It was wonderful to finally stay inside a shelter. I sat mesmerized as the sleet fell.

When I awoke there was a dusting of snow on the ground. The six miles to town was long, but relaxing. Everything was peaceful. The fog that had hung in the air day after day finally had vanished.

Once I got to the road, I saw Uncle Johnny's Hostel. It may have been April Fools, but it was no joke that I was done dealing with my hiking group. Now I found myself searching for another group as if I was playing partner tag. *Mile High*, *Llama Legs*, and *Data* were there. They greeted me. It would have been fun to hike with them, but they were heading out just as I arrived.

I saw *Found*. "So you're a solo female hiker now? Don't worry it won't last long. A guy will be hiking with you in no time. That's just the way the trail works," he said with a wink.

I gave half a smile. I couldn't decipher if I was to be concerned or glad.

I bought my own AT guide. With it I had the knowledge of when I'd pass the four-hundred mile mark, and where the grocery stores were in towns. I'd know where all the hostels, hotels, and motels were, along with their prices. I'd know where the next resupply places were, so I could buy enough food. With the guide I could find water; know how many people fit in the shelters, and see the elevation profiles. I was past asking for stats. I was independent.

A boy introduced himself as Harry, I later found out his trail name was *Shit Huffer*. Great name…it all came about when he took a picture of himself pretending to get high off human waste, known as Jenkem. It was a joke. He showed it to his friends, and before long his picture swept through the Internet like wildfire. Not limited to being broadcast on the News. The guy on the trail that named him did a double take and recognized him. "Hey you're that shit huffing kid!" He had one of those names you hear about before you meet the person. I knew he hated the name, but it just stuck to him.

I joined *Trighten, Ducky* and Harry to an all-you-can-eat pizza and salad bar! *Trighten,* an English 101 professor at a community college, was complaining about how immature some of his students were. They would raise their hands to go pee, make excuses for being late, and complain about their grades.

When Harry heard I was a Pennsylvanian he asked to see my driver's license. I told him I didn't have it. He explained he had a fake Pennsylvanian ID. He made me check if his looked legit. It looked real to me. I was surprised that he had ordered it from China.

The price for the meal was four dollars. I piled my plates with a variety of pizza slices and got a heaping plate full of salad. I was so full I didn't need to go out to eat for supper, even if it was dirt cheap.

I saw everyone but Andy from "my" group. *Diva* was happy to see me. *Peach* told me that she hadn't gone to the movies after all, since they were closed. They got a four person cabin at Uncle Johnny's. I asked *Peach* if I could see what the cabins looked like. She let me in. I felt like an intruder. They were all snug, watching Jurassic Park. I stayed long enough to see a dinosaur eat a man.

The bunk room was just fine. There were four of us. Harry and I attempted to make a fire in the stove. It was smoky because the chimney seemed to be clogged. Then Harry attempted to start an ancient VHS player. It would have been a miracle had it worked.

□■□

I wonder if Andy and *Peach* will keep writing raps...

I'm going to keep raps a tradition,

Hopefully the words flow like ammunition.

Perhaps I won't play with the same cast,

But that doesn't mean this show won't be a blast.

Well so far we made it safe and sound,

To our first trail town.

Andy said if there wasn't a piano he'd cry,

The next day he'd rather say good-bye.

We hiked a long ways,

Had three twenty mile days.

I had fun hiking with *Diva* and *Butter*.

Thankfully their pace doesn't make me suffer.

So nice to have a bed and a pillow,

And to be completely filled yo.

What will happen in the future I can't measure,

But pizza I know is my town pleasure.

Ups and Downs I won't fuss,

I'm soon going to be in Damascus.

□■□

SIX

Solo Female Hiker

April 2nd – 9th

Day 29

I was the only one who took Uncle Johnny's complementary shuttle for breakfast. My driver was almost toothless. He dropped me off at a convenience store. He said he would be back in an hour. I made my way past shelves of food to the counter in the back. I took a stool next to town folk, and then ordered a small biscuits and gravy for eighty cents.

To kill time, I consumed two pints of ice cream. When I hopped back in the car, Toothless asked if I had been waiting long.

"No, I'm just cold," I said.

"Did you have the large biscuits and gravy?" he asked

"No, I had a small, but I had two pints of ice cream." I grinned.

"No wonder you're cold!"

When the man dropped off some boxes at the post office, he asked for a hand and gave me a Snickers in return. I asked him what he thought of Uncle Johnny's previous competition, Miss Janet. He used some crude language to insult her. I didn't believe a word he said. I already heard legend passed down of her overwhelming generosity. I just didn't understand why Uncle Johnny's crew had to be so hostile.

I hadn't even seen Uncle Johnny in person. When I got back to pay for my stay, they lost my receipt. Then they charged me a good deal over the total. Later I heard that Uncle Johnny's crew were tightfisted swindlers. For example when I was there, they had announced that they had fresh brewed coffee multiple times during my stay. Once they even said they had complimentary danishes with the coffee. I had looked everywhere for the them, but it was only later I realized the danishes were just bait to get more hikers to come, because there was an unspoken fee for each cup of coffee.

I hit the road in a foul mood. I was also aware of the fact that a mother bear had thieved food recently in the vicinity. The bear had entered a tent and grabbed a food bag underneath a hiker's head.

When I got to the first shelter, I considered staying. It was only four miles in, but *Trighton* was there. He had a fire going and had a whole BBQ set up for dinner. He told me I should stay. Then he went into a spiel about his very low mileage schedule. In the end, I decided loitering around would be a waste of a day.

When white haired Dave passed, I joined him until he fell behind. For lunch, I ate a Snickers. As I ran into Brownie, I thought about camping with him. He wanted to camp where he had in 2003, when he was stuck several days in a severe snowstorm. He said his dog acquired dreadlocks of frozen fur. Ever since that incident he won't make an animal suffer the trail again.

I then passed two hikers and they both jumped. They confessed that they thought I was a bear.

For the majority of the day, I was out of water. I made the mistake of passing two streams, knowing I had little water. Afterward, there wasn't a stream for miles. I remembered Mr. Toothless telling me many hikers had to be rescued from severe dehydration. I felt like an idiot.

When, I met a southbound thru-hiker. I asked him if he had seen water; he said he hadn't paid attention. He was too happy about finishing the trail. He said I was the 21st thru-hiker he had seen that day. He was happy, and I was happy for him, for almost completing his hike. Later, I got so thirsty that I went survival mode by scooping up snow that lay in patches. I followed the trail onward.

Ahead, Harry was at the shelter and so was *Skippy* and *Ducky* along with some other hikers and kids. I impressed the hikers when I ate an entire packet of bacon. Then I poured bacon juice on the fire, which it gobbled up in a plume of flames.

One man was talking about how he snored and used to have trouble getting passed stage two of sleep. He was fired after he had been too drowsy at work. After extensive research at sleep research clinics, he decided to pay three thousand dollars for a dentist to make him a mouth contraption. He said it helped. He even demonstrated how it worked. His son commented, "See, he looks like a *special* person."

Day 30

I was sad to leave the warmth of friendliness in the morning. I later took a break and *Skippy* passed. I told him, "Only two more miles 'till the next shelter!" I would have liked to join him, but I had just sat down and had my possessions scattered all over the ground.

Several minutes later *Skippy* walked back. I wondered for a moment if he decided he wanted to hike with me. "Was I on the right trail?" he asked. I thought it was correct, but it turned out that he had gone down the wrong way. I was glad I wasn't the one getting lost for once. I thanked him for saving me the extra mileage, and then joined him on the correct trail.

I asked *Skippy* if he knew anyone that quit hiking. For some reason, I felt accomplished when people quit. I guess I felt that I had a better chance of finishing. *Skippy* named off quite a few. One was a guy doing twenties the first week. He churned his feet into hamburgers and called his mom to pick him up.

"Oh, I know another. *Found*. He's off the trail."

"No way!" I said.

Skippy explained that *Found* had received a job offer to introduce wanna-be thru-hikers to the Pacific Crest Trail. It was his dream job and he was competing against another hiker who got off the trail for the same job. "He said, he'll come back and hike the rest of the AT if he doesn't get the job."

At the shelter was Kelsey, the girl who has been hiking with *Skippy*. We divided out some Kool-Aid packets left behind. We were so excited. "Why would someone leave Kool-aid behind?" But apparently Kool-Aid without sugar tastes awful. I bet the next set of hikers would do the same thing.

The path up Roan Mountain was covered in snow. When I didn't see a blaze, I just followed the footprints. I got bored of the dark tunnel of pine going up and up and up.

Finally, at the top it was sunny. The view wasn't great and the parking lot with locked bathrooms didn't help. There was a shelter nearby, which I was thinking about going to, but I missed it.

I hiked down an icy trail that turned to gravel through the evergreen forest. Next there were two balds, where many pedestrians were walking about. There was a young couple dressed up, holding hands, and laughing. My heart sank in envy as they passed. The views from atop the balds were astounding. The wind blew fierce. I felt on top of the world.

After the glorious views was a nasty long slosh of mud. It was so slippery, it was like skiing. Had I fallen I would have been covered in mud.

I was exhausted when I found a rinky-dink shelter. *Skippy* and Kelsey were there, too. *Skippy* told me how he realized the only way to complete this hike was to treat hiking as a job. The wind gave me some trouble making a fire. And the wind continued to howl in the shelter the entire night.

Day 31

Skippy groaned when the sun lit up the shelter. Instead of getting up he pulled his sleeping bag over his face, saying he felt sick. I left.

On the balds I was blown about like a kite. I had to walk sideways, to keep from being blown off the narrow trail.

After the beautiful balds the trail went through a four-wheeler park. I squinted at the low sun, straight ahead was a sharp climb, I could see the top so I huffed and puffed my way up as fast as I could. Then something nightmarish happened. Standing at a cross section with five different paths, none bearing a white blaze, I stood scanning one trail at a time for clues. The flattest trail looked most promising, but I stopped short when I noticed the absence of footprints in the soft ground. Turning about, I heard deep motors growing louder. I waved down two guys on four-wheelers and asked them which trail was the Appalachian Trail.

"None. You must have missed the turn off at the bottom of the hill. But, if you follow this trail on the right: it'll meet back with the Appalachian Trail."

Before I left, the one guy asked, "Have you got any good weed?"

"What? No," I said, shocked. I hiked on contemplating why someone would ask *me* for weed. *Perhaps hikers are known for carrying weed,* I thought.

The last part of this day's hike was long, much longer than I had anticipated. I was relieved to arrive at the three story shelter. It was crowded with hikers. The group of four including *Peach* were there. I wasn't planning on catching up to *Peach* and wasn't sure what to do.

I could have acted stand-offish towards *Peach*, but instead I just said, "Hi."

Taking a space next to *Peach*, she told me about a place where the host was Jewish and did odd things. She went to take a shower, but the shower only dripped. She said they slack-packed over Roan Mountain, then she proceeded to ask me if I had hike Roan Mountain.

"*Yeah*," I said half confused. *Did she think I skipped it?*

When she saw me studying my guide book, she asked, "Is that mine?"

"No, I bought my own."

"Nice. Well good for you." She said.

Andy, on the other side of *Peach*, didn't say a word to me. There was no need to make excuses for him, because that was just the way he behaved.

Mile High was there without the rest of his group. He had an injury and couldn't keep up with the pace of his group. He was chipper and fun to be around. His group had a thing where they all carried something unnecessary. *Mile High* had found a shovel without a handle that he was carrying in hopes of presenting to

Llama Legs. *Llama Legs* was known for breaking or losing his spoons. *Mile High* had the shovel declaring, "He won't be able to lose or break *this* spoon." He told us of a time *Llama Legs* had broken his one plastic spoon and in attempts to fix it he glued a triangle of wood supporters to it. The only problem was that it would not fit in his peanut butter jar. So he ended up eating with a tent stake.

There was a powerful thunderstorm. During the night I was woken up to cheering coming from a bunch of soaked night hikers. They were *BackFlip*, *Patches* and *Yogi*. While they were changing into dry clothes, *BackFlip* explained that he got his name because he always wanted to do a back flip. *Patches* was named from his beard's growing patterns.

I dreamed of family and food all night. I was at a family reunion with my mom's thirteen brothers and sisters. In my dream, I sat on a crowded bench, leaning on a plastic covered table, peering at my aunt Verna cutting up a cake. I remember thinking how wonderful that piece of cake was.

Then I appeared at a bible study. It was the same bible study held when I was a child. We would play tag outside near the fenced-in cows. The charming Scottish farm boys had always said they loved the smell of manure. At the end of the bible study we would all have snacks and dessert. There I was in my dream, searching the snack table for food to take on my hike.

Day 32

I woke up to rain, and then all of a sudden it turned to snow. Some decided to wait it out, while others like Andy and *Peach* didn't waste time. After I saw them leave, I felt urged to follow. The romantic feel of snow falling through the air ended when pellets of snow cascaded from the sky. I would have enjoyed the beauty of the white balls bouncing all about the forest floor, had I not had my face pelted in the process.

Mile High's injury of a hurt toe brought him to say his pace was really slow, but he hiked faster than me.

I hiked with him a bit and he told me *Data* got his name from always knowing exactly where they were and how many miles they had hiked. When *Mile High* asked how many miles we had gone, I gave him an optimistic answer instead of a concrete one.

I had lunch and ate everything I had left. It was a terrible lunch, compared to *Mile High's,* who was sitting next to me. He was gorging on tortillas with Nutella and trail mix. He complained that his Nutella was stiff. All I had were scrapings off the bottom of my peanut butter jar, grated Parmesan cheese and a pinch of trail mix with all the M&M's already picked out. I told him how I was out of every ounce of food.

"That's wonderful," he said, in a congratulatory way. "I love going into town with all my food eaten."

Contrary to him, my stomach twisted into a knot when I thought about not having any food. He asked me if I was going to the hostel named Kincora. I didn't know what I was doing. I had heard *Peach* and Andy were headed to a hostel. I supposed Kincora was the one they were talking about. I knew I needed food, and they knew where to go. So that was where I went.

I was walking on a road leading to Kincora, when a car slowed down, the window rolled down, and a man asked, "Need a ride?"

"Uh, do you know where Kincora is?" I asked.

"No," he said.

"Thanks, but I think it's close. I'll just walk there," I said to make him leave.

While I was walking along the road, I saw a mailbox that read Kincora. I was walking up the house staircase when someone grabbed my attention. It was *Llama Legs* with *Data.* "The hostel is this way," said *Llama Legs.* They were packing up to leave.

"Hey! I was just hiking with *Mile High* today." I said.

"Really?" they marveled. "Where is he headed? Is he feeling better?" they asked. I was glad to answer their questions.

I went inside and was expecting *Peach* and them to be there. I asked a group of hikers chatting on the sofas, but no one saw them. It was relieving in a way. I then took a seat with the hikers. When they asked how I was, I explained to them my deepening hunger, with no food to tame it. They offered me cold pizza, without asking anything in return.

I hadn't met any of them before. The majority of them started in February. They calculated my mileage and told me I was speeding through. That was the first time I heard someone say that. I had always felt slow.

A girl named *Steady* asked, "Are you hiking alone?"

"Yeah. I guess," I said.

She beamed with excitement, "You're the first solo female hiker I've met! Other than me," she said, as if I was winning an award.

Bob Peoples was the owner of the hostel and he maintained a section of the AT for years. He was a wonderful man, who brought the atmosphere of Christmas day. Inside the hostel, the walls and ceilings were covered with pictures of hikers on Mount Katahdin. I found it remarkable that such a large number of people had thought of him after their thru-hike to send him a picture of their finish.

Hikers compared Bob Peoples to Chuck Norris. They even carved their own jokes about him in shelters.

"Bob Peoples doesn't hang bear bags. He hangs bears."

"When Bob Peoples goes to shelters the mice bring him food."

"Bob Peoples gives his boots blisters."

"The AT took six months off to hike Bob Peoples."

"Bob Peoples was infuriated because Paul Bunion took his ax."

I was upset with the way some hikers treated the generosity of Bob Peoples. They stole the toilet paper and donations. He only asked for five dollars of donation – enough for him to keep hikers.

Bob Peoples took us to town. We sat in the back of his pickup with a cover from the wind and pillows to sit on. I got breakfast foods for the next morning. And a bunch of baked good, bagels, and cream cheese for the trail. I got an ice cream carton of moose tracks for dinner. I started eating the ice cream in the back of the truck.

"Don't you love it," a fellow hiker said. "We can eat *anything* and still lose weight. I've already lost fifteen pounds." I smiled and hoped he was right.

Bob Peoples invited me to take the couples room. I felt very honored. "When there are no couples, I lend this room to a lady," He told me. It was the most privacy I'd had for a long time.

Day 33

I woke up at six to make breakfast for everyone. There were blueberry muffins, pancakes, bacon, and eggs. There were at least seven of us who ate. After I made a bunch of food, I got hungry and *Yogi* volunteered to work the grease popping fry pans. I was hoping for a bit of compensation, although none came, it was nice to finally cook up a full fledged family style meal. I had been dreaming of cooking a real breakfast for some time.

I started off, happily filled. I walked along the road with the sun's warming light upon me. I had a major mountain to climb. Part way up, I decided to try going barefoot. The moss and soft dirt were a trifle of bliss. The rocks weren't so welcoming. It was a great way to air out my feet for once.

I wasn't able to fit my shoes in my pack, but I had picked up a clip from the Kincora hiker box, so I could hang them off my pack, along with my krocs. I left my gators in the hiker box, since they became more of a hassle than anything else. The useless things outweigh the useful things in hiker boxes. The winner in this particular box for the most useless item went to a pair of five pound ankle weights.

At the top of the climb, I sat down to put on my shoes when *Patches*, *BackFlip* and *Yogi* showed up. I told them I hiked barefoot.

"And? Why would you wanna do that?" was their reaction.

I fell in line, taking the caboose. They were hiking fast, but I could handle it, since it was downhill. They were talking about hiking until sun down, to make it to Damascus faster. I thought that was a good idea. They stopped at some registration place and were trying to figure out if they should fill anything out. I just kept going without them.

So, chugging along, not taking long breaks, I ran into *Llama Legs*, *Data*, and *Mile High* taking a break. *Mile High* yelled out, "Hey Broseph!" And they started chanting my name, "*Feisty*! *Feisty*! *Feisty*!"

I joined them, scattered along the trail.

"Are you still hiking with *Peach* and them?" they asked.

"No," I said.

"Aren't they slack packing?" *Llama Legs* asked as if it was a crime.

"*Peach* told me they slack packed over Roan Mountain." I answered.

"So are Andy and *Peach* in a relationship?" they asked, intrigued.

"Well, I couldn't say for sure. Last I know *Peach* was frightened that Andy might like her, and she didn't know what to do," I responded, to the best of my knowledge.

Llama Legs and *Mile High* were really enjoying this. "Is Andy *always* in a bad mood?" *Mile High* asked.

"Yeah, why is he so hostile?" *Llama Legs* asked in agreement.

"It's not that he's in a bad mood. He just doesn't talk to people he doesn't know. He doesn't like wasting his time on a conversation to later find out that they aren't worth his time."

They didn't even like *Butter*. She was dead focused on her speed, and would pass other hikers without much more of a greeting than, "Excuse me, let me pass."

After I had finished my snack and the interrogation was over, I moved on without them. At the next shelter, they caught up again. As I was leaving, *Llama Legs* yelled out, "You won't make it to the next shelter, because *you're a girl*."

I couldn't understand why he would say something like that; I wanted to prove him wrong. But in fact, what he said actually came true, in a very bad, awkward way. I was hiking along when I had a sudden urge to take a leak. I was in a tunnel of bushes and spotted an open area ahead. I just didn't see the guy that was already there. Just as I squatted down, he warned me of him being there, and then said he wouldn't look. But it was too late. It was super embarrassing. I hiked a bit further, but was just so miserable. I stopped at a nice outlook. The guys passed and said I looked distressed. I got that a lot. I decided to stay, and let my things air.

Day 34

I slept well, under the sparkling stars. I could see the town lights all over the valley. Early in the morning, I kept hearing rustling, which had me worried something would steal my food. One time I wanted to look over, but I was half asleep and my body wouldn't operate with the command, *Look over there, you might lose your food.*

I was trudging along with the thought in mind that I couldn't make it to town; that was until I ran into *Legion*. I had first seen *Legion* at Uncle Johnny's Hostel. He had walked in with a loud voice that made the bunk room echo as if it were a cave. His hair style had been just as loud. He had a mullet of curly hair faded green, and he was too joyful to dislike.

At the shelter for lunch, *Legion* had the biggest grin, while he was entertaining more than a dozen of elderly folk, all the while stuffing his face with yogied food.

"I barely slept last night. Some shenanigan had a horrible snore, when I say horrible, I mean the shelter literally shook.

Since I couldn't sleep, I just hiked until I got to the next shelter. I was found sleeping on the picnic table, I must have been a sight to the hikers that were staying there," said *Legion,* all happy with himself. "I'm going to hike thirty-five miles today," he boasted. "I only have eighteen more miles to Damascus."

With his overwhelming enthusiasm, I was inspired to try for Damascus myself. It was eight miles to the next shelter. When I got there the guys *BackFlip, Patches* and *Yogi* were there with *Legion.*

They said they were impressed that I could keep up. I said, "What's so impressive? *Peach's* group is way ahead."

"Yeah well, *Peach* and her group cheat. They slack pack."

I was surprised no one liked my former group.

BackFlip gave me some much needed water, which they retrieved from a really steep climb. *Legion* shared his peanut butter and Nutella. I ate most of my food then headed off before the others. I was compelled to keep going since I felt like I was burning daylight.

Ten miles of downhill hiking was all I had to hike until I reached Damascus. Damascus was the king of all trail towns. To kill time I kept myself occupied by reciting movies; I had recited over half of Shrek earlier in the day. I also tried to teach myself to roll R's.

I passed the border into Virginia! The sign read 3.5 miles to Damascus. I was ecstatic. I hadn't been so excited since getting to Springer.

When I got to town, my legs and feet ached and my legs cramped. I wondered if I'd be able to walk in the morning. I was so drained, but so happy to be in town. I had to keep myself focused when I first made it into Damascus. The sun was setting and I still had to find the hostel.

I didn't go to bed until one in the morning, silly me. We went to a karaoke bar, where there resided some very drunk, very happy thru-hikers. They kept saying, "Four hundred and sixty five miles!" Since that was how far we had come from Springer. They poured me a glass of beer. "Have a drink." I sipped mine as they guzzled through pitchers. After they poured me a second glass, I found a young hiker who eagerly took the drink.

One of these drunken hikers was *Ice Ax*. He had hiked the entire Continental Divide Trail. He told us that sometimes he had to bushwhack his own trail. We asked him how he knew which way to go. He then pulled out his compass from under his shirt, and said, "You follow the arrow."

The second drunken hiker was very personal. He repeated his story to whoever showed up. He slurred, "I have been off the trail *three times*, three times, and three times I have come back."

I asked him why he got off. What he said was all over the place. I assumed perhaps his being overweight may have been a factor. This guy would get very close to me and ask, "Why are you hiking?" For a while I could get him distracted on something else, until about the third time when he finally got an answer from me.

"To get in shape," I said.

BackFlip, whom I assume was only there to mooch beer, scolded, "If you want to get in shape go to the gym. The Appalachian Trail is for the adventure. I came out to see the raw beauty of nature. I keep imagining the Whites. They will be so wonderful." He then went on about the Whites, in New Hampshire, and how he would wait days for the perfect weather to saunter across the ridges.

Day 35

Being unable to sleep in was a bit of a bother. I was up at sunrise and went right to the Dollar General. For my meals, I got a box of chocolate cheerios and a gallon of milk. I was quite busy most of the day; resupplying, organizing food, picking out gear at an outfitter, using the library's internet, and doing my laundry.

Almost all the people at the Laundromat were hikers. The guys were using up their quarters on an old arcade game. We then walked to subway for lunch, which tasted amazing, but I felt betrayed because mine wasn't a 5-dollar foot long.

I got drizzled on as I walked back with a laundry basket on my hip. Outside the hostel called "The Place" I ran into *Peach's* little brother, who was using the Wi-Fi. I snapped a picture of the two of us. He told me his family was staying at the neighboring house, with the rest of the group. I felt a wee bit jealous. *Why wasn't I invited? Why didn't my family visit me?*

I saw *Peach's* Dad sitting on the neighboring porch. I gave him a wave as my stomach turned sour. I felt like I got heartlessly seared off. I decided to keep a distance. They were planning to start hiking the next day. It was hard not to make it a competition. It's a status thing; hikers always talk about the hikers ahead. I knew I should be grateful for their help to survive the start, but things hadn't gone all together peachy.

Steady was at the hostel, sitting on the picnic table. She was on the phone with her boyfriend, and she said, "Oh and by the way *Feisty* is standing right next to me." That was weird; apparently her boyfriend was reading my blog.

Availability joined us at the picnic table. He got his name from a man who told him, "God needs your availability." He was cooking up a storm. He had steak, greens, eggs, and tomatoes, all wrapped up in a tortilla. He offered me two eggs and let me fry them in his stove. I made an egg/cheese/tomato sandwich. I wasn't exactly hungry, but free delicious food just can't be turned down. Talking about free food, *Steady* came out with coupons for a free cup of soup. So I jumped up, and joined her to the restaurant. I order a grilled cheese. Then, as if I wasn't full, it was my idea to go across the street and get ice cream cones.

We chatted with a couple who were interested in our hike. It was hard to concentrate, as they talked on and on. I didn't think it wise to stuff myself so much, and I hoped in the future I'd have more control. I tried to read on the couch, but instead, just decided to go to bed early. The night before we got hit with a thunderstorm and *Availability* talked in his sleep.

Day 36

There were a bunch of signs posted in the hostel "two-night stay only." I wanted to stay the third night, so I asked and the house keeper said I could since it was so empty.

I lightened my pack by sending my hand-saw home. At the outfitter, I picked up a large map of the AT for my family to track my progress.

BackFlip invited me to a funeral right outside the outfitter for his pet snail, Albert. Albert's trail name was Stealth, aka Rolling Thunder, but only those who knew him well could call him Rolling Thunder. As *BackFlip*, the keeper of Albert, spoke of his favorite memories with his snail, a harmonica was played by *Mile High*. There was a whole slew of people attending: *Llama Legs*, *Data*, *Harry*, *Yogi*, *Patches*, *Brownie* and *Skippy*.

At "The Place" we played a bunch of card games. There was a rule that if you messed up you had to pick up the pile. Then time after time, I would mess up. In unison the guys would say, "You messed up," with beaming grins while handing me a huge stack of cards.

While we were still playing cards, Noah's flood arrived. Rainwater gushed through the windows, getting the floor drenched. Our whole card game disbanded. People were running all over the house.

"The stairs have water running down them!"

In the middle of *Mile High's room* was a stream of water coming out of the wall.

"The downstairs bathroom has a leak," *Legion* pointed out as I went to look out from the porch. I stared at the torrents coming down.

After the storm, *Ducky* showed up and helped *Steady* finish a puzzle laid out on the floor. *Ducky* and I joined *Steady* for supper, although we had already eaten. She bought us artichoke dip to share. Afterward, we picked up a tub of pecan ice cream. We all dug out our spoons and gorged.

As I sat on the couch snuggled in my sleeping bag, we discussed how young I was compared to *Legion*. They thought it nifty that I was a fourth grader during 9/11, while *Legion* was working at a bar after graduating college. He thought it was brilliant I was out hiking so young. I found what *Legion* had to say intriguing. There are only two ways with *Legion*: either you're best pals or can't bear to be in a mile of *Legion's* presence. This is because *Legion* is *loud* and opinionated. I've already heard *Llama Legs* complain that he's around. I told *Llama Legs*, "At least he's nice."

Legion shared his trail rules. They were:

#1 Always know where your spoon is.

#2 Never stick your foot in a fire.

#3 Your Headlamp works better on your head than in your pack.

#4 When in doubt the trail always goes up.

#5 Poop before you leave.

#6 Never turn down Trail Magic.

SEVEN

Count & Smurf

April 10th – 19th

Day 37

In the drooping heat, I started off with *Steady*, but she was just too fast for me. The AT joined the Virginia Creeper Trail, where I felt like the creeper, while bicyclists swooshed past at incredible speeds.

Next was a multitude of zigzagging. There was a fancy word for zigzagging, called switchbacks – Just back and forth up a mountain. I liked it when the zigzags were short, going back and forth rapidly.

I found it intriguing to see two guys zigzagging beneath me. I stopped to look for them as they disappeared and reappeared through the barren trees.

I was aware I'd be passed soon. When I finally hear the first one, I turned around to see him a good distance behind. It gave me three options: the worst was to stop right away and wait for him to pass. The second was to speed up and try to delay the inevitable. Third was to be patient and in due time step aside. Rude people don't step aside. However, once in a blue moon, I would be in complete bliss of peacefulness, when all of a sudden I would panic – die for a split second – when someone behind me would demand. *"Please* move aside." I then would glare at their vanishing back, yearning for at least an acknowledgment for their disruption.

The two passed me separately, and both said hello. I was glad to see them on top taking lunch. I plopped down beside them. I got to know the two as *Count* and *Smurf*. They were comparing each other's peanut butter to see which had more calories.

"Mine has more," said *Smurf* proudly, inspecting his jar of Peter Pan peanut butter.

"I bet it's just because yours has more sugar," said *Count*, holding his *Skippy* peanut butter. "Mine has only three grams per serving."

"So does mine," answered *Smurf*. "What about protein? Mine has eight grams."

"No way. Mine only has seven. Let me see that," said *Count* taking *Smurf's* jar. "I'll have to get Peter Pan next time. Look, it even has less sodium."

They had heaps of food, and were eating donuts. They were from Maine. Both were eighteen, handsome, blond, and polite. I wondered if we would become friends.

As we were eating, *Steady* came by. *Steady* was visiting the shelter a ways off. She could have saved herself the backtracking by skipping a small section of the trail, but she was a purist. She claimed that she had to go past every single blaze.

The rest of the day's hike was on a ridge. I liked how *Steady* and I had a girl's side to the shelter. *Count* and *Smurf* were on the other side reading their kindles. The heat ruined our appetites. We thought taking out our food would help, but we just stared at it, unmoved.

Day 38

It was so warm that I didn't cling to my sleeping bag, in the morning. On the trail, I cleared a long section of spider webs. The thin threads tickled my arms. I could feel the webs slide up my arms as I moved forward. Then the webs would wrap around my face, causing me to constantly be pulling them off. It didn't take long until I was thoroughly peeved, so I started to hold up my hiking stick to catch the webs. Most of the webs were caught, but some would slide up the pole and tickle my hands. I then started scissoring the hiking sticks up and down, which worked better, but made my arms ached. I was relieved when a southbounder passed me. I thanked him for clearing the way. Fortunately for me, he was taller so I didn't have to deal with the webs any longer.

The two big climbs that day were the two tallest mountains in Virginia. The one, named White Top, made me feel like I was conquering something substantial. The other was Mount Rodgers.

I was excited to have service on the summit of White Top. My dad informed me that my family was coming to visit for Easter! He thought I might be around the Shenandoah National Park by then.

In the Grayson Highlands everything looked like a dream world. There were beautiful wild ponies nibbling on the open grassy fields. Out of the fields, powerful rock terraces jutted upward. The sky was full of fluffy clouds, like the ones painted in the rooms of infants. The views were fabulous in every direction. I could see far mountains and valleys.

At the shelter was a baby mouse. I held him. *Smurf* named him Ricky. The mouse still had his eyes closed. I tried to feed it cheese, and held it, even though *Count,* and *Smurf* weren't sure it was a good idea.

There were ponies ripping up grass near us. One pony had long blond hair; *Smurf* named her Charlene. We heard stories about ponies eating backpacks and biting a man's leg, because he had a snickers wrapper in his pocket.

I made a campfire to roast hotdogs into sizzling delicacies. That made *Count* and *Smurf* jealous. I told *Smurf* to roast his honey bun on the fire, which he actually did.

We went for a dip in the stream. It was freezing. Afterward, I felt like an idiot when I was drying my socks over the fire and melted holes in them.

Smurf and *Count* liked to make fun of the fact that I didn't carry a raincoat and that I had a trash bag for a raincover. However, they were fascinated at my light pack. I, in turn made fun of how much food they carried – however, extra food can't ever be a bad thing.

Day 39

There was another thunderstorm the night before. Ricky the mouse kept squeaking so I let him free. He was gone in the morning. I started a half-hour before the guys again. It was still drippy, so I put on a coat, but I got too warm and peeled off the layers fast.

When I took break, the Maine boys caught up and joined me in the shelter. Afterward we walked as a group. They make me laugh when they speak in Celtic accents. They even had names to go with their alternative personas.

We ran into a guy giving rides to a restaurant. He called his offer trail magic – that sent up a red flag. We took the offer anyhow. Rule number six: never turn down trail magic. I gorged on a bacon-lettuce-tomato sandwich with sweet potato fries. *Smurf* and *Count* both got double bacon cheeseburgers.

In this vacant, southern restaurant was an old television. We were only interested in watching the news. People were discussing Japan's nuclear leakage. More specifically, they were discussing if such a thing could happen in the States. I felt like they were just yapping; saying things like, "We will make sure such a thing will never happen here."

Who can promise something like that? I thought.

I was saddened when they panned pictures of Japan's destruction. I had heard of the catastrophic tsunami disaster via a text from my mother. It wasn't until now that I got an idea of the devastation.

Smurf got a six-pack of beer and *Count* got a Green Apple Smirnoff. They could get away with buying alcohol by looking older with their scruffy boy beards.

On the way back our driver asked for gas money. He said how he had forgotten to gas up and wouldn't be able to make it back. He went on about how he would have to buy some gas from a local farmer. He had *Smurf* and *Count* feeling bad and they both handed him cash. I didn't give any. I didn't feel bad. Later we found out he taxied a lot of other hikers and had asked for gas money from all of them, all the while telling them it was trail magic.

I've heard horror stories of people getting hitches. While on a drive back to the trail, the driver would stop miles from the trail and tells his passengers, "I'm not driving you any further unless I get twenty dollars from each of you." Most of the time the hikers pay. They don't know the area and they don't know how far they are from the trail.

Back on the trail, I got rained on a bit – that was chilly. I could keep up with the Maine boys for a bit longer than usual, since *Smurf* was carrying a six-pack. He kept complaining, but he would not let us help.

I made it to the shelter right before it started raining. The shelter Trimpi was like a miniature stone house, complete with an indoor fireplace that we got going, which toasted up the place nicely. *Delaware Dave* was assembling the fire. I told him I could make it, since I was *experienced*. Instead he took it as a competition.

I couldn't believe how naive *Count* and *Smurf* were about alcohol. I didn't know *Smurfs* objective was to get drunk. One can barely get a buzz off a six pack, plus *Smurf* shared his beer with *Count* and I. It was really funny to watch *Count* grimace as he gulped down the beer. "Why are you drinking it if you don't like it?"

"For the buzz, of course," he answered, annoyed.

"Oh, had I known that, I would have told you to get more. Anyhow, *this* is light beer. It's what six percent alcoholic?"

He looked at the can, "It's three."

The place soon filled with section hikers. They were funny, since they were all proud of their high mileages, which only added up to twelve miles. I liked talking to them, because they made me feel accomplished. They were also friendly and full of energy. Their leader was *Snickers*. He was a past thru-hiker. One in his group had a rich relative in Denmark. I advised him about how to act around the Danish. I even gave a futile attempt to teach him some Danish.

Snickers, who thru-hiked hiked last year, said he started on Valentine's Day. He was slow in the start, but sped up when he got to Virginia. He said that many hikers make the mistake of hiking too fast through Virginia and end up injuring themselves.

Delaware Dave sat down next to me and mentioned how his hands were still sensitive to the cold. "From the terrible weather in the Smokies," he said. Another hiker said his hands hadn't fully recovered either. "Yeah, I thought for sure I was going to have frost bite."

"What was it like?" I asked.

"Well, every morning I had a routine of thawing water. My boots were always hard in the morning, and I couldn't get them on until I thawed them out. I had to deal with knee-high snow and I had to break the trail by myself. I found it difficult to follow the trail, especially since the blazes were white. It was slow progress. I managed a few miles each day. I was scared about freezing to death. I thought for sure I wouldn't survive with all my fingers, intact. The worst night was when I was soaked and I had no dry clothes to change into. I was forced to get into my sleeping bag wet. Thank God I had a zero degree bag."

When *Delaware Dave* got to Newfound Gap he finally had access to a road. That was where an older couple picked him up. "Long story short, I found myself with a free room at a resort, in a hot tub with bikini clad women. It was so amazing I kept having to tell myself it was real." He stayed three days. The older couple liked him so much that they invited him to join them to their next vacation spot. He declined, but was still in contact with them.

My pity for *Delaware Dave* dissipated after he kept telling me of his wonderful knack of getting special treatments. He was planning on visiting an old friend in the near future where he more or less was going to be hand fed. Plus he had Girl Scouts sending him boxes of food. He read me a letter that the girls had sent him. I was delighted when he handed me M&M's, saying, "This is from the girls."

□■□

I've been independent for all it's worth,

Ran into Count and Smurf.

In a day it gets cold and warms,

We've been through multiple thunderstorms.

Hiked through the Grayson Highlands,

How it made my eyes scan.

Found a mouse all alone,

I wanted to make it my very own.

As picked it up, it didn't bite,

But Ricky the mouse left in the night.

I pet a pony eating grass,

Atop a mountain with a view so vast.

When I listen to music of a guitar,

I think of my family from afar.

◻◼◻

Day 40

It was chilly, but the pancakes *Snickers* made warmed me. They had M&Ms in them. When I saw *Snickers* making pancakes with his stove, I decided right then, that it was time for me to get a stove, so that I could make pancakes in the woods, too.

We headed off to the next shelter, where hikers were able to order pizza. I called up the restaurant and ordered for all the hikers. I got a small cheese pizza and a sub for supper. We paid as a group. I told them I would pay the remainder of the tab. When the lady came to deliver she didn't give me change. I ended up paying three times the price of my order. I was so distraught that I couldn't take the merry laughs of the other hikers. I didn't want to ruin their glee however, so I left.

At the top of a ridge, I called home. My mother wanted to send a package. I told her to send it to Woods Hole Hostel. It was eleven days 'till Easter when my family was coming to visit me. Sadly, depending on what day they chose, one of my siblings wouldn't be able to come. My mother wanted me to choose what day, but I couldn't make that decision.

Count and *Smurf* later caught up and joined me. They were excitedly chatting about their shipment for 4/20.

"So you're telling me you never tried weed?" *Smurf* asked.

I was skeptical. "Don't people die from overdosing?"

"Actually no, there haven't been any cases of someone dying from only smoking weed. Although there have been times when people mix in alcohol or other drugs and that's when people start dying," said *Count*.

"Well, isn't it unhealthy?" I asked.

"Good question," said *Count*. "No, it isn't unhealthy. It's natural. In fact hospitals are using weed for medicine. In Maine people can use medical marijuana. It's so much better for patients than all the pain medication they give these days."

I had to admit, "Well you give good points, but I'll have to research it myself." They told me how a friend was sending them weed for 4/20, the marijuana holiday. "I don't like the idea of smoking," I said. "Isn't smoking harmful?"

"Matter of fact, cigarettes smoke is worse than smoking weed," said *Count*. "I used to have an inhaler, but after I got baked a couple times I haven't used my inhaler since."

"So why then is Marijuana illegal, if it's as good as you say it is?" I asked.

"Marijuana is illegal only because the drug companies are making a killing from prescription drugs. Marijuana is a great pain killer. It's natural. It comes from a plant, not a mixture of chemicals. Weed helps a much wider range of illnesses than any other kind of drug on the market, without the terrible side effects. The drug companies are influencing the government to keep weed illegal to keep people from using it."

"You are more than welcome to join us for 4/20. I would be glad to teach you how to get baked." *Smurf* flashed a smile.

I smiled back. "I don't know...just so you guys know, my family is coming for Easter. You are more than welcome to join. There will be *food*," I said, to make meeting my family sound more appealing.

At the shelter a guitar was being played in junction to a harmonica. There were eight people staying at the shelter: the

Maine boys, *BackFlip*, and *Patches*. There was a group of three older guys that I hadn't ever seen before. The others seemed to know them. The older guys each carried out a bottle of bourbon that they shared with all of us.

Patches pulled out the shelter log and started reading a post. Everyone listened to the trail drama about to unfold. "Dear *Blue Moon*, I am glad to have been acquainted with you. I wish you a good hike... -*Spartan*."

Right below it was another post. *Patches* read, "*Acquainted*, question mark, exclamation point, question mark, exclamation point, question mark, exclamation point, exclamation point, exclamation point."

"That's what it actually says," commented *Patches*.

He read on, "What do you mean acquainted? *Spartan* is too much of a high and mighty name for you -*Blue Moon*."

Patches then told us all how he had seen *Blue Moon* before we arrived. "She seemed very upset and confused. She decided to hike on to the next shelter, hoping to catch up to *Spartan*, I suppose."

"Was she pretty?" asked one of the guys.

"Decently," replied *Patches*. "She's in her mid-twenties."

"They were dating, but I think *Spartan* felt she was slowing down his hike, so after she got an injury he just hiked ahead without her."

Day 41

I took my time meandering in the morning's general splendor. I walked over rolling hills and grassy fields, and gazed at the flowers and frosted grasses. When I came to the road, I was anxious to resupply. I searched through the two gas stations, noted in the guide as short-term resupply options. I was picking out things and told myself to chill about the high prices – that was up until I found a chunk of cheese for five dollars! I was livid. *I can't do this.*

So I asked for directions to the nearest grocery store from the lady at the counter. She said, "Go down the road, then take a right and it'll be on your left." I had no idea what kind of mileage it was, but I just started walking. Part way there, I stuck out my thumb. It took about a dozen cars to pass until I got a ride.

I threw my stuff in the back of the pickup and we were off in a rush. That was my first time hitch hiking alone. The guy was a volunteer firefighter. I guess he was on duty, since his walkie talkie was very talkie. I was so happy for the ride. As the ride became longer, I became even more grateful. The man was a bit worried about how I would get back to the trail, but I didn't let his worrying damper my spirit.

Finally at the grocery store, my mouth watered as I gazed into the glass paradise. I wanted to shout, "Look everybody! Food in every direction!" But the place was vacant. I smiled the biggest smile while running around like a chicken with its head cut off, grabbing this and that: fruit, sausage, cheese, tortillas, Fig Newton's, and chocolate.

After I checked out, I took a parking spot to organize my food into Ziploc baggies. Immediately after I put on my pack, the hose from my camel back peed on me. Then I saw I lost the bite piece. *It must have come off when I unloaded my pack,* I thought.

I walked down to the baking road to work my thumb. I got annoyed when people passed. It took half an hour until I got picked up. My driver was in a rusty truck on his way to visit his mother at the trailer park. He said not to worry about the gas running out – his gas gauge had broken years ago. He made sure that I had my seat-belt fastened, then told me how he had been taken to court for a seat-belt incident in the past. I asked him if there was anything famous about the area. He said yes for what they see in the sky. He spoke of UFOs being spotted, and the air force being out every day, even Sunday.

Back on the trail, I was feeling bloated. I stopped a lot. I even hiked a bit in my Krocs because of some enraged blisters. I put on some Hello Kitty Band-Aids, but they fell off. Then I tried duct tape – which worked. I hiked for hours. On one break, right before a big climb, I was in the midst of encouraging myself to move on and half debating if I should just stop, when *Count* showed up with the rest of the crew following behind from the night before.

Since they were all there, I just wanted to stay put. I had no reason to want to go further. My loaded pack was hurting my back. Plus it was eight more miles to the next shelter. So all I had to do was persuade the others to want to stay.

The place was a pleasant camping spot, surrounded by mountain laurel. The water source was a gurgling stream just yards away. I built a fire, and set up my bivy, while the others mulled over the idea of staying. The consensus was to stay until *BackFlip* showed up. They explained that they had celebrated the completion of a quarter of the trail. In celebration, *BackFlip* had downed his Four Loco beverage much faster than the others. When they started to hike, he fell behind. I told myself, *if BackFlip takes a long time to show up, we might all stay. Count* kept repeating, "This is such a great campsite. I always wanted to stay at a campsite."

The guys gathered around the fire, talking about aqua blazing. *Smurf* was playing a ukulele. I loved the atmosphere, but it bothered me that *Count* was smoking. "I bought this packet of tobacco to teach myself how to roll a joint," *Count* explained.

"But what about your asthma?" I asked.

"Oh I won't get addicted," he said, "I'm just learning for when we get our 4/20 package."

I didn't think it was wise to keep arguing, so I held my tongue. When he talked about his girlfriend, I thought, *Well, I guess she'll get him on the right track.*

It wasn't as if smoking was rare on the trail. Heck, it was a hiker's pastime. Many hikers had started smoking or reverted back to smoking since they had started the trail. Perhaps some thought living in the wild would be the perfect place to quit, but it was quite the contrary.

Smurf watched in fascination as *Count* rolled the tobacco back and forth until it was packed, then licked the paper to secure the hold. He held it up for us to inspect his work, saying, "Not bad for a first try."

We grew quiet as we heard someone coming down the trail. It was *Hermes*. We asked him, "Have you seen *BackFlip*?"

"Oh, that's who that guy was," he laughed. "What happened to him?"

"He downed a Four Loco," the others said. "We're waiting for him to catch up."

"Well, last I saw him," *Hermes* said with a smirk, "he was lying on the ground, mumbling something about taking a nap."

Later *Delaware Dave* hiked by. We waited eagerly for *BackFlip's* new status. "Remember that sharp climb with steps?" asked *Delaware Dave* while soaking up our undivided attention. We all nodded in unison at what spot he was talking about. "Well," he said with a smile, "*BackFlip* was at the foot of it. Something seemed strange since he was lying with his head downhill and his feet uphill. I would have said something, but he looked so peaceful."

With this news the guys started pitching tents and cooking up dinners. I learned one of the guys in the older group was named *the Cops*. After he was offered marijuana from some kid, he declined and said, "I don't smoke, in respect of my job."

Then the kid nervously asked, "Are you with the Cops?"

Another guy was named *Scavenger*. He was German. I was told he carried a two-man tent and his pack weighed over fifty pounds. *Trail Mix* was the friendliest of them all.

Patches told us how he went to the doctor because his heart randomly would speed up – similar to a motor. The doctor diagnosed him with conduction abnormality. *Patches* was all worried. "I hear it when I'm hiking." He mimicked the sound.

"Dude, that's a grouse, not you. I've heard that motor sound, too," I said.

"How do you know I wasn't hiking behind you?" *Patches* said, raising a brow. Then they heard the quickening beat. "Hear that?"

"Yeah I heard it," said *the Cops*.

"See, I'm not lying and *BackFlip* can vouch for me, he has heard it when we were hiking together," said *Patches*.

"I heard the same thing before," I protested. I had heard of people mistaking this bird for a lawn motor, but a heart condition – that was just crazy. They sat, hushed to hear the sound over and over again.

"Maybe *Feisty* is right – it sounds like it's coming from that direction," said *the Cops*.

Patches had a game, called rootball. They all got serious about playing. It was much like horseshoes. They split into teams of two. The first player threw, the root tied in a hoop, trying to ring the stick. The second player tried to get the ball in the hoop. Instead of a ball, they used a pine cone.

Finally, when *BackFlip* showed up, he was surprised to see us. He said, "If I had known you guys were waiting here, I would have come sooner." He had his headlamp around his head, all set for a night hiking excursion. This inspired some of the group to night hike. By the time day had turned to night, the Maine boys, *BackFlip*, *Patches* and *Trail Mix*, all decided to hike eight more miles. It seemed too epic of an adventure to pass up. I also didn't want to miss the pancakes *Count* and *Smurf* mentioned making in the morning. I decided to go, but then my logical side argued that I wouldn't be able to keep up. I imagined myself gasping for air while running after their vanishing lights. *Count* and *Smurf* tried to persuade me to go, but I was afraid. I watched them slowly take down their tents, then march off into the darkness.

Scavenger and *the Cops* were the others who stayed behind. They were planning to get up at 4:00 in the morning to catch up and surprise those who had hiked ahead. They wanted to know if I wanted to join them. I told them to not wake me up and see what happened.

Day 42

I didn't like the thought of being alone in the morning. I decided I wanted to join the other two on the night hike. All through the night I was too antsy to get decent sleep. Every time

I looked at my clock I was surprised how slow time passed. Finally at 3:00, I got up to hike alone in the dark.

I left a note for the guys. I followed my trusty headlamp as the moon vanished into the horizon. The climb I was so worried about the day before wasn't so bad.

I got disoriented once when I turned around by accident, thinking I was on a switchback and headed exactly the way I had come. I had no inkling of my blunder until I came across a bridge in the exact replica of another I had seen not half an hour ago. I stood on the bridge, inspecting every detail. When I noticed that I had climbed over a fence just like I had before, I turned back to climb a third time over that stupid fence.

In the woods, I was spooked by stirred leaves. My heart started beating loud and I looked towards the direction the sound came, but never saw anything. What really gave me the heebie-jeebies was when my headlight reflected a pair of close-set eyes staring at me. I was nearing this creature with every step. The thing would not flinch. Panic set in as was rounding a corner. It was only a couple yards away. In attempts to scare this animal, I uttered, "Boo," and suddenly I saw a deer jump back. It then stood still, just staring. There were two other deer faded into the darkness, joined with three more sets of eyes behind them. As I walked passed, I thought I should probably take a picture of my first deer sighting on the trail, but I was too jittery.

The moon had disappeared over the horizon by the time I made it to a field. I marveled in the huge open space, where I had a jaw dropping view of the stars. It was the most awesome view of my trip so far.

On a grassy slope of the field, I had a hard time finding the trail. The only clues of the trail were posts with white blazes every so often. At one particular post, I could not see any indicator of the direction of the trail. I would guess and start walking. If it didn't seem right I would come back and try again. This happened for some time until I spotted a tent, which directed me in the correct direction.

One of my favorite parts of night hiking was watching night become morning. It took me four hours to get to the shelter, eight miles away. I was expecting pancakes when I got there, but all the boys were asleep. I knew I had a big day and was thinking of moving on, but the thought of pancakes was enticing. So I went over to the guys, and asked for the items to make pancakes. The pancakes turned out to be a total fail. First off, the pancake mix was nasty; second we had neither butter nor oil. Third, we had only spoons to flip with, so the pancakes ended up being scrambled. We cooked them in a pot where the batter burnt on the bottom. I only grew frustrated, but *Count* patiently cleaned his pot and tried time after time. *Delaware Dave* later lent us some olive oil, but we still got scrambled pancakes.

Soon I hurried on. I planned on taking a nap at the next shelter, since I was exhausted from hiking eighteen miles before lunch. I saw more deer as I headed in the door of Chestnut Knob Shelter. I got my sleeping bag out and got comfy. *Hermes* was the only one there. I chatted with him before curling up to sleep. Then *Blue Moon* came in. She was complaining that her hiking partner left her without a water filter and asked sweetly if she could use my Aqua Mira. I drowsily gave her some drops. I didn't know if I should mention her break up. I threw out the whole idea of sleeping when the shelter became infested with hikers. The conversation was about the coming thunderstorm. The thought of camping in a thunderstorm was enough to pull myself out of my sleeping bag.

I had ten miles to go. Halfway through, I thought, *you idiot, you are killing yourself, why did you leave that shelter?* I was grumpy as I walked up and down, and up and down, over and over more and more rocks. Everything was bad. I was on a ridge susceptible to blustering gusts. My feet hurt. I was at an annoyed point of exhaustion. I yearned for the shelter. Over and over I thought, *this has to be it,* but there was always another hill.

By a forest road, a putrid smell caught my attention. It was a pile of abandoned animal carcasses. There were deer and bear mingling. It made me sad. I bet the poacher had no idea he left the bodies in such close proximity to a national scenic trail.

I felt better when the trail headed down the side of the mountain. I was still grumpy as ever when I heard something dashing through the forest. I turned to see a bear, running quickly out of sight! I didn't even have time to take a picture. I was so happy. I went from being so unhappy to happy in that moment. As I walked near the guys at the shelter, in giddy excitement, I asked "Guess what I saw?"

"You didn't. A bear?" asked Smurf.

"Yes," I said with my arms in the air. "I saw a bear," I said, literary jumping up and down.

"No way!" they said, jealous. "Where? How big was it?"

I became "the girl that saw a bear." To see a bear was one of the top goals of us thru-hikers, mostly because that was the first question we got asked.

The last spot in the shelter was open. I was the ninth person in an eight person shelter. There was a post in the middle of my spot, but I was happy. It was too bad for *Trail Mix, the Cops,* and *Scavenger,* who had to camp in the pouring rain. I was sandwiched between two old guys. The one reassured me, "Now, if I snore just punch me, that is what my wife does."

Day 43

At first I just wanted to take a zero. I hurt so badly. It didn't help that the weather was beyond dreary. I said goodbye to *Count* and *Smurf,* who were planning a twenty mile day. *Count* assured me that I would see him again.

I dragged myself out of bed and started out in the rain. When it poured I shivered, but tried to be positive, *whoopee. I'm getting a shower. All I need is some shampoo.* I regretted leaving the shelter.

By the time the sun came out, I was chaffing. I stopped to dry out and change. *Trail Mix, Scavenger* and *the Cops* passed individually. They said they were going to take lunch by the road. I decided I would join them for lunch. When I got there, they were all sitting in the back of a pickup truck headed to Bland. The truck pulled out soon after I hopped in the back. We were dropped off at a gas station. While I got chips and salsa, the guys got hamburgers and soda. There was a very talkative girl who was perhaps six years old. She made us play hangman. *The*

Cops had a hard time guessing the last letter in one of her words, but that was because it was spelled wrong.

We hitched back. We were delighted when the wife of the driver gave us cupcakes. The guys brought out Four Locos. *Scavenger* got an illegal one, containing caffeine.

At the shelter were three guys who hadn't moved from their sleeping bags the whole day because of the rain. They had started in February and were taking their jolly time.

Skippy and Kelsey showed up near dark. The reunion of *Trail Mix* and *Skippy* was entertaining. They said, "Hey," simultaneously. "Last time I saw you was at Neels Gap, a month ago."

They called each other by their real names and I said, "Use your trail names."

"I'm *Trail Mix*."

"Oh, you're *Trail Mix*. I'm *Skippy*."

Day 44

I loved to see the trees begin to bud. Flowers were blooming and butterflies were floating through the air. The spring I saw in the valleys of Georgia had finally made its way to the mountains in Virginia.

When I arrived at Trent's grocery store by walking a quarter mile on the road to get there, *Trail Mix, the Cops*, and *Scavenger* hopped out of a pickup truck. After eating a pint of chocolate ice cream and two bananas, I wasn't quite full, so I got a half gallon of chocolate milk. That did me in. I lied on a bench like a beached whale. *Trail Mix* scoffed.

Then I decided to try hobbling into the woods. It was flat! A seven mile stretch of flat, it was weird. Whenever the guide book read flat I never ever let myself believe it, because it was undeniably a lie – except this time. But even though it was flat it still took a long time, and there were so many muddy spots. There were also a ton of bridges.

I walked as the sun dimmed and sank into the horizon. I was worried I had missed the shelter, so I got my guide. Then a couple steps further, I saw the sign for the shelter: what a relief. *Skippy* and Kelsey were there. I had brought marshmallows and hotdogs to roast. So I made a fire with the help of *Skippy*.

Kelsey freaked on her way to the privy. She saw eyes looking at her. "Come look. It's a coyote!" She said. We went over, but the coyote was just a deer.

I got a magnificent fire going, something to be proud of. As we tuckered in for the night, *Trail Mix's* group showed up and polished off the remainder of the fire and food.

Day 45

I got up. Right off the bat, I had a steep climb, but I booked it. I wanted to get to the nearing hostel and rest. On top was a wonderful view. I finally got to the gravel road and walked down to Woods Hole Hostel. I said bye to *Skippy* with whom I had hiked the last couple miles, since he was slower on downhill rocky sections.

As I made my way down the road to the hostel, I crossed paths with *Butter*. She told me I should take a zero at the hostel, since in her opinion, it was an amazing place. I asked about *Diva*. I was shocked to find he was off the trail. He got serious shin splints when *Peach's* group hiked thirty miles to get pizza. Agitated, I thought, *how could they do that to poor Diva*. It seemed so selfish of them to run dear *Diva* into the ground like that. *Butter* said, "*Peach* has been getting pressure from her parents to get the hike finished early for college. Andy and *Butter* are dealing with it. I'm glad I can relax once I get to the Shenandoah National Park."

Indy was hiking with *Peach's* group. The day *Peach's* group did thirty; he hiked thirty-six miles to keep up with them, or rather *Butter*. *Indy* was what the trail community called a pink blazer – for hiking after a girl. It was no secret that *Indy* liked *Butter*, since he had told me himself.

After talking with Butter, I had no regrets in leaving the group. It sounded like they were using the trail as a raceway, and I wanted no part in that.

Count and *Smurf* were at the hostel. They had taken an unplanned zero. *Patches* and *BackFlip* were there, too. They walked around in their rain gear because their laundry was getting washed. *Count* was sporting a towel. I couldn't help but tease him.

We played some rootball. I gloated a bit about how good I thought I was. It turned out, I wasn't very good. Lucky for me and my ego, *Patches*, my partner raked in the points and I scored the winning point! I danced about happily. I could gloat safely, even though they pointed out my short comings.

"You wouldn't have won without *Patches*," they said.

"Yeah, but we wouldn't have won without my last point." I smiled.

I got a ride into town with the Maine boys. We went to a jumbo supermarket; way too big for a deprived hiker like me to handle. I knew I had been getting too little food. So I told myself to get more than normal, plus even more because it was a longer stretch. I ended up getting eighty dollars worth of food. It weighed a hefty eighteen pounds: cheese, hotdogs, tortillas, bagels, pita bread, peanut butter, Nutella, chocolate, nuts, and fig newton's. *Count* and *Smurf* were freaking out.

"You have *so* much food."

"Yeah, well you guys carried unnecessary amounts of food, too," I said to calm them down. Inside I was freaking out as well. *How in the world would I carry eighteen pounds of food, as well as the rest of my gear?*

Supper was great. We had homemade bread, salad, pork chops, pasta and ice cream. We had meditation for twenty minutes. It was hard for me to keep still. With a group that large, I think there are better things to do than meditate. The best time for me to meditate was right after a hike. It just came naturally.

Day 46

I did anything I could to help out. I did the list of chores in the bunkhouse and cleaned up breakfast. Neville and Michael were the owners. They were a young couple. Michael was happy to see me help out. Later in the day, I helped rake the backyard of sticks and leaves, and chip them up. Then we hauled the mulch. We had to wear ear plugs. I told Michael how I was used to chipping brush from working with my dad. When the chipper got clogged, he said, "This is why people hire guys like your dad. When can your Dad come over?"

"Well, he's coming for Easter."

Michael then yelled to Neville, "*Feisty* is staying 'till Easter, when her dad comes!" The funny thing was I had thought about staying.

We got free dinner for helping out. Many people helped make pizzas with the homemade dough.

Michael delivered a package to me. "This feels like it has drugs in it." He squished and smelled it. The package was from my mother. "I didn't know you were the cocaine type," Michael went on. There was a crowd in the room all listening.

I rolled my eyes. "I'll open it for you, if you'd like."

"You don't *have* to, but I sure would like to see what's inside."

I opened it to find a huge bag of homemade trail mix. It didn't excite me, I already had enough food. Then I pulled out a baggie of green sheets. "What's that?" Michael asked.

"Seaweed," I said with a smile.

Their faces were horror stricken.

It wasn't the first time that someone thought I had drugs. One evening, *Legion* had seen my baggie of parsley. "Either you are really cool, or you're not." I had a feeling he wasn't getting excited over some parsley. I was tongue tied on what to say because I had a feeling I was on the not cool side of the spectrum.

Ducky and I sat on the porch watching the pizzas being baked in the outdoor brick oven. "So why are you hiking?" I asked.

"Every year one of my friends has died. One got hit by a train. Another got killed in crossfire, that he had nothing to do with. It was one of those wrong places at the wrong time moments. I'll never know when my time comes, so I'm doing something I want to do, you know other than education and career related things, before it's too late. You're the first person that has asked. *Trighten* would never ask me questions. He assumed everything."

Ironically, the supper question was, "Why are you hiking the trail?" So I got to explain how I couldn't get a treadmill, but then decided to hike to get in shape, besides the whole adventure of it. A couple there were hiking for college credit. They had to do a bit of homework like taking water samples, but all together were doing the same thing.

For supper I ate and ate and ate. It was so good. No lie, I'm pretty sure I put on five pounds. All the young guys out here are poles. Guys lose weight. Sadly, I found out that girls gain it.

EIGHT

Humored

April 20th – 24th

Day 47

I was up by early dawn, I was still incredibly stuffed from the previous night's supper. I decided to keep hiking, before becoming obese. I felt bad for leaving, since Michael was pretty excited about me staying to help out around the place. When I said goodbye, I was surprised that Neville gave me a hug; perhaps she was used to hugging stinky people. Hikers never hug. We don't even shake hands.

I was getting worried about lugging my nineteen pound food bag, so I gave Michael and Neville half my resupply to hold until my family came to pick it up.

I called my mom to figure out where we would meet for Easter. I had to map out my miles, and I decided on lower mile days. I didn't want to deal with getting myself into a rigid schedule. Before she hung up, she prayed the short prayer, "May God bless you and keep you. May his face shine on you and give you peace."

I was thinking about my gluttony, when I came to a widespread view on the ridge and watched eagles soar. *V8* came by. He's Japanese. "I'm so sorry about the tsunami that hit your country," I said. "That must have been sad to hear, right after you started hiking."

"No, actually I left right after it happened," said *V8*.

"Did you know anyone that died?" I asked.

"No, I didn't live close to where the tsunami hit, but it was nice to leave."

"So, you were like, see ya Japan. Have fun with that," I said with a wave. He laughed. I impressed him by reciting the Japanese I knew. He said I had very good pronunciation.

"So, why did you choose America to hike? You could have gone to New Zealand. It's so much closer to Japan," I said.

"No. Japan isn't close to New Zealand. It's in the southern hemisphere. Japan is in the northern hemisphere," he corrected me.

"Oh, but the traveling time is shorter," I said.

"No, same time."

"So why the US then?" I finally asked.

"Well, I have hiked the CDT…"

I had never heard of it. "Where is that?" I wondered.

"Western USA," he told me.

"Don't you mean the PCT?"

He smiled at my ignorance. "No, but I hiked that last year."

"No way!" I said with giddy excitement. "You're a Triple Crowner!" as if he didn't already know.

Then I took notice of his tiny pack. "So that's why you have such a light backpack. How much does it weigh?"

"When it's full, it weighs fifteen pounds," he said, taking it off to let me lift it. "I sewed it myself."

"Wow! That's super light. Can you make me one?" I asked

"It's a Ray-way backpack. You can make your own."

I noticed he had an umbrella and thought, *How do you hold an umbrella and hiking sticks at the same time?* "Wait a second." I realized. "You don't have hiking sticks!"

"Yeah, I don't need them," he said.

We were heading downhill by that point, towards town. I started walking faster. "I like to run downhill," I told him.

"You must have very strong legs."

What a delightful conversation this is, I thought soaking up the compliment, and made sure it continued. "When did you start your hike?" I asked.

"March 24th, twenty seven days ago," he said.

"Wow man, you must be cranking out the miles. So, you do what? Thirty's?" I asked.

"No, I haven't done any thirty's."

"I have," I said with a smile.

"Wow, that's remarkable."

"I guess you don't take any zeros." I said.

"I've taken one."

"Damascus, right?" I assumed.

"How did you know?" he inquired.

"Because Damascus is awesome. Who wouldn't stop in Damascus?" I said. "So tell me, were there a lot of people when you started the trail?"

"One day I counted ninety people," *V8* answered. Before I knew it, our paths split, and our parting was abrupt. I was sad to say good-bye, but knew he would catch up.

I hiked a bit more before I was out of water. I was starting to get very concerned. It took a long while before I found a little dirty stream. This was one of the few times I decided to use my Aqua Mira. I detested using the stuff. I had two bottles of drops I had to mix, and then I had to wait for it to turn yellow. After mixing it in the water, one is supposed to wait fifteen minutes. As a thirsty hiker, I walked while shaking it and cut the time in half. What really annoyed me was when I decided it was safe enough to drink; I came by a stream that was perfect for drinking.

At the shelter, *Count, Smurf, BackFlip,* and *Patches* were all strewn out sound asleep. Apparently they had taken a zero day. *Trail Mix, the Cops,* and *Scavenger* were there too, as well as *Skippy* and Kelsey. It was like a reunion. I was glad to be back with my friends.

When the guys finally got up from their slumber, I ordered them to make room for me. They more or less ignored me. Instead they drowsily gobbled down food. *Patches* was eating peanut butter and jelly straight out of the jar. He scoped half a spoonful of peanut butter, and squeezed jelly on top.

We were told it was a long hike to the water. I volunteered to fill up water. The guys were still helplessly out of it. I repeated myself and *BackFlip* responded. I then had to wait for him to find his water filtration system. They weren't lying about the walk being insanely long and steep as well as containing sharp rocks. At the water source *Scavenger* was filling up. I stepped above where he was getting water and made it all dirty. "I'm so sorry," I said.

"That's okay." Then he added, "Go ahead and fill up your bottles. Mine takes longer anyway."

Count and *Smurf* both bought hotdogs off me. I made three dollars. Apparently they had been eating all day long. *Patches* complained about how *Count* would casually eat his food without asking. I figured their cause of hunger came from celebrating 4/20. *Count* and *Smurf* had taken their opportunity to teach me all they knew about weed. They said weed makes every situation better, except hiking uphills on hot days.

Smurf came next to me saying, "Now it's time for you to get baked." He wore a face of sincerity.

"Are you sure it's not addictive?" I asked. The last thing I wanted to be was judgmental or hypocritical.

Smurf was grinding up the plant in a small contraption. "Ever since I've been smoking it hasn't made me dependent on it," he said.

I imagined him getting annoyed, but he wasn't. I loved how comical he always was, but now he was very serious. He just continued filling his glass pipe with bits of grindings. Then he patted them down with his thumb. "You probably won't feel anything the first time. It's different for everyone. Okay, this is how you light it." He held the pipe in his teeth and lit the grindings with his lighter. "See these two holes? You need to hold them while you breathe in." He then proceeded to show me how he breathed in, held it, and then blew out. "Okay. Your turn," he said.

I thought, *Well, this is most likely a once in a life time thing. I bet no one will ever be so eager to teach me as Smurf. If anything, at least I can humor him.* "Uh, okay." I took the pipe and mimicked what he did. He coached me the whole way through.

"Hold the holes. Breathe in. Let go of the holes. Hold it. Hold it. Okay. Feel anything?"

"I don't know, it's not too bad. It kinda burns my throat."

"Oh, you'll know when you've had enough."

I had some more before the pipe started getting passed around communally. Then *Trail Mix* lit up a joint and people gathered around to take hits. They kept passing it around until the roach was too small to be meticulously passed around anymore.

Everyone was relaxed. *Smurf* and *Count* said their favorite places to get baked were at magnificence views. They found the experience multiplied in brilliance.

I considered marijuana to be safe, but for some people, marijuana can become a gateway drug – and that's when people get into trouble.

I felt rather sheltered knowing that I had such a brainwashed view of weed beforehand. I thought marijuana ruined lives and messed with people's brains. Sitting there, I thought I should change my name. Feisty, was a name I had made up for myself, spur of the moment. The thought was that I had to be Feisty to hike the trail. Over the miles, it felt weird to be called feisty. I didn't feel feisty anymore, anyhow. I felt worn out. I thought if I was going to change my name I better do it now. I wanted a name that could be remembered. The older men on the trail seemed to forget my name and call me sassy, or sassafras.

I changed my trail name to *Amish*, since people would ask where I was from. I told them that I was from Lancaster, Pennsylvania. Then without fail, they ask if I was Amish. I thought the name was fitting, not because I was Amish, but because I was naive about many things in the world. And some of the other hikers wanted to prove that I was Amish. In the logbook, I wrote that *Feisty* was changed to *Amish*, so everyone after me would know my new name.

News traveled down the grapevine by *Mile High*, announcing that *Llama Legs* was off the trail. I couldn't believe it.

I loved *Llama Legs*. Everyone adored his humor. They said he ran out of money. I had been there when he had lost his wallet in Damascus. I suppose he was running out to begin with. Then I heard *Data* got off the trail, too!

Day 48

We had a ridge-line walk most the day. I was videotaping an interesting blue bug, when *Skippy* came by and told me I should pick it up for bug battles. So I did. I then picked up a centipede, too.

Later I came across a small snake. I tried to catch it without touching it. I was chasing it around a bush when *Skippy* came by and asked what I was doing.

"I saw a snake," I said excitedly.

"Okay, but what are you doing?"

"I'm trying to catch it."

He gave me a funny look. "Why would you wanna do that? I hate snakes."

We took a break at the shelter's picnic table. I pulled out the centipede that I named Charlie and let him crawl about. *Trail Mix* kept asking where Charlie was. "Oh, he's climbing underneath the picnic table," I would say. I then gathered leaves and sticks for Charlie.

I chatted with *Trail Mix*, until I got too fatigued to keep up. He told me how he had been a naughty school kid. By the time he reached high school he wasn't given any classes with his friends, because they were so bad. He said there was a time he handed a second grader laxatives, telling him it was chocolate, which landed him with three days of suspension.

I was frying a tuna melt on the fire when *V8* stopped at the shelter. I told him to stay and join us, but he decided to keep walking until dark. I found it odd that he kept going, especially after he had told me he wasn't making friends on the AT as easily as when he had hiked the PCT and CDT.

We played rootball. During the first two games, *Scavenger* and I lost terribly to *the Cops* and *Trail Mix*. But the last game we played in the dark, after drinking some bourbon and we won.

Day 49

I made it to the shelter and relaxed for lunch. *Trail Mix, the Cops* and *Scavenger* showed up. *Skippy* ate spoonfuls of peanut butter for his lunch. *Skippy* and Kelsey left right before the rain started to increase.

I asked the guys if they would like to play a card game. They studied the falling rain. *Trail Mix* sat silently with his hands together as if to say something. "Do you think your family could drive us to Catawba?"

"Yeah, they probably would." I replied. "I would say you got an eighty percent chance."

It was enough assurance for them so they decide to stay. We got out our sleeping bags and played game after game as the rain came down.

Scavenger had some cider mix he warmed. The guys collaborated the rest of their bourbon to make hot spiked cider.

"How's Charlie doing? Is he still alive?" *Trail Mix* asked. I got out Charlie from his container and petted his smooth body as he slowly crawled around the shelter. *Trail Mix* randomly asked for Charlie's position throughout the evening. It usually took a bit of searching to find Charlie, but I didn't lose him. Whenever I picked up Charlie to relocate him, he would curl up into a disc.

I wanted to play poker, but we weren't sure what to use for chips, until we realized *Scavenger* had plenty of change in his pockets. He had collected mounds of change. He was planning to use it to buy a bottle of champagne for the summit of Mount Katahdin.

Most hikers got rid of their change, since it was extra weight. There was a time I didn't pick up a quarter because of the weight. Of all the change, quarters and dimes are worth the most for their weight. I would have picked up a dime before a quarter, but ironically, quarters and dimes are exactly 22.68 grams per dollar. Nickels are a hundred grams. And pennies are a whopping 260 grams per dollar – that is equal to the weight of four and a half snicker bars. We usually made fun of *Scavenger's* change jingling in his backpack, but we were glad for his heaps of quarters, nickels, dimes, and pennies.

We then gambled our snacks, since we knew resupplying was just a day away. In my case, I had a whole other half of that eighty dollar resupply waiting for me, plus whatever my family would bring along. I lost the first two poker games, but I was unflinchingly serious about the last game and won! I got my first Cliff Bar from the stash. Two things I didn't mind losing were nuts and nonfat strawberry cream cheese. Which I didn't know was nonfat, until *Trail Mix* started complaining about it. "Why on earth would you get nonfat cream cheese?"

"To be honest, I had no idea," I said. "I was more interested in the flavor, but it turned out to taste bad anyway."

"You totally got jipped, think of all the calories you're losing."

Day 50

The excitement of seeing my family made sleep difficult. Halfway through the night, I couldn't get comfortable. I was also thirsty with no water. So I stumbled in the drizzling rain toward the sound of gurgling water. Luckily, I found my way back.

The other three wanted to catch a ride to Catawba, so they got up early to join me. We didn't get up as early as the couple that had shown up the night before. They had complained the night before that we were loud. But they got their revenge: they had an alarm clock, and as if *that* wasn't bad enough they spent half an hour noisily eating and packing up in the dark. They were grumpy sort of people. I was glad I didn't have to rush like them.

Finally a bit after it became light, I got up. The others had their first cold breakfast. They usually spend hours cooking up a nice breakfast. Although they liked my style of eating in bed, *Trail Mix* mourned for his morning cup of tea. He came up with a solution: "I'll just put a tea bag in my mouth."

Trail Mix randomly asked where Charlie was. When I went to look for him, he was gone. The guys teased that he must have not liked his accommodations.

They were still slower than me in getting up and out. "I know why you get ready so quickly; you don't brush your teeth," accused *Trail Mix*. So I brushed my teeth before I left.

It was beautiful in the valley with blooming dogwoods. At the top of the mountain was a cloud that made it foggy and drizzly. I got to a shelter at 8:20 am, two miles before the meeting point. That's where the three guys caught up to me.

Down the mountain were a ton of switch backs, which *the Cops* and *Scavenger* cut straight through. I watched them fight their way through the brush. I was a bit annoyed, but then I made it a game by trying to stay ahead of them. Eventually they got ahead. The landscape beyond the forest was beautiful with fields of grazing cattle. The trees were just getting their spring leaves.

We played rootball while we waited for my family to show up. At 11:30, a green van swerved by. Next came hugs and laughter, then introductions. I opened up the trunk to find lots of food. "Look at all the food I got. I didn't even have to carry or buy it!" I teased my friends. I then gave handouts to *Trail Mix, the Cops* and *Scavenger*.

"You were right about your mom making good muffins," said *Trail Mix*, as he devoured a banana muffin. My dad kindly gave them a hitch.

I later heard the ride was an awkward one; neither my dad nor the guys knew what to say. They just sat in silence and watched the miles fly by.

My family wanted to hike. *Hike? That was the last thing on my mind.* "But I've been hiking *all* morning." But they complained that they had been in the car all morning.

We got lucky with a beautiful section of green hills to hike. I taught my folks rootball. It wasn't a complete fail. Isaac would just throw the pine cone at people, not knowing he couldn't even get points that way.

That night we roasted steaks on a fire. Isaac my youngest brother fried his on a hot rock. The intense sizzling made it sound like it was thoroughly cooked in ten seconds.

"Isaac, you better flip that before it burns."

He flipped it, but it fell into the fire. He poked it to get a hold of it and ash covered the steak. Eventually he pinned the sucker and held it in the air to see the damage.

"Mom, can I wash my steak in the stream?"

I cut in. "Are you serious, you wanna eat a cold wet steak? You'd probably end up losing it down stream."

"Yeah I guess not." He got himself a paper plate and sat down.

My older sister, roasted hers on a leafy stick. I believed it turned out better than Isaac's, but she looked so funny, I couldn't help from laughing.

We cowboy camped under the stars. None of my family had sleeping mats. I feel a bit sorry for them, but not enough to give them mine. I had a blast joking around and educating my sister in how to use a headlamp and what a privy was.

There were bugs everywhere. One bug was on my pillow – that scared me. My mother and sister laughed. "Haven't you been around nature for like over a month now?"

"Yeah, but the bugs are new."

Day 51

It was a cold night. Dad forsook the hammock and waddled inside his sleeping bag to join my mom on the ground. In the morning, I got a fire going. Serena and Isaac took their time getting up. Serena would complain in an incomprehensible, groggy fashion and roll over.

We had a little sunrise service around the fire. Mom sang some ancient Easter songs and started catching up with all the kisses she missed giving me.

We packed up and drove back to Woods Hole to get my food. My dad seemed somewhat annoyed to drive all the way to

Pearisburg. At Woods Hole, we waited for Neville and Michael to come back from church. My family liked the place. My dad *really* liked it. He liked the shed for hikers and the fire pit inlaid with stones. He liked the stone wall that was built by hikers when I was there. My mother looked at the newly planted fruit trees and my dad named the varieties. The dog, of course, was loving fetch and was following Isaac everywhere.

Legion was there and gave a spiel about his name and how the world had issues. *Legion* showed Isaac his tattoo. He then explained how it signified him being one of many in a broken world, similar to the demon possessed man in the bible. Isaac responded with, "So you're demon possessed and waiting for Jesus?" My mom burst out in laughter. Ironically, *Legion* started complaining that he hated being in the south, because everyone wanted to convert him. It seemed like he was asking for it.

Legion entertained my family for some time and my father found him to be very intriguing. *Legion* had a fifty pound pack. I tried it on with his help. It was practically insane to be carrying that much. I teased him by offering a banana. He said, "No thanks, can't you *see* I have enough food already."

"What's the hiker rule about trail magic?" I prodded.

"Right." He cleared his throat. "Rule number six – never turn down trail magic. I guess I can't break my own rule." He grinned, finally accepting the banana.

We had ham, black olives and cheese cake for Easter dinner. Soon Neville and Michael showed up. I organized my food and Michael got advice from my dad on his tree. On our way back to the trail, we stopped at a dollar store, where I picked up a frying pan and rope for my hammock.

Having to say goodbye was hard. It brought tears to my eyes. I was so happy my family visited me. Too bad my brother Dan couldn't make it.

So I hiked, like hikers do. There was a bunch of uphill. It was hot and I was running out of water. I listened to music on my newly obtained iPod. When I got near to the first shelter, I was out of water. Unfortunately, the shelter, and more importantly the water, was half a mile downhill. First I thought I could do without water. Then I let myself think rationally. The next water source was seven miles away. So I threw down my pack and ran down the switched-back-hill to the water. I found the water hole, which was a pathetic water source, but water is water.

Once I got back on the trail, a mile later of walking to and from the shelter, I ran into Jeff. We chatted for a couple miles. He didn't know any of the hikers I asked him about since he took several weeks off the trail recently. He also didn't know many people since he preferred not to stay at shelters.

Later, when I was hiking by myself, I decided I wanted to listen to music and I reached for my iPod, but it was gone. I searched all over my pack. Gone. I dropped my pack once more and backtracked. It was a good thing I found it and not all that far back. That really scared me.

I got to the next shelter where *Blue Moon, Spartan, Turkey Feather* and a man named *Super Dave* were. *Blue Moon* and *Spartan* had gotten back together at Woods Hole. Our group had watched them curiously, because we had heard of their dramatic shelter entries. We ask each other in hushed voices, "Are they back together?" We sneaked glances at them, while they conversed with laughs and smiles as if nothing had happened.

They were nice, but I would have rather been with *my* friends, like the Maine boys, *Trail Mix, the Cops, Scavenger, Skippy,* Kelsey, and so on. I made a fire and offered them marshmallows. I asked them if they got any of the bananas my mom had set out as trail magic. They were like, "You rock! That was from your family?" When I asked them what was the most special thing about their Easter, *Spartan* said the bananas were the best part. Then it dawned on me how very special it was that I got to spend Easter with my family.

NINE

Rain Fly

April 25th – May 1st

Day 52

I found the hammock so comfortable that I slept deep into the morning. My mother had given me a bite piece for my Camelback, but it clearly wasn't working, which was apparent by all the random squirting. While signing the register my water leaked all over the page. *Super Dave* assisted me by holding up the tube so I could scribble an entry. Before leaving, *Blue Moon* insisted on giving me her water because she was concerned by the profound amount of leaking.

After a couple minutes of walking I felt something at the toe of my shoe. Assuming it was just my shoe falling apart, I didn't stop. I walked on until my toes became irritated. It was a good thing I stopped, because inside my shoe was Charlie's cousin. The centipede was more than alive when I flung him to the forest floor. I found it curious that the tip of my sock had turned green from the centipede.

After a steep climb that made me thirsty and sweaty, I sat on a bench chatting with *Spartan* and *Blue Moon*. We spoke of Audie Murphy, since his monument was a mile up the trail; near where his plane had crashed. I felt uneducated since I hadn't heard of him before. From what *Spartan* said, it sounded like Audie Murphy saved us in World War II.

I grew weary in the exhausting heat and desired a rest in the shade, so I went down a long trail to a shelter. I took off my sock and to my surprise the tips of my toes were black! I worried that my life was in danger and just wanted someone's reassurance that I would survive a centipede bite. I debated hitchhiking to a hospital, but decided I would talk to someone first.

Back on the rocky trail, I met *Trail Baby*. She was more like a grandma than a baby. I showed her my black toes and she thought a creature from the water had sucked the blood to the surface. She told me I shouldn't fret about it, unless it started to hurt or if the blackness started to spread. I imagined myself becoming slowly engulfed by blackness.

Later I met southbound thru-hikers coming back after a snowy winter. The girl named *Rambler* looked ridiculous since she was wearing a mosquito net over her head, as if the mosquitoes were so severe back in Maine that she was too petrified to remove it. The guy named *Fifteen* told me how he consumed massive amounts of food at the Home place in Catawba, which was the restaurant where my dad had dropped off *Scavenger, the Cops* and *Trail Mix*.

These southbounders told me that Dragons Tooth wasn't a big deal. Contrary to their report it turned out to have legit rock climbing, except *I* was descending. I had to throw down my hiking poles to use my hands to grasp the metal rungs hammered into the rocks. After the ladder were skinny ridges similar to long steps so that I had to walk downhill backwards, while trying not to fall to my death.

When I found a campsite, I was ready to pass out, but there was no water. I watched a day hiker offer a hiker water and I seriously hollered, "Hey! Why are you giving *him* water? I need water." Luckily he wasn't offended and had more water that he graciously gave.

After cooking on a fire, it took me three times to find the correct distance to hang my hammock. I fell asleep hoping that I wouldn't get cold.

Day 53

I woke up sweating and was up and out by seven. The trail went through a pasture where the cows stared me down, but I liked them because I felt at home.

It was baking hot and I felt like an idiot because I had missed the water source. A section hiker who noticed my piteousness gave me a half liter of water. He said he didn't have his trail legs yet, but he sped past me like the energizer bunny.

At the Catawba parking lot were coolers of trail magic. All I wanted was water, but only empty bottles were left. So I scavenged water from the parking lot puddles. I sat cross legged in the parking lot eating my lunch and adding the last of my powdered milk to my purified puddle water.

There had been outbursts of rain, but on MacAfee Nob I found it surprisingly sunny. Some day hikers were fascinated at my endeavor, "How did you know what to pack?" the one girl asked. They offered me granola bars, but I declined since I was already brimming with food. They were happy to take my picture on the cliff. I felt blessed with a clear view, since everyone liked getting their picture snapped there.

After a short walk to the next shelter, I sensed rain and decided to stop early for the day.

▢■▢

I had my kicks

With *Scavenger, the Cops* and *Trail Mix*.

They would take their time,

Having a break before a big climb.

When it started to rain,

We found the weather lame,

So we played a game.

Then decided to stay the night,

Oh what a delight.

We played rootball,

While waiting for ma and pa.

My dad became an angel on the side

By giving my friends a ride.

My family wanted to hike with me more

When I just wanted a relaxing session galore.

Hopefully they still wish to hike,

Since there are many more days in sight.

My mommy gave me a kiss for everyday

That she missed when I was away.

My toe turned blue

What should I do?

Mommy can you kiss it, too?

□■□

Day 54

A couple came in late the night before. I groggily asked for their names, but I hadn't heard of them, so I replied, "Sorry, I don't know you," and rolled over.

Rabbit and *Tortuga's* alarm clock went off early. I guess they wanted to get to town as soon as possible. I asked them what their plan was. They said, "Get to town by two," so I made that my goal, although I didn't need to rush since I was supplied for another weeks excursion. They hiked a mile, and then stopped for breakfast. I passed them and climbed some never-ending slopes going higher and higher. Finally at the top, to my dismay, I got confused and lost. To get back on the ridge, I had to jump up a crevice in the rocks and use my arms to hoist myself up through the tight squeeze.

Looking out from Tinker Ridge, I saw a wicked view when the opaque fog opened a moment, revealing a town nestled in the valley.

On the descent, I picked up an orange newt. Later I found out that they come out after it rains.

At the shelter, the couple caught up to me. I got water, a snack, went to the privy, and signed the register. An entry by *Back Flip* read, "If anyone got lost on Tinker Ridge, raise your hand." He had two stick figures depicting *Scavenger* and himself with their hands raised. So I joined in by drawing a sick figure with its hand raised, too.

Rabbit and *Tortuga* stopped not even a mile down the trail to gather more water. Apparently, it was the last water source before town. I thought, *My water is unstable*, but I didn't feel the need to stop. I placed the hose behind my ear to keep the unstable water contained. With so much of my stuff falling apart it made me feel like a mess.

I could hear the sound of traffic a couple miles before town. It sounded so loud that I told myself it had to be close, but the sound only grew stronger as the miles increased. At the highway, I had a relativity short walk to town, which was literally a shopping center.

On the sidewalk, I bumped into *Yogi:* that made me happy to be catching up with people. He happily showed off his brand new backpack and shoes, then gave me Daleville shopping advice.

I couldn't resist the grocery store, but I got totally overwhelmed by so much food and so many choices. I had the hardest time looking through types of butter. First, all I could find was fake butter. Then I was astonished that the least amount of butter I could purchase was a hefty pound!

Next stop was the outfitter. Many purchases were made. I got new shoes and insoles. Then I spent big bucks on Smart Wool socks, to replace my melted ones. Then I bought a new bite for my Camelback. Finally, no more leaking!

Yogi had warned me of a severe thunderstorm, so I hit the road. I got drizzled on a bit, but made it to the shelter before the storm. The new insoles made my feet hurt like crazy. They say insoles need broken in, but I didn't have much of a choice.

Yogi had his tent set up, which made no sense to me, but in the end he actually managed to stay dryer. The only person in the shelter was a fellow named *Rain Fly*. He was shocked to see the mammoth amount of food I dumped on to the floor. I ended up selling him a dollars worth of summer sausage.

Day 55

During the night the frigid wind blew rain into the shelter and the shelter floor got drenched.

Rain Fly had said that he hiked slowly, so I wondered if we hiked at the same rate and I decided to follow him. I noticed his unique way of hiking right away. He held his hiking poles out as if skiing. Not far down the trail he stopped to dig debris out of his boot, so I passed him and led the rest of the day.

At a shelter we joined Yogi at the picnic table. I was enjoying my carrots dipped in hummus immensely, when I noticed *Yogi* watching me intently, "I'll trade some M&Ms for a carrot dipped in hummus," he proposed. I didn't want him to suffer, so we traded.

Rain Fly and I passed a lot of wildlife. We saw lizards, some deer, and many newts. *Rain Fly* was scared when I made a fat snake coil before he could pass. Unaware I stepped over a skinny, green snake that laid perpendicular to the trail. *Rain Fly* called me back and I got close to the snake, but it didn't budge. I told *Rain Fly,* to try making it move; instead the snake climbed up *Rain Fly's* pole. I laughed, "How are you going to get it off?" He tried pulling the snake off by the tail, but it held on tightly. Of all the snakes I saw on the trail, this one was the prettiest. I thought this was the perfect pet – finally a snake I could catch. I told *Rain Fly* I wanted to keep it, but he insisted that I let it be. We watched the snake slide off the pole and climb up a bush.

Rain Fly was happy to have a hiking buddy. He told me story after story. He had climbed up a tree to escape an angry mother bear, twice. He attempted a thru-hike in '08, but spent all his money partying during Trail Days. He explained how he was adopted and when he was fifteen he ran away from home. He traveled America by camping and working part time jobs most his life. He said he got his GED when working at a church. Then he joined the same church for a mission trip to Mexico and stayed in Mexico for a month or so, until the church came back for their next mission trip.

I found out *Rain Fly* dubbed himself when he was a kid with an invented superhero name: Rain Fly. He only realized his word creation was already in use on the trail when hikers asked about his tents rain-fly.

I enjoyed all of *Rain Fly's* stories and hoped I would have a slew of exciting stories when I got older. I felt bad for him because he had no family and in the back of my mind I hoped that I wouldn't end up like him.

We quit hiking at four. I was a bit hesitant to stop early, but *Rain Fly* insisted.

The privy there was wonderfully large, lighted, and clean. I marveled at its large size, similar to a handicap bathroom. Most privies were dingy, spider infested, smelly, cramped places. Sometimes the contents were filled to the top and sometimes there were no walls what-so-ever – just a john in the air.

Day 56

We started off by getting lost. The rest of the day I learned more about *Rain Fly*. He told me about how hurricane Katrina affected New Orleans – where he was from. As he was working on his mother's house, he watched the cost of building materials triple. When the storm was about to hit, he was told there would be hurricane winds for eleven hours, so he decided to shelter at the nearby high school. He stayed three days before leaving early to get home to his starving dog. This time, the dog who would usually frolic when greeting him just lifted his head off the floor. He said that when the dog recovered it looked at him as if saying, "Never do that to me again."

Near the end of the hike my feet hurt and my legs felt strained. I couldn't wait to be done. Ironically, when I was about to sit down, I saw the shelter hiding on a hill just a couple yards away. The shelter was uniquely made with two floors and a porch. I made some pancakes for supper.

I calculated that at our rate it would take us six days to get to Waynesboro. I told *Rain Fly* I would supply pancakes for his suppers and that he could buy any other food from me.

Day 57

I had yet another day with *Rain Fly*. I was banking on hiking eighteen miles to a certain shelter, which I later found out was actually twenty-three miles away, but I still thought, *Hey, we should do that*. I really didn't expect that we would make it, but we did! We climbed a whole mountain from end to end. It was a *long* up in the morning and a *long* down in the evening.

I enjoyed talking about the Bible when *Rain Fly* asked about my New Testament. He told me how he thought all churches were the same, but after going to several churches he realized his misconception. One church he liked up until the pastor came up to him and advised, "I don't think this is the right church for you. See we are the First Baptists. Perhaps you should try the Third Baptist church down the road."

Rain Fly suffered. All the downhill terrorized his knees. He became famished before I wanted to stop for lunch. I kept having to tell him, "It's just two more miles to the shelter."

We passed through the guillotine; a part of the trail where there was two rock walls with a large rock stuck on top.

On the downhill to the shelter, I got way ahead of *Rain Fly*. I then found the shelter and chatted with the group of hikers. When I saw *Rain Fly* approaching, I yelled out his name. The fellow next to me excitedly hollered, "*Rain Fly*" *Fat Jim* and *Rain Fly* had hiked together before, but *Rain Fly* had fallen behind. It was funny watching them talk. *Rain Fly* would say, "If it weren't for *Amish* I would be *way* back there, but she keeps me going, although she's a bit slow uphill."

Fat Jim was losing weight. He used to wear an extra-extra-large, but now only wore a large. He was anticipating his trail name to change to *Slim Jim* by the time he finished.

Day 58

Once again we had a steep climb. The higher we climbed, the worse the weather became. We climbed into a cloud and the vertical rain was bone chillingly cold. We had disputed over where we should stay; *Rain Fly* wanted to go twelve miles and I wanted to go further to the next shelter, twenty-two miles away, but I knew I couldn't get him to do two twenty mile days in a row. It was hard to motivate him, plus I was still a bit sore myself.

Rain Fly was repeating himself a lot. He even told me the same story twice, about how he won Leki hiking poles in Damascus during Trail Days.

I asked him to not swear around me anymore since it was bothering me. I have a tolerance for swearing when it's used properly, but *Rain Fly* would describe everything with swear words and I thought it was time he should work on his vocabulary.

On our last hill, I was surprised to see Kelsey coming up behind us. She had taken a zero in Glasgow. *Rain Fly* fell behind as I hiked with her and caught up on the past week. At the shelter, *Skippy*, *Scavenger*, and *Yogi* showed up. The couple *Rabbit* and *Tortuga* were present as well. I wasn't sure what to say, but I thought *Tortuga* talked too much for not really knowing the others.

They were all headed to the next shelter. I was happy to see them, but decided I had better stay with *Rain Fly*. I told *Rain Fly* I didn't have enough food to supply him anymore, so he figured out where to resupply and saw that it was near the next shelter. He hinted that he wanted to go further. I didn't want to deal with mind games so I took the hint and we were off.

I hiked with *Scavenger*, while *Rain Fly* fell behind again. *Scavenger* explained, "*Trail Mix* and *the Cops* are off the trail, because *the Cops* had a bachelor party. They will be skipping up to Front Royal, since they have hiked this area around Virginia Tech." He told me how he wanted to do two twenty-seven mile days to get to Waynesboro. Big miles sounded refreshing. I told him I was up for the challenge.

To save future time I cooked up the remainder of my pancake mix. The fire was partly dead when *Rabbit* offered his stove, because he wanted to get rid of his fuels excess weight. I made a leaning tower of pancakes. *Yogi* wanted one so badly. He even pleaded, "I'll eat one of the burnt ones."

But I was too stingy to give up any.

TEN

Scavenger

May 2nd – 10th

Day 59

At the crack of dawn I awoke ready for big miles, but
Scavenger was still hibernating. I tried whispering, "*Scavenger…
Scavenger…*" but it was to no avail. So I pinched his toes, like I
had seen Kelsey do to wake *Skippy*. I watched *Scavenger* slowly
awake and then collect fire wood to get a pot boiling for a brew.
He then invited me to have a cup. I sat there, giddy to get going.
Rain Fly woke up the entire shelter of people that I had worked
so hard not to disturb by announcing, "*Osama Bin Laden has been
killed and thrown into the sea!*"

I couldn't believe how poor his hiking etiquette was, but at
the same time I was astonished at the news.

Rain Fly was so excited to see and smell coffee that *Scavenger*
charitably poured him a cup. I felt slightly guilty for abandoning
Rain Fly, but I was ready for a new chapter.

I was feeling sick. I presumed the culprit was the slimy
hotdog I had the night before. We planned to do a thirty mile
day. Tired of waiting, I started off without *Scavenger*. I had a
couple miles climbing up an elevation of 3500 feet. I kept
thinking, *When is this trail ever going to reach the top?* I did try to
enjoy the scenery, because if I always thought of the trail as a
raceway I would miss the beauty. It was sad that hikers tend not
to care about nature the more they are in it. "Oh, another flower.
Oh, another waterfall." Everything tends to blur.

These long climbs had become a morning routine in these
northern mountains of Virginia. At the top, I climbed up
boulders and reached up to the sky with my phone in hand,
hitting send with no success. The last message I had received
from my mother had sounded concerned, but there was nothing
I could do. In the midst of this conundrum, *Scavenger* arrived, so
I slid down the rock and joined him getting baked in the sun
while walking along the balds. We talked about hiking, his

career back home, his next adventures, the Bible, beer, and the number of miles to the next shelter.

Late morning we ran out of water. I could hear water down a steep mountain side and pondered searching for it. The guidebook informed us of a long side trail to water. After watering up we cut down to the AT where the stream passed right by. I felt like an idiot – all that extra walking for nothing! We backtracked to our packs, where a third backpack was laid. I figured it must have been Jeff's, too bad we couldn't tell him the climb was avoidable.

Nearing the shelter, I saw a large white object and wondered what it was. "Maybe it's a horse."

"Nah, I doubt it," said *Scavenger*.

But sure enough at the shelter was a lady with two horses. "I used to ride horses for a hobby, but now I get paid for it," she said.

There were two middle aged men lying in the shelter. All their moaning and groaning indicated that they were still in the beginning stages of their trip. One mentioned that he had attempted to thru-hike years ago, but quit after eight hundred miles due to an injury.

I worked up a constant beat of slapping my arms every time a black fly bit me. Once I finally got grossed out at the number of smashed bugs up and down my arms, I asked for bug spray. *Scavenger* pulled out a bottle of 100% DEET. I thanked him and stared wide eyed at the directions. This stuff was potent. It warned, "No contact with skin." So I cautiously sprayed once on each sleeve. Next I saw *Scavenger* bathe his arms in DEET. I warned him that burning sensations could occur. I imagined him jumping around as if his arms caught fire, but it shocked me that all he said was, "I don't feel any burning." Then he slapped his arm and exclaimed, "I hate these bugs!"

I was eager to go, but I patiently watched the tall German man with his thick black beard tend to his fire. He then sat back, pulled out his pouch of tobacco and rolled a cigarette. While smoking, he crouched by the fire and lifted up his pot of boiling water and placed it on the table. He then stirred in the grinds. *Scavenger* had the build of a solider with broad shoulders on a tall frame. He spoke in a soft rumble. I suppose *Scavenger* could be scary if he tried, but he was nothing but amiable.

"Want some coffee?"

"Uh, yeah thanks," I said.

It was getting late so we cut the day short. There was no shelter at mile twenty-seven anyhow, so we settled for a twenty-two mile day. I still had a sickly feeling at supper time so I wasn't eating. *Scavenger* cooked up some couscous and gave me some; it was delicious. I was so touched by his generosity that I felt compelled to share. I gave *Yogi* and *Tortuga* each a pancake which they lathered up with butter and honey. I was entertained to see that *Yogi* was still ridiculously happy for a cold, day-old pancake.

Day 60

We planned to hike a thirty mile day. We started at 7:20am and ended at 10:25pm. First was a steep down for miles, then like a V the trail went up for miles. I passed three loud girls going ballistic because of some mud. I found it funny, except I felt conscious of my stench and overall filth.

Around five in the evening *Scavenger* caught up. By that time I had noticed I had dropped my phone, but he hadn't seen it. I decided not to worry about it.

After a ridiculously rocky section, *Scavenger* stopped to take a break near a road. He was hoping someone driving by would take him to Waynesboro. I suppose if I had tried hitch hiking it could have happened, (because I'm a girl) but I didn't want to skip miles. *Scavenger* said all he wanted was to watch a game of hockey with a beer in his hand.

We came to a campsite atop a high exposed place where all the other hikers planned to stay. We had hiked over twenty miles and *Scavenger* and I were thinking about calling it quits, until I remembered there was no water.

Monstrous thunderclouds blocked out the sun, causing darkness to fall prematurely. I tried denying the coming torrents as long as possible. I would joke about it as the cold wind began to blow. All of a sudden it was upon us. In frenzy, we stopped to cover our packs. We were drenched in seconds. Lightning began to flash and thunder roared. Most distressing was that I couldn't see. I was forced to remove my glasses because they were wet and fogged up. Things got worse when I acknowledged my headlamp was dying. I was constantly stumbling over the rocks that I was straining to see. I remained in this condition for miles. I felt like a poor wet puppy, who was too tired to care if it fell asleep in a puddle.

Thankfully, *Scavenger* watched out for me. He led the way. Whenever an obstacle was on the trail, he would yell, "Big rock," or "steps" or "this is extremely slippery," and he would turn around and shine his light so I wouldn't trip. He mentioned that he did the same thing for *Trail Mix* and *the Cops* when they had had even worse headlamps than mine.

I mentioned to *Scavenger* that I was glad I wasn't staying atop the exposed campground in this storm. *Scavenger* agreed that the other hikers were probably getting soaked. *Skippy* was in a hammock with only a tarp to keep out the wind and rain. We later heard that his tarp came loose and he woke up chilled in the icy rain. We knew our goal of staying in a shelter would be much more accommodating – if we ever got there.

We were both rot with thirst. We stopped at a spring, but it was dry, so we went on tripping like blind zombies.

Scavenger calculated that we were close to the shelter – I hoped he was right. He calculated with his watch that we were only a couple minutes away. After a large stream crossing, we lost the trail. He kept on searching back and forth as I followed, groggy and confused.

Eventually, out of the dark of night, a light shone in our direction. It was someone in the shelter who had heard our distress. We got inside the shelter before the rain picked up. In the shelter I changed into dry clothes. As I listen to the constant rain beat on the roof, I ate a bagel and fell asleep like a rock.

Day 61

The raining cats and dogs were still gallivanting on the tin roof when I awoke. I was glad to see the rain tamper off and stop. Yet again *Scavenger* took his time in the morning. While he spoke to a hiker named *Thru*, I left. The five miles to town felt forever since I was impatient. I ran into a hiker's dad; he asked for Joseph. I raised a brow. "Huh?"

"Oh, uh, *Yogi's* my son!"

"Right, yes of course."

At the road, *Scavenger* showed up and we walked to the information center in search of a ride. There was a long list of names to call for rides into town – over three miles away. I got a lot of, "Please leave a message," and a bunch of, "sorry but," before a sweet older lady came. She took a liking to *Scavenger*, so the conversation was mostly about Europe.

We were dropped off at a motel. *Scavenger* got the room under his real name and I found out he was named Benedict, which I found to be a wicked boss name.

I got a package from a friend. I was impatient and opened it on the way to the library. Inside was a massive bag of jumbo marshmallows. I was dumbfounded. "Wow, this is like two pounds!" I wondered how to fit them in my pack. Taking a seat next to *Scavenger* at a computer, I got confused when I didn't know what to type as my password. Apparently I needed to get a visitors pass, sign in to the mother computer, and then be assigned a seat. Oops! I used up my hour and then hit the grocery store.

At the motel, *Thru* left a note and came to join us. While organizing my food I spilled some natural peanut butter on the bed covers. I rinsed out what I could in the sink. When *Thru* went to wash his hands, he asked, "Did someone upchuck in the sink?"

Scavenger had a beer in his hand and the channel was turned to hockey. I was somewhat surprised that he actually accomplished his goal.

We chose Chinese for supper. Walking in I noticed the large population of overweight customers. Chubby children balanced towers of food on their plates. I thought up strategies for eating at the buffet. Small portions made the food appear gourmet. And it was better to not have pudding in my pizza or meat balls in my pudding. The most difficult strategy was to not over-eat. Naturally, one is going to over eat, but the trick is to stop before the nausea sets in.

Day 62

Scavenger and *Thru* went to the Laundromat while I used the sink. I found it shocking to see the dark, nasty water being wrung out of the clothes, but nonetheless it was satisfying to witness the murky water rush down the drain. I tried installing a dryer by duct-taping a blow dryer to the wall. I thought it was amazing, but in all honesty it wasn't effective, so instead I used the fence to dry my clothes in the sun. I had my laundry washed and hanging before *Scavenger* and *Thru* returned.

To my dismay, the refrigerator was actually a freezer, so all my fresh items froze. My yogurt was fun to eat partly frozen, but my carrots were solid and my mangoes later got squishy. We left our overfilled packs in the lobby as we ran around town.

We didn't want to leave so *Scavenger* and I stayed at the YMCA's free camping. I loved how near to the library it was and spent my time reading luxuriously on their couches.

Scavenger was in a whole different league in his affection for literature – to the degree that he became a walking library. I found him with his nose in a book and a stack of newly purchased books at his elbow. I couldn't believe it. "Did you finish your book that is as thick as the Bible?" I asked

"No," he replied, without being phased. "I love stories written by Steinbeck." He lifted up several for me to see. There was *Mice and Men* as well as *The Little Red Pony*. "Have you read any of his books?"

"No." Feeling like a poor soul who couldn't appreciate literature, I looked around. I found a book and bought it, then sat there just reading with *Scavenger*.

We went back to the Chinese buffet. I hadn't even noticed that they had sushi! My favorite! So this time I ate plate loads of

126

it. I made sure to eat properly with chopsticks, soy-sauce and wasabi.

Day 63

In the morning my things were drenched with dew from the nearby pond. I hung my things on a bench to dry as I sat in the sun and watched robins yank up earthworms. I even saw a beaver sneak a look at me before diving pack into the water.

My day was spent lounging in the library.

At the YMCA, they gave me a towel and a piece of bar soap. The shower was warm; I went mostly since my head was producing flurries. The shower was nice but a bit of a downgrade, since I had to press a button literately every ten seconds to keep the water flowing.

Back at the campsite, *Scavenger* was reading. I joined him, reading in the sun while munching on carrots.

A gray bearded man pulled in and walked directly over to our picnic table and took a seat. Rusty was his name. He seemed a bit down. "To be honest, I miss hikers. I used to have a thriving hostel for hikers. It served more hikers than any other hostel on the trail."

I asked him, "Well sir, if you miss hikers why did you close your hostel?"

He explained that hikers had trashed his place. They stole his valuables and didn't donate. He simply couldn't afford having guests anymore. I felt bad and upset at how greedy hikers could be. "Why don't you set a price everyone has to pay?" I asked.

He explained, "If I set a price, I must have an inspection by law and redo everything to standard. But I can't do that. My place isn't meant to be up to standard." He began describing his place in great detail. I asked if I could come see it.

He was uncertain. "No hikers have been to my place this year. I'm not even in the guidebook."

"I would really like to see your place," I insisted. *Scavenger* wanted to go, too. Rusty relented with the condition that we would pay for gas. Some hikers came by and were setting up tents. "Don't let them know," Rusty whispered. "I'm experimenting if this can work with only a few people."

We waited in the car as *Scavenger* cashed his traveler's check at Kroger. I saw *Llama Legs* in the parking lot. That was weird, since I was told *Llama Legs* was off the trail. I wanted to hear the story, but all I could do was wave my arms and holler, "Hey, *Llama Legs!*"

Rusty made us get out at the top of his long driveway. He told us every other hiker had walked to his place, so we would, too. He explained that he had special signs that we could only fully enjoy by walking. One sign read, "Triple crowners have big heads" There were signs about blue blazers, yellow blazers, and purists. There were signs cautioning falling rocks, mud, and snorers. Overall there were around a hundred signs. By his house one read, "No nudity in this area."

"Every sign has a story behind it," Rusty said.

An old man named Bob gave us a tour of Rusty's Hard Times Hollow. There were goats, dogs, chickens, and a potato patch surrounded by woods. Rusty said he was the only owner of an address on the Blue Ridge Parkway. "No other person has a driveway on a national park."

I prepared a nice, little meal with soup inside a bun's hard crust. The two old guys, Bob and Rusty, were both avid chatterboxes. They persisted as the day slowly diminished.

Day 64

I cooked up bacon and eggs and invited everyone for breakfast. I attempted to clean the kitchen, but the place was a complete mess. There was stuff everywhere. Rusty had all sorts of odd collections. Out of date food was randomly placed about the house. I figure I couldn't blame him, since not many people grow their own food.

An Amish family adopted Rusty after his parents kicked him out, so he spoke Pennsylvania Dutch. I knew a couple of phrases, but he would just keep speaking Pennsylvania Dutch to me as if I understood. He had a lot to say about the Amish being hypocritical. Like having a phone wired to their house from their neighbors; or hiring someone to drive them around. He eventually left the Amish since he couldn't stand that they took advantage of him, since he didn't have to live by their strict standards.

Bob was weed-whacking even though Rusty tried to stop him. Bob eventually butchered Rusty's garden hose. Rusty was sure the man was losing his mind. The problem was Bob didn't stop talking. If you changed the subject, he would just talk about something else. Bob's wife and daughter went on vacation to get some space. They intentionally went to places Bob disliked to insure that he wouldn't join them.

On our drive to the trail, Rusty stopped to talk to a park ranger. Rusty told us to never mess with a park ranger. "They have access to the White House and their cars are armored like tanks." Evidently parks need their service because criminals tend to run and hide in national parks.

Rusty dropped us off a bit further from where we were picked up. He gave us each a bear hug before leaving. I walked back to reconnect to where I had left the trail. It was a really short distance – just over a bridge. *Scavenger* teased me for being a purist. I told him, "I'm not *that* much of a purist."

"Then why did you walk over there just now?"

"Because I could," I said.

We came to the start of the Shenandoah National Park; there was a registry for hikers coming through. We had to put a tag on our pack listing our home address, the next shelters we were going to stay at, and how many days we would be in the park. It was a bother to fill out. *Scavenger* made up an address, like the time he got a cell phone and looked up a random address on Google Maps when he was forced to list an address in the States.

We got drizzled on as we discussed energy, and passed many cell phone towers. *Scavenger* complained that the towers were unhealthy. I didn't believe him until I saw a yellow bio-hazard sign. He told me Germany was shutting their nuclear power in 2030. I defended, "Hey, it's cheap."

"Yeah, but it kills you."

"Good point."

Scavenger forgot to bring any water and was regretting it, but luckily there were water bottles left for hikers by the road. He downed two.

On the trail to Calf Mountain Hut, *Scavenger* voiced his concern that the hut would be full, from all the tents already set up. I considered, "Perhaps they all snore and are just being considerate." When we arrived, only two people were staying in the hut. I asked why the others didn't use the hut.

They replied, "Oh, they snore."

We hung around the crackling fire and I had my first ramen on the trail. I tried to get the Shennie-section-hikers to eat my monstrous marshmallows, but only four were taken.

Day 65

When I awoke in the hut, a man was awake and he told me his wife normally snored louder then she was snoring at the time. I found it comically odd and left. I crossed the Blue Ridge Parkway a dozen times. At one particular crossing, a man yelled out from his car, "Hey you want something to drink?"

"Yeah," I said as if it were obvious. He handed me honey-buns and oranges. Ironically, I left the sodas, but I knew *Scavenger* would love one. He never showed, so we left him some near the road.

The guy handing out the food had attempted to thru-hike last year, but got sick before finishing. He seemed to really love the trail and wanted to finish the section he had missed and try thru-hiking again.

When I told him I was *Amish*, he continued, "From Lancaster PA."

My forehead wrinkled, "Huh?" Apparently he read my blog and knew all sorts of things about me. He knew I needed fire starters and handed me some candles. Before leaving, the man mentioned how the park rangers were trying to get rid of a homeless guy.

Back on the trail, I stopped for lunch at a hut and was scared by a man hidden in the corner of the hut. His stuff was scattered about and he was lying in an old sleeping bag. Something seemed fishy; *This has to be the homeless man, people we were talking about.* The guy would not stop talking about his ex-girlfriend or girls, or hiking – it didn't matter what. He did say that when he hiked Springer Mountain, which in my mind was questionable, some dude quit halfway up the mountain and threw his pack over the side before turning around to go home. The homeless guy was frustrated, "Hey man, you had food you could have shared," but the pack was too far down to retrieve. My theory is that this man made up this story or someone made it up for him.

For some reason, I introduced myself and he asked, "So since you're Amish, does that mean you don't smoke?"

I told him perhaps *Scavenger* had cigarettes and left.

In the pitch dark, I could make out a fire at Pine Field Hut where two section hikers were. I treated them with marshmallows and roasted some honey-buns to share with them. The guys were very impressed. I didn't think *Scavenger* would show up, but he never ceases to amaze me. He had left the shelter at ten and had been talking to his girlfriend in Germany for hours.

Day 66

During the night I woke up to see light surrounding a man's upper body. When I recognized *Scavenger* I asked, "What are you doing."

He twisted in his seat, "Cooking breakfast."

I shielded my eyes from the light, "What time is it?"

"Four."

I sat up, "What! Why are you up cooking breakfast at four?"

"I want to get to the halfway point by my birthday. Ive calculated that I need to hike thirties every day."

He spent his early morning cooking, and I fell back asleep.

He left at seven.

Five miles down the trail, I caught up. He was taking a break by a road. After hiking a bit together I noticed he wasn't in the best condition for such gruesome mileage. He said he had gotten six hours of sleep. Aghast, I told him that wasn't enough, but he insisted it was. He was complaining that the tops of his feet were hurting. I thought, *No wonder you're hurting. Your pack weighs fifty pounds.* I had told him several times to get rid of some pack weight, but I bit my tongue because I knew he wouldn't do anything about it.

I hiked alone; there were a lot of steep climbs. I had just run out of water when four happy old ladies greeted me. They asked questions about my trip. Of course we got to the topic of food, and they asked me if I wanted anything, to which I admitted, "Well, I really just need water." And they poured me some wonderful icy water – that surprised me, ice. *How unnatural.*

It was odd to be able to hike faster than people without packs. Some of these folk stared at me in wonder when I told them that I was hiking the entire trail, not just the Shennies. The one acted as if I were some hero, with her jaw on the floor. "How do you do it?"

It was three when I took lunch. I kept it short. It was hard being motivated after that. But twenty miles before lunch isn't shabby. I felt better when I read *Skippy's* post in the logbook: "Hurry up *Amish* and *Scavenger*, we feel threatened by the other German group."

Later I ran into Kelsey! "I caught up," I rejoiced.

She was glad to see me and was surprised that I had hiked thirty miles. "I have your cell phone. Found it in the middle of a stream on top of a rock. Still works!"

She told me about her frightful stay in Waynesboro. "A lady invited us to stay at her home when we were shopping at a grocery store. *Skippy* and I didn't see anything wrong with staying at someone's house. In fact we were glad to have a free place to stay," she remarked. "But then the lady started to behave odd and it only got worse over time. She mentioned that police had been at her house earlier in the day. We asked why there were police her house. She told us a neighbor had given her death threats. Plus, she started acting insane from her medication that helped her alcoholism. As you can imagine, we didn't get much sleep from being first being scared of living in a lunatic's house and the death threats. So we stayed another night, this time at a motel."

Kelsey also saw her first bear, which made *Skippy* jealous.

We walked past a campground and got invited by a family eating at the picnic table. They called out, "Would you two like something to eat?"

I beamed. "Oh yeah!"

Kelsey was indifferent. "I don't know, I already ate."

"Are you kidding? I'm starving," so we both took a seat. I was treated with all sorts of goodies. They would keep on pulling out more and more food, while asking if I wanted it. Most of what I said was: "yup, yes, yup, mm-hmm, that would be nice, yes thanks, mmnm."

Kelsey and I made a great team: while I was stuffing my face, she did all the talking. The man there had hiked the Appalachian Trail decades ago. They had been looking for someone with which to share Trail Magic. It was great – I didn't even have to yogi. I loved being a girl. They let me use their phone to speak with my mother, and then invited us to stay and set up camp there, but we moved on. They gave us food to take with us, as well as their phone number to call for more trail magic in Pennsylvania. It was an all together delightful experience.

We got a little lost in the dark before arriving at Rock Springs Hut. *Skippy* was happy to see me. They asked where *Scavenger* was. I told them, "He was planning to do a thirty like me, but I doubt he'll make it, it's been dark for awhile now."

Before I knew it *Scavenger* showed up.

I shared my new treats with *Skippy* and *Scavenger* and ate some more myself. *Skippy* was a bit sore about us girls being so lucky. "The only reason they gave *you* food is because you're girls. I saw that same family and they didn't say anything to me!"

"Well," I advised. "If you weren't always listening to music and smiled once in a while you might get lucky, too."

I told *Scavenger*, "Yeah, I'm not doing a thirty tomorrow."

After a little he looked up and agreed. "Yeah, I don't want to do a thirty, either."

Day 67

The day was chill. We read all morning. Kelsey and *Skippy* slept in late. Near lunch time we walked four miles to a restaurant. The prices were high and the portions were low. We hung out for hours and read some more. We felt bonded as a group.

The "other German group" as *Skippy* called them, showed up. We started to debate over whose German was better. The guys were talking about having a drinking contest between the Germans, called Edward 40 hands. The rules were to duck tape a forty ounce beer in each hand. "*Our* German could win hands down. Have you seen him drink?" we taunted.

When the Germans finally met face to face, the rivalry only grew. They lived on opposite sides of the country. It didn't help that *Scavenger* was from Bavaria, the wealthiest part of Germany. Bavaria actually tried to split into their own country. *Cologne* was from northern Germany and his English wasn't as developed as *Scavenger's*.

Llama Legs and Harry were at Pass Mountain Hut. I made a sizzling bacon wrap and Harry let me finish the rest of his Mountain House. It was great to see him again. When it started to rain we packed up for bed. I felt bad for the other hikers who got to bed at sundown and had to put up with our noise. Although I helped a tad by giving the one hiker ear plugs. *Scavenger* didn't show up, perhaps he stayed at the shelter four miles back.

ELEVEN

The Other Germans

May 11th – 16th

Day 68

I didn't know if *Llama Legs* waited for me, but somehow we started off together. It wasn't in my nature to talk to guys blessed with being tall, dark, and handsome like *Llama Legs*.

I took the opportunity to ask the pending question; "Why did *Mile High* say you were off the trail?"

"You know how I lost my wallet in Damascus? Well, I was waiting for my new credit card to be shipped when I got a text from *Mile High* asking if everything was okay. I sent a text, "Actually, I'm going home. I ran out of money." At the time it was a great joke because I thought I'd catch up quickly and his reaction would be priceless, but it's taken me much longer than I expected."

"How long did you think it would take you?"

"A week."

"How long has it been?"

"Over a month." There was a pause. "You're a Christian right?"

"Yeah," I said.

"In Damascus I went to church for the first time. And it raised a lot of questions. I never gave much thought about religion until I started hiking with *Mile High* and *Data*. *Data* was raised a home-schooled Christian and *Mile High* is a Jew."

"Yeah, but he's not a *real* Jew," I interjected. "Remember how I had a debate with him about the New and Old Testament? I understand that he doesn't believe in the New Testament with Jesus and all, but he doesn't even believe in the story of Adam and Eve."

"Who are Adam and Eve?"

"They were the first two people on earth," I exclaimed, blown away at his lack of knowledge about the Bible. "Let's start with the basics then. Do you know the big deal behind Jesus?"

"No not really."

"Oh, well all in all, he was the one that made it possible for people to live in heaven."

"Oh."

"So why did you go to church in Damascus, anyhow?" I asked.

"Well I was told the best place to ask for odd jobs would be at a church."

"Yeah, I can see that."

"I made a lot of money without having to work hard. Like at one of the homes, I was mostly preached to and didn't really work. Then I was astonished when they handed me a hundred dollars."

"Wow! Yeah, Christians can be very generous people," I said.

Over the miles we talked about all sorts of topics.

"So, what do you think about me marrying a Canadian friend simply for the health care benefits?" *Llama Legs* asked.

"Probably not the best reason to get married."

"And by the way I don't ever want to have children," he said.

"Why forever not?"

"Because there are too many messed up kids in this world. I don't think I would make a good father, so it's best for me not to have children."

I agreed that if people were going to be fathers they should be good ones, and immediately respected his way of thinking. But I knew I would probably disagree on his opinion of sex before marriage. After he dove into the subject, "This is awkward." He weaseled his way out of the awkwardness by altering his wording. "I like candy and I don't see why I shouldn't have it," was his way of putting it.

"It's a lot worse for the girl, she's known as a slut, is stuck with the baby, and can't afford a place to stay. If you're going to get married why complicate it before it's even started," I pointed out. "Did you know that statistically couples that wait to live together after they're married have a lower divorce rate than the couples that live with each other before marriage?"

After conversing for ten miles straight, we stopped at one of the park's shops where we got the famous blackberry smoothie along with the rest of his group.

After five miles we got to the next hut. I noticed *Llama Legs* had a pocket in the back of his shirt.

"Oh, it's just my biking shirt." Then he spoke about his long distance biking races. I felt unqualified for the conversation, so I broke out a deck of cards and started shuffling.

A kid in the shelter looked at me with a huge grin and a twinkle in his eye. "Can I play a hand?" he asked. So we played. He was with a sick friend hiking a section of the trail for their graduation project, and I thought they were ingenious because they got to miss school for it. He had been stationary for several days while waiting for his sick friend to recuperate.

Soon *Llama Legs* left and I had to make the choice between staying and leaving. The kid with a twinkle in his eye begged me to stay longer. I had been enjoying my time so I stayed. They shared their food with me and I thought I could share some beef stroganoff with them, but they were vegetarians. We played until the sun set and then I took out candles and we playing by candlelight.

Day 69

I bid farewell to my new friends. The happy kid was uberly grateful that I had decided to hang out with him. The sick one announced that he felt like a spring chicken and was ready to get hiking again. They were studying a map when I left. I wouldn't be seeing them again, because they were going southbound.

I walked out of the Shennies and came to fences along each side. Dogs barked as I passed the backyards of homes. I hitched to town. Next time I'll resupply at a dollar general since *Skippy* said they're cheaper, but I went to the Food Lion and the moment I got the bill I regretted it. I ate my chips and salsa on a bench like a homeless person. I then hitched back – that was my fastest resupply!

I had all sorts of pets on the trail; Charlie the centipede, Nelly the snail and Ricky the mouse. I tried to catch a snake back in the day and a grouse yesterday, but that day, I found a mouse sitting on the trail. I knew I wanted to catch it, but I didn't know where to put it. I quickly decided I could sacrifice my water bottle for the time being. I threw down my pack and chugged some water before dumping out the rest. After a game of cat and mouse, I had a new, little pet in my water bottle.

I hiked along to the shelter, where the "other German group," also known as Mannschaft Schlampenstempel, were. Only *Cologne* the German could pronounce their team name. The people in the group were *Llama Legs*, *Fin*, and *Cologne*.

Cologne insisted that he didn't think *Scavenger* was a real German. "I spoke German to him, and he spoke back in English; I doubt if he can even speak German."

And then there was the whole Bavarian thing. *Cologne* enjoys calling Scavenger *"the Bavarian"*, so *Llama Legs* and *Fin* teased, "*Cologne* you only wish you were Bavarian."

The guys were positively disgusted when I dumped out the wet mouse on the picnic table. The mouse, whom I named Eleanor, shivered so intensely that she had a wobbly walk, so I placed her in the sliver of sunlight cast on the table. I would lose track of Eleanor and *Fin* did not approve when she got in his dining area, "Is the mouse eating my hotdog?" he asked dramatically. They all were feeling sorry for the shivering mouse and accused me for its piteousness. I put the mouse in my coat pocket which dried her out fast.

When *Cologne* asked, "Where's the mouse?" I pulled out Eleanor and she ran up my arm and jumped off and hit the ground running. Unfortunately, the sun had set and it was too dark to see.

The guys liked to discuss the hardships in life, including getting up to pee at night. "Did you hear of the guy that peed out his tent and then hit his Croc?"

"Did you know there was a girl that started the trail with a contraption to pee on trees? At Neels Gap they told her she didn't need it."

"Yeah, it's definitely better to be a man," they concluded

Next they discussed the countries where the hottest girls lived. *Cologne* thought Californian girls were the best in the States.

The others replied, "Yeah they're hot, but they're too emotional." *Llama Legs* thought girls from England were hot.

Cologne disagreed, "No way! Girls from Scandinavian countries are far hotter."

Day 70

It was Friday the 13th and motivation was at an all time low. The weather was so foggy and humid that I felt like I was eating atmosphere. I saw a box turtle and a dead deer in a stream. Then on a road I saw a deer skull with 'cursed be *Llama Legs*' written on it.

Cologne left as I arrive at the shelter and that was when the rain kicked into high gear. *Fin, Llama Legs,* and I waited out the rain and eventually took naps. *Fin* found some tobacco, but there weren't any papers. They mentioned New Testaments have rice paper. After they couldn't find any in the shelter, I offered *Fin* a page of mine. He seemed a bit uneasy, "Just don't give me anything saying I'm going to hell."

□■□

Good thing it rained since:

I was about to snap.

Oh man this is a perfect time for writing a rap,

Right before taking a nap.

I'll start all the way back in Daleville,

Where I got new gear and relocated my snail mail.

I hiked chill days with *Rain-Fly*.

I felt bad, since I abruptly said goodbye.

I made enough pancakes to feed a pig and a hog,

Yogi stared at them long and hard.

My sickness of low mileage, I needed a cure,

It was fixed by our German, *Scavenger*.

We hiked entire days through,

And weariness slowly grew,

I knew to do thirties forever, I'd turn blue.

I had a group for a bit and thought them my crew,

But it's good to meet people I never knew.

◻◼◻

The rain cleared and I meandered through the green tunnel once again. I whistled to keep from boredom and *Fin* behind me, whistled back. On the way to the shelter *Llama Legs* educated me on hallucinogens. He explained that people either have good trips or bad trips – similar to dreams. *Fin* remarked that because he had a bad trip he hasn't had the desire to try, again.

"The guy that wrote Alice in Wonderland was definitely tripping balls. And you know in the Matrix when Mr. Anderson touches the mirror and it stretches? Things like that happen. The bad trips are filled with your worst fears. They are worse than nightmares, because they feel like reality." I thought of *Skippy* and thought, *I bet he'd be surrounded by snakes on his bad trips.*

The shelter was filled with soaked clothes hanging from every open space. I got to watch *Yogi* and *Llama Legs* reunite. "Hey, dude!" *Yogi* exclaimed giving *Llama Legs* a hug, "I was told you were off the trail! How have you been?"

Day 71

I awoke early to the sound of heavy snoring. Bleak was the forecast, but I was ready to finally leave the state. Virginia made sure that I knew her state was no cakewalk. Virginia was not flat and I don't know where that notion ever came from. Even with the last couple miles, she gave me the beat down. The section was known as the roller-coaster and there was a sign cautioning that the section was insanity. All I could think was, *Why Virginia? Why? I thought we were friends.*

There was a parade of boy scouts on the trail. They didn't seem very friendly since the lead kid shouted, "All to the right!" at the top of his lungs, like an army commander. It made zero sense to have the whole troop stop and stand in the bushes and whatnot, since it would have been much easier for me to move aside. As I passed the kids, I eavesdropped on some knee-slappers conversations. The one kid was telling a riddle and told the other kid, "If you know, don't tell."

The other kid replied, "Well logically, it's..." speaking too quietly for me to hear.

The child scolded, "I told you to not tell if you knew."

The next several miles, I tried to piece the riddle together from what I had heard. I figured out it must have gone something like: There was a *couples* retreat on a cruise ship. The ship wrecks and every *single* person died, but there weren't any casualties. How is this possible?

On the trail there were many people who stopped to talk to me. They would ask, "How are you?"

"Fine, I just wanna be out of Virginia."

"Wow! You're a thru-hiker! Are you having a good trip?"

"Yeah, it's been good." They would wait with their mouths open and eyes bright, waiting for me to elaborate, but I wouldn't say much more than, "I'm really tired right now." I felt bad for not being able to match their enthusiasm.

I breathed a sigh of relief at the border of Maryland. "Virginia, you were beautiful, but you were never flat! Goodbye." Virginia took me thirty-five days to beast and I was not looking back. *Skippy* showed up right as I got to the 1000 mile mark sign.

Skippy had stayed by a shelter with a snake, but was too freaked out to remove the thing or to sleep in the shelter with it. He wished I, "the snake wrangler" had been there to take care of business. I agreed. *Skippy* also mentioned that not far back he had seen a baby snake; he admitted it looked somewhat cute, until he noticed the rattle. Then he freaked out because he remembered that baby rattlers can't control their venom and therefore can be extra deadly. All he could think was, *I don't want to die. Not me, not now.*

Kelsey commented that *Skippy* was airing his socks, but they smelled so bad that she didn't hike with him all day. She asked if I had noticed the ungodly smell since she didn't have the heart to tell him.

I was glad to be with *Skippy* and Kelsey again. Apparently, *Scavenger* was behind us. I hoped he would catch up by his birthday. We stayed at the Blackburn Trail Center, where we set up camp on their porch. I was surprised when the lady that lived there made us a spaghetti dinner with awesome sauce and brownies for dessert.

There was a scale there and *Skippy* was enthusiastic that his pack *only* weighed thirty pounds. Mine weighed twenty.

Day 72

We had a nero day and saved Harper's Ferry for the following day. I was excited that my mother and brother were planning to hike Maryland with me and that I would be going home for a couple days.

We asked if anyone had seen *Scavenger*. One guy mentioned that he saw a large tent south of us, two miles away. I got excited. "That must be *Scavenger*!"

But *Skippy* disagreed, "Scavenger never sets up his tent." As we were waiting for *Scavenger* I read his book, which *Skippy* had previously been reading. It was, "The Red Pony" and *Skippy* read, "Heaven is for Real".

On our three mile trudge of the day, *Skippy* told me that throughout history people have seen the same things, but called them different things: angels being mistaken as elves, fairies, or whatnot. But he believed people's stories of heaven were all from a hallucination set off in their brain when they die, so I guess he thought heaven was a bunch of boloney.

At the shelter were tons of stink bugs. They kept landing on me, so I cleaned out my peanut butter jar and collected them.

Prescott arrived. I had seen his name in the shelter logs, so I asked, "Why are you way back here?" Apparently, he enjoyed taking zeros. He commented that he hiked with *Peach* and *Buddha*, which was Andy's trail name. *Skippy* was really excited when he found out that *Prescott* lived fifteen minutes away from him. "There are so many people from Boston on the trail. Every year a different part of the world hikes the Appalachian Trail. This year it is clearly New England."

I asked a section hiker who was finishing in Harper's Ferry if he had any food he didn't need. I was so happy when he gave me some tuna. This man had helped me before by giving me water way, way back; he told me how he was disgusted at the bubbly residue of powdered milk at the bottom of my bottle and remarked that at the time, I had looked like I was on the verge of collapsing.

It was pouring, but I still needed to make a fire to cook my food. I thought I would at least give it a try. It didn't work. I was sitting under the pavilion eating tuna, when three men appeared. They asked how far away the water was. The one guy had just broken his brand new carbon fiber hiking pole by falling on it, but they were incredibly happy just to be out on their first day of their hike. I felt bad, since rain was in the forecast for the next week. They left when they learned that the water source was half a mile away.

We were so unlucky because a drippy man showed up and instantly fell asleep and began a dreadful snore. It was unlike any other snore. While the others were wondering how to get any sleep from the sporadic sawmill going on, *Skippy* and I impersonated the sound and broke out in to fits of laughter. One of the guys suggested removing the man by chucking him onto the picnic table. Every once in a while his snoring would stop and silence fell until loud snorts of nasal clearing erupted. "He almost choked to death like four times now," complained the one guy. Soon they became desperate and decided to make lots of noise. They lifted their feet inside their sleeping bags and banged on the floor until the snoring ceased. I was glad for ear plugs and fell asleep.

Day 73

I had to hike swiftly to keep up with *Skippy,* who was going to a gas station to resupply. I took the opportunity to consume two pints of ice-cream, and then shared his french-fries. We came across graffiti that read, "It's 5-4-2011. *Trail Mix* and *the Cops* found a teleportation device. Shout out to Blue Team *Amish* and *Scavenger* hurry on up." Although the note was defacing property, I was happy to be remembered.

At the Appalachian Trail Conservatory headquarters, in Harper's Ferry, I got my picture taken like all the other hikers. I wasn't impressed with my photo, my hair was cropped around my head funny, and the stretchy blue shirt I wore since Georgia still clung a bit tight. I looked at the book full of pictures taken of the hikers and recognized speedy people like *V8* and *Hermes.*

The ATC had an extra room set aside for us to keep the place looking clean, since hikers tend to reek and lounge around like mange dogs. I liked the place since they had sticky-buns and sofas. The computer was the item in demand, so we graciously took turns and we became Facebook friends. "Wow *Amish,* you look great with long hair," *Skippy* complemented.

I found a hefty jar of *Skippy* crunchy peanut butter in the hiker box. I showed it to *Skippy* and he immediately lit up. He hollered, "This is my *absolute* favorite kind!" He then went around telling everyone that he found it.

I knew when my relatives showed up, because of my mother's traveling voice. They held their breaths as they gave me a hug. Right off the bat, I wanted to see the food they brought me.

Eventually *Scavenger* showed up. I gave him the slice of cheesecake I had asked my mother to bring, with three candles and wished him a happy birthday.

144

When I realized my mother and brother were ready to go, I felt like I was skipping on my Harper Ferry experience. It was hard to make my brain think "hike"; logically all that came to mind was to be whisked away and given the royal treatment. I told myself, *You can do this, just a couple more days before you rest.*

Before long we were over a bridge and out of Harper's Ferry, known as the unofficial halfway point. Then we had a long section along a river, which was so flat that it became dull. I was relieved to see my two new hiking buddies didn't over pack.

But the man at the shelter did; his pack weighed sixty pounds. It didn't surprise me that he had the name *Tortoise*. He pulled out a bear canister. "These things are great," he declared, beaming, "No bear can get my food with this!"

I thought it looked ridiculous and I tried not to say anything harsh. He began lightening his load by cooking all three of us mashed potatoes with salmon. He even gave me his harmonica and commented, "I thought I'd have time to learn."

In the Ed Garvey shelter log, a scandalous lie was written about me and the person didn't leave their name. I was glad my mother was oblivious of the entry and she kept talking cheerfully. I scribbled it out. I had been leaving slightly in-depth entries for friends, but after this incident I refrained from writing anything. I noticed an abnormal celebrity reaction came from people who caught up. They would say, "I've been following your entries for weeks and wondered when I'd meet you." Then they would give an awkward introduction before speeding off. Perhaps the same thing had happened to *Llama Legs;* people were constantly giving him feedback on his funny jokes and comments, which he had quit writing. I hadn't understood at the time why he quit and actually wanted to be like him, but now I could only wonder what happened.

Skippy and *Scavenger* showed up late and partied on the second floor of the shelter. They brought beer and were loudly playing cards in celebration of *Scavenger's* birthday. Part of me wanted to join them and the other part wanted to yell in frustration, "Be quiet! Can't you see my mother is with me?" But I was content that *Scavenger* could celebrate his 27th birthday.

TWELVE

A Bit of Home

May 17th – 29th

Day 74

The rain was still coming down in the morning. *Nocello* left early; he was part of the Mannschaft Schlampenstempel, but I never got to meet him. He had been leaving graffiti signatures all over the place. His name was hard to remember until *Llama Legs* told me he was a cello player, but couldn't carry a cello on the trail, hence the name no cello. It was nice to be able to pronounce his name since I kept calling him something that sounded more or less like Nutella.

Carby, my brother, stated, "*Tortoise* wasn't lying when he said that he snored."

"They never do," I answered. As I looked out into the dreary weather, I said, "Let's leave after the rain stops." We chatted while *Tortoise* packed. He had trouble making everything fit back into his pack. He made us coffee from the water he had hiked to retrieve that morning. I was shocked at how inefficient he was to hike that section twice. I needed to use every ounce of energy I had to get through the miles.

We had tried catching rain water during the night, but it wasn't any good with unwanted tree droppings in it.

When the rain stopped, we packed up and left by the time *Tortoise* was ready. He rapidly fell behind and began to say his adieus when he suddenly wiped out. He got up and hollered that he was okay and immediately took a second spill.

Throughout the day, Carby needed my assistance to fit his trash bag over him and his pack. My mother had a trash bag with a hood. She had the appearance of an elf whenever she tucked the hood behind her ears. At one point, she wore the poncho over her pack, and looked like a hunchback. I couldn't stop laughing at her.

A park that was situated on the other side of a stone archway was where we utilized the restrooms and studied our reflections in the mirrors. While my mother pumped out rusty water, I informed her of a hiker who had traced back his giardia from a spigot.

We went back to the trail through the archway, but were only teased when the trail went through the very park where we had just been! Stupid mistakes happen, but family has a way of making it exasperating. "You should know that the trail went this way. Haven't you been living on the trail for months now?"

Throughout the day, Carby and I quoted Shrek and Lord of the Rings. Some parts he would nail and that made me happy. Other times he would say a wrong word and I would catch it.

At only four miles to go, I was pooped. I sat on a stone wall while listening to this and that. When I looked to the sky, I saw ominous, southern clouds swiftly moving toward us. The others put on their silly trash bags and asked me, "Do you need help putting on a trash bag, too?"

"No, don't worry."

All of a sudden the rain was upon us. Again I was asked if I needed a trash bag. "I'm fine," I insisted. "See, I'm dodging *most* of the raindrops."

As the sky continued to dump on us, we ran gaily down the trail, passing other hikers. One man sincerely tried to start a conversation with me, but all I had time to say was, "Sorry, bye."

After several minutes, the rain died down and a lady told us the next section was flat. She must have been joking, because the only part that was flat was the footbridge over the highway. I waved at the traffic and got honks in reply.

I was in awe at the rate my mother was booking. She was worried about getting room at the "5 person" shelter. I had them guess how many people were at the shelter. Mom guessed two and Carby guessed twenty. I guessed one and he happened to be an intriguing individual. We referred to him as *Carrot.* He had an afro of bright, orange hair and he had a thing for carrots, which he was constantly peeling to eat. He was young, probably high school age and had tattoos all over his face, arms, and legs. We were glad to see that he had a fire going. I thanked him for his hard work and capitalized on the flames. I made quinoa in a can, and added tuna and cheese for my gang's supper.

I found the fellow *Gas Cap* to be interesting. He was a thru-hiker who started in late December. I couldn't wrap my head around why someone would do that to themselves. Perhaps he was too impatient to get hiking. I suppose it must have been his Christmas present to himself. He said he rarely shared shelters in the deep of winter when the snow was piled high. *Gas Cap* was a real gentleman. Although I thought it was odd that he had a sack filled with pill bottles, he smiled a lot and was really charming.

Day 75

It was pouring when I woke up, but it slowed to a drizzle. Poor, poor Carby said he woke up to the roof leaking on him.

Mom watched in awe as I inhaled three packets of oatmeal.

We started with an abrupt incline that resembled a wall. *Carrot* marched past us with a scooter under his arm. As he scampered up the trail, I thought of the story *Carrot* had told us about riding down a hill towards town on his scooter and not being able to slow down. The road was slick and he was gaining momentum fast. He decided his best option was to roll off his scooter. He got a bit banged up, but survived.

I felt so exhausted and my knees operated like rusty hinges. While we scrambled over rocks, I dreamed of sleep. By lunch I could have passed out in seconds, so I proposed that we all take a nap, but Carby was full of energy and Mom claimed that it was too much work to blow up her mattress.

Since I had a thousand miles under my belt, I felt like I should be able to dance around my family while carrying their packs, all the while beaming a laughing grin. *But that today was definitely not that day, if that day would ever come.*

This time when it rained I meekly put on a trash bag, since my shirt was finally dry and I couldn't bear having it wet again. We circled around dozens of puddles and unfortunately, I slipped into one and soaked both my shoes. My mother thought it the most hysterical thing. I didn't see the amusing side of the incident. However, falling into the puddle *did* give me the liberty to continue walking through puddles. At the end of the day, I marveled at my incredibly wrinkly feet and invited everyone to witness how white and wrinkly they were.

The brand spanking new shelter had a polished wooden floor. But the water source was a mile round-trip. My mother was frazzled about the water situation, but I told her to hang loose and let the guys offer us water. I was right, before long *Gas Cap* gave us a liter of his water and others offered to fill up containers. Carby made a fire, which I cooked on and toasted pop tarts for dessert. I went to bed as soon as possible. *Skippy* smirked at my pathetic state of exhaustion. "You're going to bed already?"

Day 76

I awoke to *Prescott* announcing that he had tons of water for the taking and warned that he was soon dumping it out. I sat up and gave orders for my peeps to fill up my water bottle and take care of themselves. I felt my head split into different personalities. The pleasant lazy side smoothed, *Awe you poor sleepy thing, just go back to sleep.*

The unfeeling logical side snarled, *Get up you smelly fleabag.*

No, I don't wanna.

All of a sudden, I had a realization. *You can do it honey it's you last day,* encouraged the sweet side.

Yeah! Get cracking it's your last day, spat the cruel side.

I ate a bunch of pop tarts and cold oatmeal; although I had a fear of making pop tarts a habit. I realized it was the first time I ate oatmeal on the trail. Oatmeal seemed so basic a food that I felt like an idiot for not eating it sooner. I remembered how I used to eat trail mix for breakfast, day after day, back in the Georgia days.

Carby found a hiking stick and called it a staff. He was against using poles and called us bi-polar. He walked ahead of us, saying, "Staffs are superior because Gandalf and Moses had them."

149

As dreary and miserable rain sounds for three days straight, it was. Believe me, it was. Ironically, I was telling my mother that *Smurf* and *Count* were days ahead, when near noon time, we came upon a pavilion just as the rain intensified. Inside were a bunch of boys lying in their sleeping bags. All five were as dreary as the weather. They were *Smurf*, *Yogi*, Harry, *Johnny Apple Seed*, and *Mango*. I felt like an intruder at a sleepover. Some of them were still unresponsive. *Smurf's* friends, *Johnny Apple Seed*, and *Mango*, introduced themselves with friendly smiles.

I asked, "How on earth have I caught up?"

"We're waiting on *Count* he's spending ten days in Maine. Visiting his girlfriend," replied *Johnny Apple Seed*. "We warned him not to go for that long, because he'll never want to come back. Other than that, we've lost motivation."

I nodded. I had lost motivation, too. The rain definitely had a part in the problem. After making it "halfway", we all felt like we deserved a vacation. I totally understood how they felt. Believe me, I couldn't wait to get home and be a bum myself.

From the pavilion it was two tenths of a mile to the Mason Dixon line. We were back to good, old PA. *Skippy* was there, taking pictures with us.

I had invited my friends to relax and eat good food at my house, but no one took the offer. Kelsey was visiting her boyfriend in a couple of days and *Scavenger* didn't answer his phone. *Skippy* thought he should catch up to Kelsey, with whom he shared mail drops. He mentioned he was aiming to hike a marathon and sped ahead of us, skipping as he went – just to humor me.

At the bottom of the mountain was a parking lot where my dad came to pick us up. On the drive home, my father had difficulty dealing with my pungent aromas. He acted as if it was so bad that while he was driving, he rolled down the windows and stuck out his head.

My mother said, "When we hiked I didn't need to have my eyes open to follow Emily, I could just follow my nose."

By the time we arrived home, I was feeling extremely conscious of my smells. I stood awkwardly in the kitchen, thinking I should be running up to family members and giving hugs. It had been thirteen days since I had taken a shower. My brother jumped into the shower while I was distracted by being home, which appeared different than I had remembered: the furniture seemed smaller and there were new gadgets everywhere. When I got to my room, I was a bit sore over the fact that my bedroom space was being used as storage.

My mother let me pick the menu for supper. We had tacos, which were absolutely delicious.

Day 77-82

I utilized my house the way hikers would use a hostel and I absolutely loved it. I was a couch potato and watched a marathon of films.

My mother drove me to my aunt's cabin in the mountains, where more aunts were gathering. During the two hour drive we passed Duncannon, a trail town, I had yet to hike through.

At the cabin, I heard my mother tell the same exact story at least three times! "And what do you know? There was a man with a tent set up in the shelter!" she remarked, as if it were extraordinary. Her inexperienced perspective of the trail seemed silly and I found it a nuisance to hear over and over. I was glad; however that she had enjoyed "her little hike."

Aunt after aunt told me to eat more, but I had already lost my raging appetite. We made mountain pies on a fire outside and I was asked if hikers used hobo pie makers, too. "No," I answered, "imagine how much weight that would be!"

Back home, I assisted Carby and Euan, a childhood friend, in grocery shopping for the section that they would be hiking with me. I encouraged them to buy clever things, but Euan still got a weighty can of baked beans and Carby purchased gobs of frosted pop-tarts.

When I took a look at Euan's pack, I immediately tried to cut weight. We got rid of several pounds right off the bat; including a leather Bible and extra clothes. He insisted on bringing a headlamp that weighed more-or-less a pound. I informed him that I wasn't bringing a sleeping bag because of the warmer days, but instead was bringing a liner. He followed the notion and ditched his, which cut another two pounds.

Day 83

All in all, I spent a week at home. It was so long that I became used to the luxuries of a house: where being clean was normality. I used to be unable to smell myself, but after being clean for so long, I could smell things that my family had, and I had to agree my backpack did have a strong odor.

Carby and Euan joined me on the car ride towards Maryland. Euan was excited for hiking big miles. He asked, "What was the most you ever hiked in one day?"

"Thirty-three miles," I grinned.

"Then we should hike thirty-five."

My mother wanted to join, but decided not to after hearing the crazy miles Euan the stallion wanted to do.

My Aunt Alice drove me and my two companions to the trail. Back at the parking lot, *Legion* was sitting on the picnic table. Then *Steady* came along. They both said, "I thought you were a week ahead." It was lovely to see the two of them. *Legion* mentioned the posts in shelter logs that were written about me. I replied that I had no idea who was writing them.

It was cool to be able to show Euan and Carby some of my trail friends.

I could hear my heart beating in my ears as I followed Euan. It was hotter than I had remembered and Euan was fast. It was not fair that he had such long legs. At seventeen he was probably over six foot tall. He didn't seem to think having long legs was great, but while he strolled along, I was hustling to match his speed.

It was odd that all the hikers we passed knew who I was. It was strange, since I didn't know them. They would tell me all sorts of things that they had heard about me. And they knew some of my friends.

We were shooting for fifteen miles, but a thunderstorm overpowered our intentions. We stopped at two small shelters, with a hiker in each, but they moved together for the three of us to have our own. They had built a fire so we immediately started cooking Euan's bacon and baked beans. We raced the unrelenting rain to cook our food before the fire became waterlogged. The beans were extra watery and the bacon was dusted in ash. With pride, I offered to use my homemade, cat-food can stove to finish cooking our dinner.

We ended the day with our sleeping pads in a circle and played card games. Euan's headlamp was so bright that it made the whole shelter glow. I was enjoying the game immensely since I was a steady winner. It had been dark for awhile but, Euan pleaded, "One more hand. Please just one more hand." Game after game he would say the same thing. After he didn't win, he started to say, "Let's play 'til I win." Eventually he won and we went to bed.

Day 84

It was hard to sleep without a sleeping bag. Euan was in the same boat, since he left his behind too, by my influence. We only had liners. Carby was the only one who got adequate sleep. All night we were on the verge of a chill. Every hour or so, I put on another piece of clothing. Finally, by early dawn, I suggested wrapping up in our tarps. We made quite a racket with our crinkly tarps, but by that time it was too late, the sun had already risen.

The guys wanted to do a thirty mile day. For lunch Euan made a fire to cook his food. I tried to persuade the guys not to do a thirty, because I knew the pain that would come with it, but I wanted to get to the halfway point at the same time. Carby was all for the thirty miles until he heard we had only done thirteen miles by lunch, and then he was a bit concerned.

After the halfway point of the Appalachian Trail was a convenience store for the half gallon challenge. I was upset that the contestants didn't get the ice cream for free anymore when they finished. We still had many miles to hike, and there was no way I would have been able to hike had I eaten the whole thing.

We shared the half gallon between the three of us as it started to pour. The rain slowed once we started walking again. There were toads all over the trail, and Carby muttered about me stepping on one in the dark. We night hiked until 10:30ish. Euan had an insanely bright headlamp, which I was jealous of at the time, since mine was so dinky.

My belly ached a bit and my knee hurt. Carby gave a great motivational speech. "My dear friends, you've both done so well, I am proud of you. We have come far, and have gone through many obstacles together. Now we just have a bit more to go." It surprised me how inspired I felt afterward.

I felt extremely bad when Euan stubbed his little toe as we were hiking. It happened several times where all of a sudden he would yell in scrutinizing pain and would kneel in a tight ball for a minute or so. Carby and I would wait there until his pain subsided. He said it felt like murder to stub a single toe.

The shelter was filled with people – one was snoring – but we all found room. Carby had to squeeze under one of the bunk beds to sleep. I told him to wake me up if he needed to get out during the night. I made sure to keep warm, by putting on everything all at once and wrapping up in my tarp.

Day 85

In the morning, I thought the one man sleeping was *Scavenger*. I kept wondering what I should say to him, and I was so excited that I caught up that quick. But it turned out to be someone else. I was disappointed.

We spent the morning playing cards. We all hurt miserably. Well, Carby was only a bit sore and only sustained a blister on his pinky toe. Euan was in the most pain. He didn't want to go *anywhere*. Plus, he wanted to wait for his five finger shoes to dry.

At first, I could barely walk because my knees were hurting so intensely. I took ibuprofen for my knee, which hikers refer to as "vitamin-I" because many are in need of it constantly. I didn't think it was healthy to pop pain killers that much, but Euan was on the opposite side of the spectrum when he criticized, "Drugs are bad for you. It doesn't fix the cause. It only changes the effect, which makes your body take longer to fix the issue."

I led the measly eight mile hike and Euan commented, "Hiking today's eight miles was harder then yesterday's thirty."

I noticed that they definitely lost some of their spunk. "Yeah guys, do you see *now* why thirties are so hard? It's not just that one day that hurts, you feel it days afterwards. And imagine doing thirties day after day. It isn't easy, just saying."

At the shelter was a couple, their two friends, and their dog. They enjoyed playing scrabble together.

When I introduced myself, they said, "Oh Amish, we heard of you."

"Really? Tell me, what have people been saying?"

"You carry uncooked bacon, you caught a mouse in a Nalgene bottle, and you started off on Springer with just a sleeping bag."

"Well, the first two are correct, but the third just makes me sound like an idiot."

Day 86

We left the mountains and plodded across the muddy fields. The hardest part was trying to keep our feet dry. Early on, Euan retired his five fingers and hiked barefoot. He triumphed in his new found freedom when crossing the saturated trail, but I got my laughs when he yelped his way across the scorching blacktop.

We were meeting my mother for lunch. We had a lofty fifteen miles to do. Not surprisingly, we were late. In a field full of cow pies, my cousin Donald ran up in his white tee-shirt and stopped abruptly to give me a hug. My mother and brother were not far behind. I was exhausted and Carby persuaded my brother to carry my pack the next mile.

We dangled our feet off a bridge while eating a lunch of strawberries, carrots, cantaloupe, and egg salad sandwiches. I was given my old sleeping bag back as well as some food. It was hard to see them go. Mom and Carby gave me a kiss on either cheek, then simultaneously spat from the salty sweat.

All of a sudden, I was walking alone. It was a hard blow to know that my friends were far ahead. I didn't mine the terrain, until I got to some shoulder high grasses. They itched my legs and the putrid mud engulfed my shoes. At the end of the grasses, I brushed off the ticks around my ankles.

Next, on a rocky section, a big, fat, ugly fly buzzed around my head for miles, causing me to be in utter frustration. I tripped and my knee smashed into a rock. I hobbled over to a log and wept silently for several minutes before I urged myself forward.

At Cove Mountain shelter a man had his tent set up in the shelter. The man woke up and asked if he should make room. He told me there were porcupines in the area and forbid me from eating in the shelter and to hang up my things because porcupines crave salt. They were known to eat backpacks and would leave nothing but the plastic clips.

When I introduced myself, the man suddenly jumped up. He was overly excited. It was *Fat Jim*. He emerged from his tent and more or less interviewed me. We talked about *Rain Fly* and how he got off at Harper's Ferry just like he had planned.

THIRTEEN

Many Visits

May 30th – June 4th

Day 87

I woke up to the sound of shouting. I soon learned that there was a porcupine in the shelter. It ran off before the guys had the chance to throw stones. I fell asleep thinking, *If that porcupine had walked under my hammock it would have pierced me!*

The hike was *mostly* downhill to Duncannon. In town, I ran into *Fat Jim*. He thought that he was lost. "Don't worry, you're on the trail," I reassured, pointing to a telephone pole with a blaze on it. He seemed excessively happy to be recovered and immediately joined me. He mentioned that he would like to resupply and eat a burger. He promised he would buy me a burger, but all the shops were closed because it was still early morning. He said that he just wanted to go wherever I went, so he never did resupply.

I questioned a lady feeding birds for the directions to the Doyle. As she was throwing pieces of bread to the birds, I couldn't help but think, *Why waste food on birds, when hikers need fed?* We went to see *Skippy's* favorite place on the trail, the Doyle Motel, but it wasn't opened yet.

We crossed the highway bridge, and then climbed up to a ridge, where we ate lunch with a view of the river.

I felt uneasy when *Fat Jim* called me a trail legend. He claimed that because many people knew me and apparently made stories about me, that that somehow made me a legend. At first I felt humored by the praise, but he freaked me out because he wouldn't drop it, so I told him to quit his nonsense.

Near supper time I was hoping we would pass some sort of cookout since it was Memorial Day. Low and behold we passed a sign directing us to a party with food galore. I passed on the ordinary trail magic foods such as hotdogs, burgers, sodas, and went for the hummus, pasta salad, chocolates, ice cream, and wine. I joined a table of ladies playing cards and enjoyed the game immensely.

We were invited to take the leftovers from the party. I enjoyed picking out my favorite foods from the smorgasbord. As I was packing up, I had trouble fitting everything in my pack. *Fat Jim* offered to carry the hummus, so I let him. We were invited to stay the night on their screened in porch and *Fat Jim* wanted to do whatever I did. He admitted he had no opinion otherwise. I wanted to stay since the party was still going.

It annoyed me that *Fat Jim* took several trips to the coolers and sneaked the beers into his back pockets. Some guys from the party went to get beer, but they were all gone and *Fat Jim* said nothing. In fact when I reprimanded him he claimed that *they* had plenty of beer back home and remarked that this was his chance to have an enjoyable evening.

Disgusted, I went inside and joined one of the ladies, Angela in dancing to the music of a talented piano player. As we were dancing she mentioned that she wanted to take me home. I answered, "That would be awesome! I would love to have a shower and be clean!"

"Oh, I hadn't even thought of that! You are more than welcome to use the shower here," she said.

At length Angela decided to take me with her. She wholly wanted to get me away from *Fat Jim*. She insisted there was something creepy about him. She wasn't comfortable with the idea that *he* was hiking with a young girl like myself. I had grown used to hiking with "creepy" guys, but I had to admit I did feel uncomfortable when *Fat Jim* gave me a wet bear hug. I felt slightly bad for ditching him, however staying at someone's house outweighed the ditching part – plus the fact that he was "creepy" made it a good excuse.

As we rode off, Angela introduced me to her friend Cheryl. They handed me a phone because their utmost concern was to clue my parents in on my whereabouts.

In town, we passed fallen trees. Angela and Cheryl informed me that there had been half a dozen tornadoes in the area last

Thursday. Similar to sightseers that cruise past the best Christmas light displays, we cruised by the biggest fallen trees and worst hit homes and gawked at the devastation. We would just keep pointing out, "Wow! Look at *that* tree! It just so missed that house!" Or even, "*That* tree did hit a house." We stopped to take our pictures next to the biggest uprooted tree. The ground was still attached around the base of the tree, along with grass, flowers, and some sidewalk still in place.

When we got to the house, I was given a spare room with a queen size bed. After I took another shower, I ate supper as if I had not eaten a monstrous lunch earlier. Last we watched a movie. It was bliss.

Day 88

I awoke around ten and made omelets by noon. Cheryl left to find a job, while Angela and I talked in the hot tub. Angela told me that when she was young she was taught strict rules about dating. She believed that if she kissed a guy that she had to marry him. She found herself in this predicament and did marry the man. Neither of them were in love at their wedding, but neither let the other know. Even worse was that the man she married was in love with another even before the wedding. They broke up and Angela remarried. Her current situation was that her second ex-husband wanted her to sell the house.

We had dinner when Cheryl came back from getting a job. She was also open about her shipwrecked marriage. She got married when she was young and naive. She was very insecure and ultimately felt used. Cheryl was left alone with her two children to raise. She showed me pictures of her children all grown up. Looking back, she regretted that her children were raised without Christian values. She feared that they might repeat her life. She had been very poor, but she looks back at her effort with pride that she raised her children without government assistance. As a single mother, she raked in the dough by working many years as a mail carrier. She endured year-round hostile weather and showed me scars from being bitten by dogs. Ultimately, it was the weight of the mail that led to complications with her back and ended her career.

After a bit of house cleaning we had a girly night of watching romantic movies and soaking in the hot tub 'til two.

Later I found out that while I had been in air conditioning all day, my fellow hikers had to deal with unbearable heat. It was so bad that many took a nero or even a zero day.

Day 89

My mother was planning to hike with me, so I sent her Angela's address so that she could get me. I was excited for her to meet my new friends.

Angela insisted that it would be better if I quit hiking and instead take a Christian seminar. "You've done plenty of hiking already. This class is fantastic, you'll learn so much more," she said. I sensed her genuine desire for my best interest, but I found it odd to have someone try to talk me out of hiking. It was inconceivable to quit and only revved me to get hiking again.

After Cheryl got background papers for her new job, we went out to eat. We sat with a wonderful view of the Susquehanna River and dined on pizza. I was so glad to stay at Angela's house and I couldn't wait to get back on the trail to brag about how fortunate I was.

My mother showed up at 7:30, entirely ready to get hiking. Her twin sister Eunice came, too. Carby was their chauffeur. I wanted my mother to get acquainted with Angela and Cheryl, but she was too flustered to be sociable. My mom was upset that she had to drive extra far and was concerned how to get back to the trail without a map.

Getting to the trail was an adventure. First Angela and Cheryl led us to the highway. Then my mother misread a wave, so we went the wrong way. When we got on the correct highway, we went the wrong direction. All in all we eventually arrived at our desired destination. My mother was on pins and needles most the way there, but I was just happy to be back on an adventure.

I went to the bridge to see a beautiful sunset over the vast farmlands. I then went down to the house to retrieve my hiking poles and got busy dumping out Eunice's excess water. I changed the batteries in my headlamp before we bid farewell to Carby. My mother was concerned that it was dark when we got hiking, but we were lucky to see two porcupines along the trail. As we walked, I saw little sparkles on the ground. I bent over to get a closer look and saw they were tiny spiders with shiny eyes.

Hiking with the twins was priceless. My mother stressed and Eunice whined. Once we got to the shelter, I tried not to wake any sleeping hikers nor blind them. It was crowded, so we climbed a ladder up to the second floor. It was a hot night. A liner would have been sufficient.

Day 90

In the morning, I recognized *Legion*, *Steady*, and *Tortoise* at the shelter. Some of the hikers expressed some bitterness because we had woken them up during the night and that they had a hard time getting back to sleep.

Tortoise wanted to make coffee for the twins, but he needed water. I was a bit nervous to surrender my water, since I didn't want to go down the steep steps to retrieve water again. But I gave up a portion. Then the water boiled over and spilled on my leg! Luckily, I wasn't burnt. He shrugged it off, "Oh its fine, I just need *more* water." Inside my head I was raging, but I gave him the water anyways.

The others at the shelter felt bad and gave me small portions of their water until I had a proper amount.

After our nap at lunch, Eunice was whining that she was tired and wanted a break. I had a feeling we were close to the shelter so I advised her to take larger steps. She didn't appreciate the advice and complained that I was acting like a slave driver. I suppose making my mother and aunt hike eighteen miles was a bit much for their first full day, but hey – they did it.

The shelter was stated to fit a dozen, but it only fit half of that. So the twins cowboy camped and I set up my hammock. Eunice was jealous of my sleeping arrangements. She wanted to sleep in my hammock, or to sleep under my tarp. She didn't get either, but I gave her my sleeping pad so she would be extra comfy.

Legion named my mother and aunt after my very own trail name. They were *Momish* and *Auntish*. The other hikers picked up the names instantly.

I went down to the fire to cook up dinner, where *Tortoise* was a nuisance since he repetitively asked, "Has anyone seen my roll of duct tape?" First off, no one needs an entire roll of duct tape and second, we were doing him a favor by not finding it, because he would have less weight to carry.

Finally *Legion* responded, "I think someone took it to the privy, saying that they ran out of toilet paper." This kick-started a full blown discussion about how that would play out. They debated which side of the duct tape would be most useful. "Well, the sticky side is better because you can wipe and remove hair at the same time."

Auntish took her first bite of the meal I prepared. I was expecting a different reaction than, "I forgot to bring salt. I'll have to tell Donald to bring some."

Day 91

While I was busy boiling water for *Auntish's* coffee, she asked for water to swallow pills. I was too busy to be of assistance and I came back to witness her spitting and sputtering all over the place. When my mother cracked up laughing, I looked at the bottle and realized *Auntish* had drank my fuel! I remembered my dad saying that having denatured alcohol in a water bottle was a bad idea. Perhaps she was a bit embarrassed or the fuel gave her energy, because *Auntish* left without waiting.

Her hubby met her on a road. *Auntish* gave me a hug and told me she had such a horrible time and couldn't wait to join me again to have another terrible time. It was sad to see her go so soon. But I was glad to still have *Momish*, who made a good hiking partner.

At the 501 Shelter, Aunt Alice came with tacos and cheesecake. Both were things I had requested. I told the other hikers there would be tacos coming, but they couldn't resist ordering pizza. I was worried that Aunt Alice's trail magic might go unnoticed by the hikers, but some more showed up later. We had a huge party going on. *Legion's* birthday had been two days ago, so I put candles on a slice of cheesecake and we sang happy birthday. He seemed very happy and gave me a hug. I could tell he was enjoying himself because he was talking more than ever with the flock of hikers. There must have been around twenty of them.

Alice had brought her three nieces and Donald. The three girls thought I was ridiculous for hiking such a long period of time, "I'd rather sit on a couch and watch TV with a bowl full of popcorn."

"Well yeah. I like that, too! But sometime it's fun to do what people do on TV, instead of just watching it." I said.

Aunt Alice joined in, "Yeah you got to live YouTube."

We walked to a nearby view, which they absolutely loved. Alice had to tell the youngest to keep away from the edge. My mother left with them. It was sad to say goodbye, but I was excited that Donald was staying.

Day 92

My aunt left all kinds of goodies, including some V8 I had requested. Donald looked at me in disgust as I poured the V8 into my Camelback. "Don't worry it'll wash out," I said.

The rocks were brutal on my cousin Donald and one time a big, fat fly buzzed mercilessly around his head. When he could take it no longer, he took off running.

It was funny how nonchalant he was about taking a leak. I would notice he stopped and I would turn to wait up on him, then instantly turn back around and trudge ahead to wait.

Soon Donald was hurting. After his whining prolonged, I persuaded him to take a seat on a log and I weaved athletic tape between his blistered toes. He claimed that it helped, but his complaints and stumbles only increased, which made the fifteen miles seem unending. Donald texted his mother, "I hate this."

His mom texted back, "I hate it too! I wish I was there hating it with you."

Donald got ahead of me and I was worried he might miss the sign for Eagles Nest Shelter. So I was all anxious until I arrived at the shelter, where he thankfully was.

When I came in, *Legion* was reading the shelter log. I could tell he was frustrated because his profanity increased. "*Nocello* doesn't think I won't call the ATC again, but I f**ken will."

"Uh, what are you talking about?" I asked.

"I hate that f**ken guy, there is graffiti up and down the trail because he can't help but sign his name on everything. *Nocello* was here, *Nocello* was there. Every hiker behind him has to see this bulls**t. You can't get away from it. I came to the woods to get away from a**holes like him."

"So what are you gonna do about it?" I mused.

"I called the ATC to stop him from defacing their property. I presume they got a hold of him. But, he must have found out that I reported him. Look what that idiot did!" he fumed.

Legion pointed to a ten foot graffiti saying, "*LEGION* was here."

Legion raved in his New England smoker's voice. "He doesn't think I'll call him up for this, but I f**ken will."

I tried not to laugh at the situation, for *Legions* sake, since he can be very opinionated.

One hiker came by and excitedly informed us that the privy was at its full capacity. "UN-freaking believable! Is it overflowing?" asked *Legion* and immediately got up to go see. He returned to get his camera, "I bet I could squeeze one on top!"

When they proceeded to talk about dull things such as mileage and places at which they were planning to stay in the next town, I got out my cards and *Legion* joined in to play the rest of the night. We maxed out at five people playing at once. Donald was getting a ride situated to get home ASAP. It took him a long time to unwind until he eventually joined in the fun.

FOURTEEN

Playing Catch-Up

June 5th – 12th

Day 93

Even though it was a measly two miles to the first road, Donald was still frustrated. "That had to be two miles by now," he wheezed. The road that we were waiting for turned out to be dirt and was blocked off with several gates. Donald called his parents on my phone to explain his location.

He then gave me all his edible food in payment for using my minutes. He reached into his pack, "Check out these delicious energy bars." He pulled out a wrapper with mouse droppings falling from it. "Yuck, sorry about that, but I have some more." He pulled out yet another with chewed holes. "That won't do. I think I have one more," he assured, reaching for the third. It was untouched. I felt bad for leaving him to find his parents alone with a dead cell phone, but I was focused on catching up to *Skippy* and *Scavenger*.

I spent the day listening to Julia Andrew's biography. I had to discipline myself to only listen to an hour at a time, because my battery was low.

I bumped into *Spartan* and *Blue Moon*. We got to see a dog reunite with its owner after being lost in the woods for a week. The owner was smiling and crying simultaneously. I couldn't pet the dog because it was jumping so vigorously that it was impossible. Only after I backed up, did I understand what was going on and I couldn't help but smile.

I was thinking about hiking a thirty, but after I parted from *Spartan* and *Blue Moon* I got tired, sore, and unmotivated. The shower at the next shelter sounded irresistible, but it turned out to be less appealing, than I thought, since it was a single stream of bone-chilling water. Only after I finished did I remember that I didn't have a towel and had to air dry.

At camp was a group I had seen before with their dog. They began yelling at each other for a considerable amount of time.

From all the yelling across the campground, I figured out that the group had gotten separated and the dog followed the one in the lead. The others searched hours for their dog. They insisted that the guy who got ahead blue blazed. "There is no way in hell, I blue blazed," he shouted back. When the shouting kept persisting I thought, *At least the dog was fine. Hopefully they can forgive each other and not put their marriage and team in jeopardy.*

"It's not worth fighting over," I coaxed the man near me.

"Sorry *Amish*, but it is."

Day 94

I hurried through the day. I climbed a ledge of rocks, a trail of rocks, and a sea of rocks. I also saw three snakes. One I almost stepped on.

The mosquitoes were a nightmare. After I got sick of slapping myself, I stopped to get my bug spray and they instantly swarmed. I hastily lathered up, which helped to keep the little buggers at bay.

As I was heading down the trail, I ran into a pack of ultra buff guys running up the mountain. I asked them how far it would be to the shelter. "Ten minutes," they replied. I couldn't wait to get to the shelter, so I timed myself. Those buff guys were exact in their guess!

At the shelter *Mousetrap,* a guy who got his name from smashing several mice, asked if my mother hated him. I stared at him, confused. My mind raced. *He doesn't know my mom. Perhaps it's one of those "your mom" jokes.*

"Remember, we kept your mom awake, when we were celebrating *Scavenger's* birthday?" he explained.

"Oh! You were there? Don't worry." I smirked. "My mom's not the hating type." I thought it was funny that he was so concerned, but I was glad he cared enough to ask.

As I was cooking up dinner, I felt like the entertainer. The hikers sat in the shelter facing me and I cracked silly stories while they laughed at me. Then I tried boiling some water over the fire, but I couldn't find a good place to balance my pot, so it kept spilling time and time again. They just sat there and laughed. Finally, *Mousetrap* the warmhearted, came to my assistance. I must have been too tired to think clearly.

Day 95

I got a move on at 6:30 and climbed Dante's Inferno out of Leigh Gap. Dante's Inferno was known for zapping hikers dry on its barren, rock face. It had me worried and I mistakenly asked a section hiker, who frightened me by blowing it way out of proportion. Some thru-hiker's rule of thumb was to divide the difficulty of what section hikers say by two. For example if a section hiker said the shelter was half an hour away you knew you were only fifteen minutes away.

I sped along as fast as my legs could scurry. I only let myself take breaks when I was too miserable to take another step. I received a text from *Skippy* telling me he was in the Delaware Water Gap just thirty-seven miles away.

The gnats and flies were unrelenting. The gnats would buzz around my face so I held my hiking poles in one hand and swatted them with the other. Soon I got tired of swatting and decided I would try ignoring them. That worked until one flew in my eye. My eyes filled with tears. I tried blinking and rolling my eyes about, but I couldn't get the bug out. I had to stop and take out my contact. *Why would a gnat commit suicide like that?* The gnats continued flying into my eyes until I resorted back to swatting.

By the time I ran into a ridgerunner, I was so thirsty that I couldn't help but tell him about my thirst. "Dude I have no water, and I think the next water source is a couple miles away. I'm just so thirty. Man just a gulp of water would make all the difference." He must have felt compassion for me, because he gave me a half liter of his personal supply. Several times he stopped to move brush off the trail, while I waited for him. He even broke out his hand-saw, very similar to the one I had back in the day.

"Is it worth it?" I asked the ridgerunner. "I'm only halfway, and it's so hot, and it's only going to get hotter. I'm so tired, but if I don't try to catch up to my friends now I fear I never will. The

167

bugs are terrible. There isn't much water. And I haven't seen many people. The rocks are killing my feet. Tell me, is it worth it?"

"I believe it is worth it. For me, Maine was worth it, it was so beautiful."

"Well then, could you tell me about Maine?"

I had him talk about Maine as long as I could.

When I learned that John the ridgerunner had thru-hiked in '07, it changed things. Not that I thought he was useless, but now he was an overflowing wealth of knowledge. He told me about the chilling yet mystifying call of a moose in the night. And he told me a story of a moose that walked around a shelter. He thought it was a person at first, with a large pack and heavy boots, but the noise kept going back and forth. He finally went out to help the "lost hiker" to find a hefty bull moose!

He added that after another encounter, when a moose jumped over his tent, ever since that event, he refrained from setting up his tent anywhere that resembled a trail. "When a beast that weighed over a thousand pounds jumped over me, I thanked God I didn't die. Sure that time I was unscathed, but did you know they have terrible eye sight? I could have been trampled!"

I was warned that the following day was predicted to be overbearingly hot, so I set up my hammock near the trail and planned to get up before sunrise.

Day 96

I got up and left at four in the morning. It was a bit scary to cross a freeway in the dark. But it didn't stay dark for long and it didn't stay cool for long either. I hiked quite steadily, until I got to the shelter, taking me over ten miles of toe-stubbing, merciless rocks. It was a pain to focus on each step, because the spaces between the rocks were too small for my shoe to fit through and many times my shoe would get wedged between the rocks.

I did notice, however, that stepping on rocks a certain way massaged my feet. And I took every chance I had through the rocky trails of Pennsylvania to massage my feet.

John said those ten miles of rocks were his least favorite part of the trail. "Aren't you lucky, you get the joy of maintaining that section," I teased.

John was at the shelter like he promised. Also there was a lady. "Years ago, I tried a thru-hike, but now I just do sections each year. I enjoy seeing hikers, but you are the first thru-hiker I've seen. It's not what I expected. I'm getting off the trail today and I'm going to the beach."

I wondered how it was possible that she hadn't seen *any* thru-hikers. After a bit of pondering, I figured we must have been between bubbles. *What a shame,* I thought. *I won't be seeing many hikers for a while.*

The lady told me the story of *Nature boy*. He was a quiet kid who had attempted to beat the unsupported speed record. He had trained for it. If anyone was going to break the record, it was going to be *Nature boy*. He flew by like no one else. I had heard of jealous people stealing his shoes and taking them a mile up the trail. But there was nothing as cruel as the night he camped near a road in a national park. People threw pebbles at his tent. "Hey! *Nature boy*! Come out here!" they demanded. "*Nature boy!* Hey! *Nature boy!*"

He told them to leave, but instead they unzipped his tent. When he peeked his head out to see what was happening, they knocked him unconscious. The next day he woke up outside his tent, with an atrocious headache. He tried to hike, but his headache overwhelmed him. He went to a local hospital and unfortunately was unable to keep hiking.

It really bothered me that people would do such a thing. It was being investigated, because the incident was on government land which bumped the case up to a federal crime.

I stayed at the shelter for the hottest part of the day while I chatted with John. We discussed all sorts of things and laughed at the nuances of the trail and the silly things people do.

After a long, delightful downhill I came to town. The Delaware Water Gap church hostel was great! The cold air conditioned room was delightful. Even the showers were warm.

I went to a market and had a hard time picking from all the delicious baked goods, but decided on pumpernickel bread with pumpkin spread.

They didn't have a no sleeping sign on the couch, so I took the opportunity to do so.

Day 97

I got out early with *Kayak*, a man who had picked up my jacket the day before. We crossed the highway bridge over the Delaware River into the state of New Jersey.

From then on, building fires would be questionable. The enforcers that prohibited fires could be a bit excessive. A friend of mine had built a fire just past the Delaware Water Gap, when a helicopter came overhead to put out the fire and drenched them all.

It was a hot day. After a dip in Sunfish pond, I spotted *Fat Jim*. He was sitting in the sun. It was hot as ever, but he explained that he would rather deal with the heat than the mosquitoes. This was logical because mosquitoes keep to the shade. I felt enlightened, because I had never thought of that.

Fat Jim was happy to see me and immediately rummaged through his pack to hand me a bunch of his food. He had brought hummus, for the very intention of giving it back to me. He decided then and there that he would hike with me to complete his section faster than originally planned.

Mid day the air turned to a swamp and soon my clothes were drenched with sweat. We decided to take a soak in a stream. I found a secluded section for myself and laid in the chilling crisp current.

Things started out good, such as a beautiful sunset that we watched for a long time. I decided to keep going before it got dark. Unfortunately we still had to hike in the dark. Then, as if that wasn't bad enough, we got soaked in multiple showers. Even more horrid, was that the swamp surrounding the shelter was a giant breeding ground for mosquitoes. The mosquitoes would have been manageable except that it was too hot to sleep inside my sleeping bag, but without my sleeping bag I had no protection from the relentless swarms. The whole night I struggled between making the choice of being overheated or eaten alive. It was the worst feeling *ever*.

Day 98

I woke up while getting eaten by vampire bugs. We got out of there ASAP and headed to town. *Spaceman Spiffy* was the only other hiker who stayed in that tiny mosquito infested shelter. When he introduced himself I immediately knew that he was new on the trail, because no one has a name *that* long. No one remembers a name like that; he was destined to be known as *the flip-flopper* with an outrageously long name. He was a flip-flopper, because he was hiking north, starting in the middle of the trail. His plan was to hike north to Katahdin and then, drive down to the middle of the trail and hike south to Springer Mountain. The whole idea of flip-flopping made my head swirl.

We hiked to a whisper of a town. *Fat Jim* got me coffee and a doughnut at a shop called Joe to Go. The man that worked at Joe to Go was like the Uncle Johnny of the north, because he hated hikers, even though they were probably more than half his business. He would not let us loiter inside. After we sat in our hiker designated bench outside, we went to a bar to get water. *Fat Jim* ordered a couple beers and *Spaceman Spiffy* was a darling by having the correct cords to charge my iPod.

Fat Jim gave me a bunch of food, denatured alcohol, batteries, and bug spray. I was so delighted to have bug spray! Then we walked a tiny little section into the woods, completing his section. He handed me a twenty dollar bill before we parted. I told him I would spend it well. After that I didn't know what to say. The whole saying good-bye and turning away seemed so unnatural. When hiking, you always assume to bounce into people up the trail. *Fat Jim* did something unexpected: he came up to me as if for a hug and instead gave me a kiss. Then immediately turned and walked away, leaving me startled and grossed out. *Spaceman Spiffy* uttered a weak, "See ya."

For hours I felt disturbed and violated. *Those ladies back in Pennsylvania were right. Fat Jim was a creepy old guy.*

Then I wondered if that counted as a first kiss. It certainly wasn't anywhere near romantic like in fairytales. I guess that's shows how misleading fairytales can be.

After several miles, I ran into a bunch of guys at the top of a mountain. They were assembling their own radio tower. They were very sweet and offered me a seat under their tarp. With a cold Pepsi in my hand, the old guys enthusiastically told me that they were in a competition. The radio tower that made the most contacts would win. This crew had only five people. They have been driving up the same mountain and setting up their radio tower longer than I had been alive.

The Mount Greylock team had only ever lost three times. Each time was a historic event for the guys. They informed me that the team on Mount Greylock had dozens of people. They mentioned that I would be hiking Mount Greylock in the future. "If you have the opportunity, you should unplug anything you find," they joked.

On the next mountain's summit, I came upon a pavilion where only two guys sat. One was a talented guitarist. The music complimented the view well. When they got up to leave I told him I liked the music. "Thanks for listening," he replied.

I asked a father and son group if the bugs were bad at High Point shelter. They attested that they were, so I decided that I would pass that shelter. But, I had to check if I knew anyone there. I dropped my pack and ran down the trail to the shelter and was greeted by three guys. They all turned out to be friendly. I asked them if they saw my German. Apparently, they had their own German. We described our Germans as best we could, and then decided we weren't talking about the same person. They informed me of a secret shelter about five miles down the trail. So I made that my goal.

I hiked some and ran some down the mountain. Next were fields and ponds below. There was a farm and a trail through a marshy area. I was tired and just wanted someone to pick me up and give me a home.

When I got to the road a man pulled over by the trail. He was taking his six dogs out for a swim in the marshes. He described for me what obstacles I had before the secret shelter, and then left with his pack of dogs. I thought about waiting by the side of the road until he finished swimming his dogs to see if he would let me sleep on his porch or something. But it was getting dark and I didn't want to chance having to camp near that bug infested swamp, so I trudged on.

The darkness slowly overtook the forest and I could see deer prancing about. I got jumpy over some gun shots. Just a bit earlier, I had seen a sign about being on hunting land. I reassured myself that my neon pink shorts and blue shirt were probably flashy enough.

Finally, I came to the sign and got to the shelter. I cooked on the porch and got spooked by a massive spider running in circles on the ground along with hundreds of its babies. The shelter was like a cabin. I opened the door to find two others sleeping. The floor was black and white tile. I set my sleeping bag down and instantly loved the warm floor.

Day 99

In the morning, I got to meet the tattooed guy and the girl with him. I say tattooed guy because when I asked people if they had seen *Scavenger*, they would ask if he had tattoos.

The Blood Sucking Bugs were fierce. Fortunately, I had spray, but I was running out. I had to reapply more bug spray from sweating it off. It was exciting to walk across what seemed miles of bog boards, but soon I was surrounded by swarms of hungry mosquitoes. I had no place to put down my pack to apply more bug spray, so I ran as quickly as I could without slipping on the slick boards.

When I got to the shelter that *Scavenger* was supposedly at the night before, I took a break. The tattooed man and the girl showed up. I watched the bugs swarming on them. They were going berserk, flaring their arms about wildly. They were constantly slapping their arms and legs. All the while trying to get food ready to eat, and checking what people wrote in the shelter log. I felt sorry for their predicament, but I had so little bug spray that I was afraid I would soon be going crazy myself. After weighing the pros and cons, I finally chose to be compassionate. They were so incredibly grateful. They even noticed I was running low and were careful to only use a little.

Later even I couldn't be sane with the bugs when, I hiked through a wildlife preservation. Most of the wildlife there was swarming around my head. I guess they didn't want the mosquitoes to go extinct. I ran half of it because the bugs were so overpowering. There were swans, ducks, and geese swimming in the marshy ponds. I took a quick picture, while the bugs pounced on me.

After a couple miles, I ran into a lady who had two other friends giving her company on her section. When I confessed my concern about running out of bug spray, each person grabbed their personal can and sprayed me down, while I twirled for them. Seeing that all three had rather large cans of bug spray, I was hoping they'd give me one of theirs. But I was touched so much by their generosity I knew I'd feel guilty if I asked for more.

All I could think about was getting to the library. My feet felt as though I was wearing shoes two sizes too small and my mental state was zapped as if working double shifts. When I got to the road and it happened to be the wrong road, I got very upset and cried a bit. I had hiked day after day with miles higher than normal and I hadn't even made it far enough to get to the stupid library! I could see people in their cars looking at me with concern. It would have been nice if they had pulled over and lent me their home so that I could sleep, eat, and shower.

Right after I pulled myself up from my misery, I thought, *Well I guess things can't get worse,* and that's when it started to rain. *This cannot be happening to me, not today, how cliché.* I felt miserable and stopped hiking prematurely.

The man in the Wawayanda shelter was named *Wild Light;* he hiked north to the Delaware Water Gap thirty-three years ago and was out to finish the trip. *Wild Light* was a very sweet man. He made me hot chocolate and coaxed me into cooking on his stove. He shared his water with me, put my food in the bear box, and even gave me some peanut M&Ms. So that made me feel much better.

One hiker named *Raisins* came in late and we talked for a long time. He got his name from starting the trail with an overwhelming amount of raisins and he didn't even like them. He hiked thirty mile days, everyday. He told me people got offended and were rude to him, because they felt insecure about their lower mileages. I asked him if he met *V8. He* answered he didn't, but hoped he would. He got really excited when I mentioned *V8* because he was Asian, too.

Raisins mentioned he got to hike with *Nature boy* a bit after the incident of *Nature boy* getting beat up. *Raisins* said, "*Nature boy* had to stop and sit down because his headache was so severe. He definitely had a chance of breaking the record and that could have been the reason why people came to beat him up."

Raison then left to hang up his hammock. The other guy in the shelter looked beaten up by the trail. He had recently graduated college and was carrying too much stuff. I named him *Denim*. He had a denim coat, denim pants, and some denim shorts. Cotton was the worst thing to have on the trail and I wasn't surprised when he complained, "All my clothes are soaked."

When I saw his dagger, I scoffed, "That thing looks dangerous!"

"Oh, my bowie knife is nothing compared to my samurai sword," grinning he grabbed the sword and unsheathed it. The shinning sword was about two feet long.

"What? That looks awesome, but it must weigh a lot."

"Yeah it does," he admitted. "I think I'm gonna send it home."

He sat down and took off his heavy boots, exposing his plastic wrapped feet. I gasped when he unwrapped his feet. "Well you see I'm allergic to poison ivy, so I thought if I wrapped my feet up it would stop spreading."

He didn't have any sort of guidebook, so I ripped out the half I had already done and handed it to him. He was so amiable and pathetic, that I wanted to join him on his trek south. He thought he might stop his hike in Tennessee near his uncle. "You know, once you get to Tennessee you are practically at the end," I said.

He was smirking as he dug in his backpack. "You'll like this one." He laid out a thin fuzzy white blanket.

"Is that your sleeping arrangements?" I asked.

"Yup."

"Hmm, white. I wonder how long it'll stay that color. Is it hard to sleep without a sleeping pad?"

"Yeah, mostly."

As we fell asleep, we renamed *Wild Lights*, since his name was so hard to remember, to *Come Again*.

Day 100

I went to the road and hitchhiked to a grocery store. It was hard to only get one item in a store with gobs and gobs of merchandise. I did pretty well. I told myself I could survive on peanut butter. With its high calorie to weight ratio, I could save weight, but then I got pancake mix, too. And then I couldn't pass up a coconut cream pie from girls happily selling baked goods. Before I got out of the parking lot to hitchhike, I was picked up by a car.

The library was beautiful, but it wasn't open yet. I had to wait until noon for it to open, which wasn't bad because I had a yummy pie to eat and a book to read. I snuggled up in my sleeping bag. I swear I looked like a hobo; however, some lady commented that she thought I was wearing a new trend in pants.

I used that computer up to the last second. I typed a ton and got the contact information of a couple who invited me to crash at their house.

The hitchhike back wasn't as easy. I walked to the main road, which was already more walking than before. I stood at a busy intersection, but no one stopped. I walked a bit and tried again. *Humph.* I guess that was the way guys felt when trying to hitchhike. So I walked while holding out my thumb. That did the trick. I got a ride from a darling lady named Lisa. She was so intrigued by my journey that she drove me the entire way back to the trail.

It was two and I had eleven miles to do. I passed some sort of large camp. The children screamed when they let off a rocket. I imagined the rocket landing near me, and that I would run back with it in hand and be awarded a prize. Never happened.

There was more than one cliff out-cropping, that the trail followed over. I lost the trail a lot, since I wasn't used to looking down for blazes. Or perhaps New York just isn't as good with marking blazes. On one cliff, I brushed my teeth and watched my spit fall down... down... down... then splatter. That was fun.

On the path to the Wild Cat shelter, I took a wrong turn. I retraced back. The shelter was visible once I looked in the right direction. Moments after I arrived, it down poured. I was surprisingly happier after the rain started for the mere reason that I was so close to getting soaked and yet didn't get wet. I made yummy pancakes and handed one to each of the older gentlemen.

I was excited because the next day I was going to Mark and Pat's house. Mark read about my hike on my blog and wanted to help me out. Before falling asleep, I asked the other hikers to make sure I didn't sleep in.

FIFTEEN

Familiarity Breeds Contempt

June 13th – 22nd

Day 101

I left by seven and after two miles, I came to the road where Mark was waiting to get me. The rest of the day was bliss.

At his house, I walked up the stairs and looked around the beautiful house. Mark was looking at my calves. "You have a batch of bug bites on your legs."

Twisting around, I looked at the back of my legs for the first time in a long time and remarked, "I sure do."

I was bombarded with food, which wasn't a bad thing. His wife Pat, was the one that bombarded me. She asked if I wanted anything before she left to go grocery shopping. I was glad that I answered honestly because she came back with a variety of wonderful dark chocolate bars.

Pat had a little kitten in her hands, "We found Mr. Kitten in the engine of a car. His tail was broken, so I took him to the vet." I saw that the kitty was missing half his tail and on the end he wore a bandage that waved around like a flag. "I'm taking Mr. Kitten back to the vet to be adopted. We don't need any more cats."

Mark and Pat did already have several cats. One was named Seven, from a time when they had so many cats, they started giving them numbers. But, I didn't see why they had to give Mr. Kitten away, especially since Pat seemed so attached to the cutie

Day 102

When I woke up, I was shocked that it was morning already. It was strange not to be disturbed during the night. I didn't have any problem with cold feet, nor an aching back, nor even obnoxious snoring. The cherry on top was that I didn't have to wake up to the horrid buzzing of nature's alarm clock.

In the kitchen, Mark asked, "So, do you mind if I talk about *Peach*? I know that it didn't work out between you two."

"No, I don't mind. Why?"

"Well, I'm reading her blog and she wrote she's going home to visit the college that she'll be going to next year. Perhaps you could catch up to her. She's only a couple days ahead of you."

I thought, *It would be cool to catch up, but what then? Be in a race to the finish?* "I'd rather not."

I ate constantly all morning. I had cereal and the second half of my Ben and Jerry's ice cream. Lastly, Pat baked homemade bread.

Mark laid out several different trail maps. He sat there reading them for a long time. "So I'm guessing you'll be able to make it to *this* shelter by today, and perhaps *that* shelter by tomorrow. Or maybe if you hike a bit extra you *could* make it to *this* shelter." Eventually he meekly asked, "Would you mind if I joined you?"

"I don't care. You may as well, since you seem so excited."

"Okay, so Pat will drop us off and then pick us up on Thursday," he announced happily. He went about the house collecting all his gear and broke out his box of dehydrated vegan meals. He let me choose one. He weighted his backpack and then mine and announced, "Mine is lighter than yours! Wait – you're a thru-hiker, so how can that be?"

On our way to the trail we had many stops. Pat got coffee and we went past a pastry shop full of cheesecakes and chocolates. I was told I could have whatever I wanted. It looked so enticing but I refrained, because I was already intensely full.

Mark and Pat insisted on getting me new shorts since they had seen my shorts in the laundry with a rip down the crotch. At a sports store, I tried on several different pairs before I settled for a purple pair. It was a relief to have functioning shorts again.

As we unpacked from the car to hike, *Skippy* came strolling out of the woods. I was ecstatic. All this time I thought that I had lost the race of catching up to *Skippy*. But there he was! I introduced him to Mark and Pat. He seemed to be a bit sleepy. After we waved farewell to Pat we left together, but *Skippy* fell behind after he stopped to tie his shoe.

The hike was an adventure. It rained on and off and there were plenty of rock scrambles. One part was titled the Lemon Squeezer, where two rock walls came together tighter and tighter. Right after the Lemon Squeezer was a steep ledge. I was too good for the easy trail that was marked with a sign, so I jumped up and hugged the tree to pull myself around it. There was a moment when my pack's weight pulled me back and I feared the worst. I suppose Mark did too, because he seemed to panic beneath me, but soon enough I swung around. Mark followed with an added precaution and threw up his pack before scrambling up the rocks.

Mark had a bit of a knee problem and his toes hurt. Although he was a bit intimidated in the beginning, to be hiking with a thru-hiker, he had no trouble keeping up.

We squeezed into the shelter, which looked more like a pile of rocks. I was cooking pancakes inside the shelter when I knocked my stove over, spilling burning fuel. It scared me as well as everyone else in the vicinity. Mark was not pleased and had me cook on his stove.

The act of spilling burning fuel was actually more common than people tend to believe. I looked around the shelter to count up the burn marks, and thought, *It's a wonder shelters don't burn down more often.* Burnt marks on picnic tables and shelters were just as common as the graffiti that covered them.

I was glad when *Skippy* finally arrived. He mentioned that he got lost several times. He chatted with Mark and it looked like *Skippy* was interested in staying at Mark and Pat's place.

I didn't get to talk with *Skippy* much, but he did mention his remorse at giving up the invite to stay at my house. "You know how *Count* went home for ten days?" said *Skippy*. "Well, soon after he got back on the trail, he quit."

I gasped, "No way? He was halfway! I remember how excited he was to hike in Maine." I looked around, expecting shock from the other hikers, but realized that none of them knew *Count*. I saw in that moment how much the past thru-hiker community had fragmented.

I missed the good old days with *Count* and *Smurf*. And I reminisced the times with *Trail Mix* and *the Cops*. I regretted that I passed on the opportunity, when I saw the boys in the pavilion back in Maryland. I knew *Smurf* and his friends were far ahead, and there was no way I was going to try catching up to anyone else.

Day 103

In the morning, Mark was up and ready, while I was ready for a second round of sleep. I had a little mental battle before pulling myself out of bed. I couldn't let Mark down. Most of the day, I was too tired to concentrate. Sleep was on my mind all day. It was a difficult morning, as one can imagine.

Some of the climbs were a bit brutal, but Bear Mountain was surprisingly nice. Mark kept warning me about its difficulty, but in the past years it had been so touristy that there were steps conveniently built on both sides of the mountain.

All day we ran into people asking if we were thru-hikers. Mark would then motion my way. "She is. I'm just joining her for a couple days." Next came a big smile followed by praises and volleys of questions, and then spews of unwanted information about the trail followed. One of these people asked me if I would like some apples. After we walked over to her car, she handed me both apples, as well as every other food item she could scavenge from her car, all the while completely ignoring Mark. I felt like a celebrity.

We took an extra detour. See, Mark would say that the trail went such and such a way and I wouldn't think twice about it. It seemed to work out until we went the wrong way and we had to hike the long way around a touristy lake. I didn't mind since we got to take a refreshing swim and later saw a bride and groom get their pictures taken.

It was the day we finally got to go through the zoo. I was excited to eat cotton-candy, see fierce animals, and watch clowns scare little children about, but there was none of that. The place was a vacant little thing. There were barely any animals to be seen. As we walked through taking glances at the empty cages, the zoo was beginning to close down, and the officials ushered the small crowds past us as we kept marching through. Many people informed us that we were "going the wrong way." The officials saw that we were hikers and let us pass.

Right outside the zoo was a massive bridge called Bear Mountain Bridge. I noticed several suicide hotline signs and stopped to look down; it would be a *long* drop.

Following the bridge was the climb when I got a most unwelcome bloody nose. Mark was impatient and suggested that I stick toilet paper up my nose. I did, and kept a brisk pace climbing up the mountain. It was a very uncomfortable experience. Ironically the mountain was called Anthony's Nose.

Skippy made it to the Monastery pavilion just an hour after we arrived and he had started hiking around noon.

The bugs were a pain as I hung my hammock inside the pavilion.

Day 104

We decided we would walk together, since we were going to get picked up by Pat at the same time. *Skippy* had a slow start. He justified his extra hours of rest by saying, "This may be the only time in your life that you get to pick what time you wake up."

I remember that I just couldn't wait for the hike to be over. Finally we got to the road. We sat in the grass as the sun scorched us and then everyone jumped up after someone spotted a tick.

Mark called Pat and got all flustered, because Pat had made a wrong turn on the highway. When she arrived Mark handed each of us a cold beer.

Back at the house, *Skippy* had a heyday discussing home brewing with Mark, who brewed his own beer. I didn't mind hearing about brewing beer since I had much to learn, but when the topic shifted to hiking I became exasperated. Mark enjoyed talking about everyday occurrences of what other hikers did as if it was the most exciting thing ever. He spoke about how people filled up shelters and exploded their things all over the place and then had to condense everything when people showed up. I could take it no further, "Can we *please* talk about something else?" I demanded, irritated.

I later felt bad, but hiking seemed so overrated. Everyone I talked to had something to say about hiking and finally, I had had enough.

Day 105

We were going to hike, but the weather was looking bad. I was more than glad to stay. I slept some more. We ate some amazing homemade cinnamon raisin bread and some interesting scrambled tofu. We played a game, all four of us.

After the game we made and ate some lovely vegan pizza piled with veggies, and some tofu pepperoni.

In the evening we had a music jam, where everyone picked out a couple of songs. Mark and Pat shared their beloved Blue Grass. *Skippy* shared Brazilian music as well as some music he wrote himself. I started dancing to a rap song that I played. I wanted them to join in the head pumping, but they just stared at me. *Skippy* told me later, "You were so red that I thought you were gonna pass out."

Day 106

As Mark cooked up some oatmeal for breakfast, I woke up *Skippy* by putting a cat in his room. It took us a while to leave. It didn't help that I didn't want to go. Mark helped me prepare by getting me toilet paper, making a stand for my stove, and giving me some food. The only thing I was excited about was getting garlic to keep the skeeters away. I heard that if I ate enough raw garlic then it would sweat out of my pores. And instead of my sweat washing off the bug repellant it'd add another coat of armor.

The drive to the trail was hard. I wasn't feeling well and I was getting homesick. Mark gave me a hug before he left. I put my headphones on and followed *Skippy* down the trail. Some drunken guy joined *Skippy* and I a bit. He asked if I wanted a soda; I mumbled no. The dude talked and talked. He told *Skippy* he thought I didn't like him.

Perhaps I didn't, I thought.

After the guy left, *Skippy* said, "I want another soda."

"Why didn't you tell me that before," I complained. "I could have given you the one he offered me."

"I always want soda," he protested.

"Fine. The next time I get a soda that I don't want I'll save it for you."

The miles went fast and soon enough *Skippy* and I arrived at RPH shelter. *Skippy* played his guitar some. I had a hard time naming a song we both knew and liked. Finally, once I named the desired song, he looked up the chords on his phone and we sang a bit.

Some random town ladies came by, when they realized we liked food, they came back with some nice things to eat. While they chatted away we ate their food.

I met some new hikers. *Crop Duster* was an amiable guy. He got his name from being constantly gassy. The name was still fitting him well. The other was *German Sheppard*. He was a rosy cheeked German, with a lovely smile.

Day 107

I made some smashing pancakes, complete with M&Ms and joined *Chainsaw* for most of the day. I asked *Chainsaw* about his snoring since his name suggested that he did. But *Chainsaw* admitted that since he lost so much weight from hiking, he stopped snoring.

Chainsaw told me about his job as a firefighter being unpredictable. He spoke of a time when he had to tell a screaming mother that her son had died from committing suicide. He also spoke of a time when he assisted a woman in deliver twins. She had been on the road on her way to the hospital when she called 911 for help.

Chainsaw continued to keep my attention when he told me of his friend's job as a kidnapper. "Kidnapper? Isn't that bad?" I questioned.

"He works for parents that want to rescue their kids from religious sects. He first has to capture the kids and then undo the brainwashing before returning the kids back home."

"That is so interesting. Why don't they have *that* on TV?" I asked.

"Well, it's illegal. Kidnapping is looked down upon and many of these kids are eighteen and older, so technically they have the right to make their own decisions. There's a lot of gray area, but ultimately he is reuniting families."

We went swimming in Nuclear Lake, where people liked to make fun of President Bush's pronunciation. After several minutes of sun bathing, a bug landed on me. I smacked it and then sat up to see that I had crippled a dragonfly. I was devastated.

Chainsaw was almost giddy with excitement when he saw that some fishermen nearby had a cooler. "I bet they have sodas in that cooler. Oh! I want one so badly," he cried.

 It never happened, but something clicked in my head, *Okay, guys really like soda.*

We were still lounging at Nuclear Lake when *Crop Duster* joined us. He told us how he was on a time constraint and had to finish the hike soon to get back home for a bachelor party. "I'm the best man," he moaned.

"That's great!" I comforted.

"No, I've been a best man before. It means that I have to pay for the bachelor party," he muttered glumly.

"You could do something cheap," I suggested.

"It's a *bachelor* party. He'll hate me if it's stupid."

Crop Duster told me that after he finished he was going to have a collapsible bike sent to him in the mail to ride home to Pennsylvania.

At the shelter, I was delighted that I persuaded *Crop Duster* and *Skippy* to play cards. *Skippy* was somewhat out of it, but *Crop Duster* was an enthusiastic player.

In the morning, I hiked with *Chainsaw* again. I felt like a sleeping zombie. By the way walking with closed eyes never works out. We didn't talk much. I found a can of seafood bisque at a pillaged shelter near a road. I tried to open the can with a knife, but after that proved worthless *Chainsaw* used his pocketknife, and meticulously opened the can for me.

Chainsaw stopped before me at a campsite and I went on to the shelter. It surprised me that *Skippy* hadn't caught up, since it was beginning to get dark. There were several section hikers. A hobo guy was carving a stick. Apart from the fact that the stick he was carrying weighed nearly ten pounds, I had to admit that he was quite skilled at carving. I found it entertaining that the hobo man liked to ramble on and on, but had trouble hearing me, even with hearing aids.

I was glad when another guy came by. He was a happy fellow. He told me about his first couple adventurous days on the trail.

"I took a zero day today and yesterday I hiked eight and a half miles in nine hours, and made it to this shelter at ten in the night," he exclaimed.

"Wait a second; you did what – eight miles in nine hours? That is *not* good. How big is your pack?" I asked.

He brought over his pack for me to see. "Well, I packed fifty pounds of food to last me a month."

"A month? You only need a week at the most," I declared. And then I thought, *Man, I'd love to have some food.* He started to munch on trail mix and let me have some. There were beautiful large yogurt covered raisins in the mixture.

Besides the four pound tent, he also carried a machete with which to bushwhack and kill bears. "I guess I don't need it because the trail seems well maintained."

"Yeah don't worry, you don't need it."

I noticed that he was exceedingly excited to talk to me. He was practically jumping up and down while speaking. Perhaps he was compensating for my lack of energy. Or perhaps he wasn't used to being by himself for an extended amount of time. He kept on using the word ludicrous. To him everything was ludicrous. I started liking the word the more he used it.

He excitedly informed me about his wood burning stove to "save weight." I had never heard of such a thing. I assumed he meant he cooked over a campfire.

"It's forbidden in the state of Connecticut to have a fire." I corrected.

"Oh yes. Yes. I know. This is a stove." He brought out the little contraption and told me he burned twigs and sticks in it.

I gave him the name *Three Bananas*, after he told me a story of hiking Mount Lafayette with only three bananas and a bottle of water. It all started when an acquaintance from school invited him to hike in the Whites. "It was only during the hike that I realized that he was totally ludicrous," exclaimed *Three Bananas*. "He was born in Britain, but grew up here secretly loathing the US. And whenever other people passed on the hike he pretended to speak German, since in his mind Germans are the most mountaineering people. Not only did he start speaking gibberish to me whenever people passed, but he expected me to speak gibberish back to him. It was ludicrous."

I noticed a group of guys taking forever to set up their tent. I informed them that they didn't have to bear bag and could just hang their food in the shelter. That probably saved them twenty minutes of finding a tree and actually getting a rope thrown. I invited *Three Bananas* and the three guys to play cards. We played Scum, which they enjoyed. They were all giddy about being out in the boonies, but I was dead tired. I tried to stay awake, since I thoroughly enjoy playing cards.

As we were playing, I saw a light coming down the trail. It was *Skippy* who finally arrived near ten o'clock. He told us about hiking by the blooming Mountain Laurel. "The flowers glowed florescent like an airstrip when my headlamp shone on them. It was freaking awesome!"

Day 109

Chainsaw came by in the morning. "Think your friend who is picking you up would take me, too?"

"Don't count on it. He likes hikers, since he wants to hike next year, but I don't know. He'd probably at least take you to town."

It was short of a mile to the road. And Mark met us on the way. *Chainsaw* asked for a ride to town. Mark didn't seem too pleased, but let him in the car. In Kent we stopped at the post office to pick up my package.

The town seemed very proper. It didn't look like a friendly hiker town.

Chainsaw had us wait for him as he resupplied and he was back in a jiffy. Then he was dropped back off at the trail. Mark had the windows down – he kept saying that he smelled something funky and blamed the funky smell on *Chainsaw*.

Neither Mark nor *Chainsaw* thought the other was safe company for me. I thought it was odd that they were near the same age and judged each other so harshly.

We drove into a parking lot and walked into an old diner. Inside there were old dolls and banana seat bicycles on the walls next to pictures of Marilyn Monroe. "I used to come here all the time to eat their wonderful massive omelets. That is, until I became vegan," said Mark almost mournfully. They indeed were wonderful omelets; however, I found it slightly odd that Mark didn't have an omelet, since he was reminiscent about their appeal. Instead he got a vegetable stir-fry and was very strict about what went in it.

Once we got to the house, I ran to the shower. Life was good. I missed having a soft bed away from mosquitoes.

At this time of the hike, my motivation was low and I had seven hundred more miles to go. I knew I would be able to finish, but it was a matter between zombiing my way through or actually enjoying the hike.

They say there are three kinds of people that finish; the first, just love every minute of being in the outdoors. The second find the woods a better alternative to the life back home and the third just won't give up. I thought the best option was to slow down my mileage, and hopefully have more energy to enjoy the rest of my hike.

It just blew my mind how excited newbies could be about hiking. I suppose that was because hiking hadn't yet turned into their everyday like it had for me.

Day 110

In the morning it was raining. *Skippy* let me choose if we were going to stay at Mark's house. I took the opportunity to zero most willingly.

Hearing about all the health benefits of being vegan, had me considering being vegan myself. Of course, practically none of my food was vegan, so I would have to post pone. Overall, I couldn't believe I consumed so much fat and thought it was doing me good.

Day 111

I ate a bunch of cereal and read a bit more about being vegan, before we rode down to the trail. Once we got dropped off, it didn't take long for me to notice that I had dropped my newly obtained bug spray. I stopped to retrace it and I called Mark after I couldn't find it. He said he would bring it, but I felt bad, so I told him not to worry about it. I was glad that *Skippy* had waited and even retraced my steps with me. I knew then and there that *Skippy* was a good friend.

The rain started up and I could hear thunder. There was a downhill section, which was absurdly dangerous. It was a twisted staircase of sharp slippery rocks. With the rain making it extra slippery, we tiptoed our way down. The last part of the trail wasn't so bad, as it was flat alongside the Housatonic River. I followed *Skippy's* fast pace. We got in around noon.

Neither of us wanted to hike further in the rain. I spotted a bottle covered with a paper bag. I inspected it to find a full bottle of Bacardi. *Skippy* looked in the shelter log to see who had left it. An entry read, "I left a bottle of Bacardi at the shelter. Whoever comes by is welcome to drink it." And that's what we did.

I thought it was funny that *Skippy* couldn't stand the taste of pure rum. He had to add flavoring to it. Every time he took a drink he made the funniest faces. After teaching each other drinking games, we gaily ran to get water. At the stream *Skippy* asked, "Do you think I should purify my water?"

"Nah. You'll be fine," I replied nonchalantly as I scooped up some water.

I taught *Skippy* a game where you have to keep your balance by not moving your feet and hitting the other person's hands to make them fall. As we were playing, a Chinese kid joined in the game. He was very friendly. He beat me. We then went to the shelter, laughing as we ran. After a bit I went outside and puked behind the shelter. *Wow,* I thought, *I don't think I've ever drank this much before.* And before I knew it *Skippy* was there looking at me.

He curled his lips into a smile. "There's some puke, right there," he pointed to the side of my mouth. "You are *so* drunk."

SIXTEEN

Back With the Crew

June 23rd – July 2nd

Day 112

I left *Skippy* snoozing and hiked the first half of the day with a Swedish guy, "My trail name is *Bombadil*. As in the last name of the Lord of the Rings character Tom Bombadil. There is no particular reason why – he is just a guy singing songs in the forest, not really caring much about anything else. Some people call me *Glee* and some people call me *The Leprechaun*, because I'm wearing all green. I let people call me whatever – it's part of having fun out here.

"I will be the second Swedish man to have ever thru-hiked the AT," he remarked happily. His back story of why he was thru-hiking was complex. It all started when *Bombadil* decided that he wanted to go to another country for a semester of college. He decided to spin a globe and wherever his finger landed he would go. He got Gambia, a country in Africa. There he met another exchange student from Pennsylvania who convinced *Bombadil* to go hiking with him. He said, "I'm doing this from a big commitment. I came later in the season to hike with my friend, but he quit early on and I was stuck with only four months to finish. I've been hiking mid-twenties ever since. I take no breaks. I just push on."

Lucky for him, he seemed to be thriving.

He was a speedy fellow, so following him was a bit of a challenge. "The only time off from the trail was actually being sick," continued Bombadil. "That was my zero day – right there. I got sick on the roller coaster in Virginia, and kinda passed out on one of the warm days and so I had to go into the Bears Den Hostel. I stayed there five days – just being sick. I couldn't stand up on my feet. I thought I had Lyme Disease. I went to the doctor. But I recovered, and I'm back on the trail again – doing good."

After lunch I hiked with *Crumbs,* the Chinese kid I met the night before. He was the same age as me. When I told him that

Skippy and I were drinking the night before, he replied, "Hey! That means it wasn't a fair match, when I beat you at your game.

I shrugged it off and asked why he was hiking.

"My dad has always loved hiking. He would force me to hike with him when I was a kid. So as you can imagine he was shocked and overjoyed when I announced my intention to hike the whole summer.

"Every time I pass a road crossing I imagine my mother pulling up and shoving me in the car," admitted *Crumbs*.

"Why? What are you talking about?" I asked

"Well, my mother never wanted me to go. My parents had split decisions and they fought constantly over whether I was going. My dad was the one who helped me prepare for my hike. But my mom still wants me off the trail."

"My mom didn't want me to hike either," I commented. "But she let me go after I did everything she wanted me to do. Perhaps if you level with your mother, she might feel better about you being out here."

We hiked together and ran into *Three Bananas*, who was exhausted. I couldn't blame him, his pack was still a massive forty-five pounds. I persuaded them to try switching up the packs. Mine was the lightest, so I gave it to *Three Bananas*. *Crumbs* took the monster backpack and I took his. I was shocked when *Three Bananas* complained, "This backpack hurts my back. I'd rather carry my own."

As I took back my own backpack, I thought, *Okay my backpack hurts my back, too.* Then a light-bulb went off. *Maybe I should get a new backpack if he'd rather carry his forty-five pound pack rather than my twenty.*

We only went a short way before *Three Bananas* wanted a break. He took a seat on a log, "You guys don't need to wait for me."

"But we want to," said *Crumbs*. I could tell *Crumbs* enjoyed being around *Three Bananas* as much as I did.

Every five minutes, *Three Bananas* needed another break. I was starting to get annoyed, because I couldn't figure out what his problem was. On one of the breaks, *Three Bananas* took out a small peanut butter packet, "All my food needs to be cooked, but everything is too wet to burn, so all I have to eat are these peanut butter packets."

"Oh! Dude, that's why you are so worn out. Here, I have a bag of nuts and chocolate. Eat up," I commanded, handing the bag to him.

When we got hiking again, I was apprehensive about when the next break would be, but it never came. *Three Bananas* had transformed into a force to be reckoned with and even I had to work to keep up with him.

The shelter was half a mile off the trail! "That means it's a mile, round trip. I would rather stealth camp, even though it's *illegal* here," I muttered sourly.

The crazy terrain didn't help my mood. The other two were ahead and lost the trail. When I finally found the trail, I was ready to explode, because it was steep downhill. Soon after we arrived, a ridgerunner showed up at the shelter. Now, after all that fuss, I was glad I didn't stealth camp. I could have gotten a fine. I turned to the ridgerunner and half whined, "Why aren't we allowed to have fires?"

He sympathized and explained, "The ash from the fires make the ground infertile for years."

I was surprisingly content with his gentle reply. He turned out to be a nice guy.

The ridgerunner bear bagged my food, just because he wanted to. And when *Crumbs* realized that he lost his wallet, the ridgerunner contacted another ridgerunner who later retrieved the wallet.

When *Skippy* showed up, he mentioned that he wanted to join me on my way to Salisbury.

Day 113

I sold my two full bags of nuts to *Three Bananas*. I was glad, since I was sick of those nuts and *Three Bananas* was in dire need of calories.

Skippy told me that he got sick from drinking bad water. He blamed me, because I claimed the water would be fine. We started off together and I led speedily since I knew *Skippy* was fast. Not far along, I looked back. *Skippy* was nowhere in sight. I walked back to where he dropped his backpack. I put two and two together and figured he ran to the privy. When he came back, I gave him the diarrhea pill I had been carrying ever since Springer Mountain.

"Thanks. Why did you let me drink that water?"

"It seemed fine to me," I said innocently.

"It definitely wasn't okay. It was tinted brown."

"Really? I don't remember that."

We walked along the road to the bustling town of Salisbury. People were in and out of shops as if the holidays were upon them. I picked up some tomatoes, carrots, beans, and cereal. *Skippy* picked up an assortment of medication and after popping several pills, he felt intensely worse. We slowly walked back to the trail, but had to stop at the trailhead, because *Skippy's* vision became unsteady and he grew dizzy. I strung up my hammock for him to lie on and he called home.

His mother emphasized that he shouldn't be hiking anymore in his condition. He decided to go home and invited me. *Skippy* also called up *Scavenger.* I was happily surprised to learn that *Scavenger* was in Salisbury and had already paid for a room, but wanted to come. He stated that he would try asking for a refund. We didn't get news if *Scavenger* was coming until *Skippy's* mother showed up hours later. It was astonishing that our direction of travel changed so suddenly.

I asked *Skippy* why he wasn't hiking with *Scavenger.* He explained, "I enjoy being around *Scavenger* and all, but *Scavenger* is apt to skip sections of the trail. And I don't want to fall into that habit."

Skippy's mother was funny. She was a bit fickle about using the privy, which was conveniently placed for *Skippy*. I never realized how big of a deal it was that *Skippy* was born and raised in Brazil, until I was in the car listening to *Skippy* and his mother banter in incompressible Portuguese.

Skippy explained to his mother where Salisbury was, in order to pick up *Scavenger*. I was excited to see *Scavenger*. He had a haircut and his beard was pleasantly trimmed. I got out of the car to give him a hug. During the car ride, I told him how I tried to catch up to him and he told me of the disappointing towns in which he stayed.

Apparently in Unionville, NY, the new mayor wasn't as friendly to thru-hikers as the previous one. The old mayor was known for inviting hikers into his house. But *Scavenger* found it difficult to even locate a place to stay: the hostel was under construction, and there was one camping spot listed in the book, but he was shooed away. Luckily, a nice guy invited him to camp on his front lawn.

He also told me how he was thinking about buying a house in the near future and renting out some of the rooms. He had a picture of a house with a cross section and was calculating how much he would have to pay per month, minus the rent he made.

I was excited as we climbed the steps to the fourth floor of the apartment complex, where *Skippy*, his mother, and his mother's boyfriend lived. They were *so* friendly. *Skippy's* mother found clean clothes for me, after I had a wonderful shower. I was a bit sore, however, that my tan washed off.

I was handed an ice cold beer right away. They also wanted me to eat. "You must be hungry," they insisted. They grilled up loads of sausage, steak, and chicken on the balcony. They also grilled up some veggies for me, since I was regrettably still on the vegan bandwagon.

I thought it was the dearest thing to see *Skippy* meet his newly born niece for the first time. He had been talking about how much he wanted to see her.

It was strange that *Skippy* didn't introduce us by our trail names. I was introduced as Emily and *Scavenger* was called Ben. We were Rui's house guests. It was all so bazaar. I felt more at ease with my trail name.

There was lots of chatter, mostly in Portuguese and I was getting sleepy. There were movies playing so I watched on the comfy sofa. When *Skippy's* mother realized that I was falling asleep, she busied herself by getting the couch ready for me to sleep upon. Then she blew up the sleeping mattress for *Scavenger*.

Day 117

Skippy was such a night owl; the night before I was dead tired and he was wide awake. Our sleeping schedules were so off that it had been hard to hike with *Skippy*. I liked to hang with him, but there was no way I was going to wait 'til noon to start my day off.

Kelsey came to visit with her boyfriend, since she happened to be visiting home the same time.

Kelsey had always believed that trail names were silly, but recently Kelsey was hiking with *Yogi* when she found a dead opossum. *Yogi* excitedly suggested that she could be called *The Dead Opossum Girl*. She matched his excitement and accepted the trail name. *Skippy* was a bit upset because ever since he started hiking with Kelsey he had been trying to give her a trail name, but she refused even the most dignified names. "And now she likes *Dead Opossum Girl?*"

Skippy invited a bunch of friends over. We were discussing the sizes of the bears that we had seen, but they had nothing to add in, "Dude, I have no combat. I saw a squirrel the other day."

Skippy's mom was a fun lady. I joined her swimming in the pool. I ended up spending most my time lying in the sun, while *Skippy's* mom conversed with her friends. My Spanish was good enough for me to decipher that the one lady asked if I was Rui's girlfriend. "No, no," replied his mom.

We slowly got ready to leave. I had looked around for a new backpack since mine had weigh distribution problems that made

my back hurt. We stopped at some outfitters, but the cost of a
new back pack was quite high for not knowing if it'd be any
better. *Skippy* was a dear, and gave me one of his backpacks. I
thought about sending mine home, but realized how much I
didn't want to come home to a smelly, lousy, good for nothing
backpack. So I merrily junked it.

We left a couple hours later than planned and got hiking
around seven at night. There was a small bus at the trailhead,
which meant the shelter was going to be crowded.

We had a bit of a tizzy finding the campsite near the shelter.
The mosquitoes were unbearable. I loosened my tarp so that it
rested on my hammock, blocking the passage way. With the
restricted airflow I started to sweat. I smashed all the ones inside,
but the ones humming outside had me uptight; I was sure that
they could bite through my hammock, and ultimately were
hindering my sleep. I decided earplugs would do the trick. As I
reached for my backpack, swarms intruded my space. It didn't
take long until I had had enough. I grabbed my sleeping bag and
pad, and then made my way to the shelter. Lucky for me, there
was space.

Then it started to pour. It was the kind of rain that instantly
drenches everything. I could only hope my stuff wasn't
becoming waterlogged. Then I got thirsty. I tried to tell myself I
could sleep without a drink, but soon I really *couldn't* sleep
without a drink. I didn't want to get wet, so I tried collecting rain
off the roof. I believe I held out my palms to collect the slow
drips. I got frustrated and searched for a water bottle on the
backpack hanging up, but I couldn't find any.

Day 118

The day was blissful, which made up for the rainy, buggy
night. I awoke at five and went to see my tarp that had a puddle
of water on it. My things were a bit damp, but nothing was
harmed. I packed up in a flash because the bugs were on attack
mode. To hamper the process of getting eaten alive; I paced like
a madman while eating a banana.

The hike was quite lovely. An exquisite waterfall greeted me
at the border of Massachusetts. On a climb, I picked blueberries

and put them in my cereal. On the top, I found a sweet view in the sun and dried out my things. On the rocks, I sat soaking up the sun like a lizard and breathed in the refreshing breeze.

I ran into some trail maintainers and recognized the ridgerunner and sat down to lunch with them. They needed suggestions for provisions and I quickly listed off a few things I wanted at that moment.

There was a flat section, where I ate a variety of berries. It was beautiful, but the bugs were bad. I saw deer and five snakes. The last two snakes were large, black snakes; both of them gave me a fright.

□■□

I passed many types of mushrooms.

Some had red tops,

Some were white,

Others were brown,

And some were orangey bright.

□■□

I got tired at the end of the day and wondered where the shelter was. After almost missing the shelter, I got in at nine. All the hikers there were already in bed. *Skippy* and *Scavenger* showed up an hour later. In the midst of falling asleep, I heard their voices. I decided I wanted to welcome them. I only found out later they were terribly lost. They said that if I hadn't had my headlamp on they wouldn't have found the shelter.

Day 119

The previous day, I had a nice solitary hike, but I wanted to hike with my friends some. That meant waiting on them to get started in the morning. It wasn't too hard, since I was groggy myself. We hiked all together. It felt like the first time. Part way through, *Scavenger* fell behind. Then *Skippy* and I took a lunch break on a tent platform. He mumbled something about not rushing and lied down; I joined him, looking at the sky. I was talking when I looked over and saw *Skippy* had fallen asleep. I decided to leave and ran into *Scavenger* taking lunch on a beautiful hilltop.

Scavenger taught me the cheapest, most efficient way to travel in Germany; that was, by train on weekends with a group ticket. Apparently if you knew what you were doing you could make a couple bucks.

We discussed government, which of course was complicated. And taxes, and how *Scavenger* slams the door on the people who collected taxes for Movement TV. "All they have to do is get inside someone's house, see their TV, and say, well, you have a TV, therefore you have the ability to watch government TV." Apparently government TV in Germany doesn't have commercials, so they have to get their money by taxes.

Scavenger found it hypocritical that prostitution was illegal in the States, but on American commercials sex was used to sell products. I was glad for his insight, because it gave me something to think about.

We were nearing Upper Goose Cabin, and walking along the pond, when I saw a boat and excitedly called to *Scavenger*, "We should ask for a boat ride to the cabin."

He didn't seem thrilled. "That would be skipping a section. I thought *you* were a purist."

"Well I'm *not* a purist anymore. Just wait a second," I pleaded, before going to wave the boat down.

Well, what do you know, we got a ride. They handed us drinks. There was even beer for *Scavenger*. Everything was splendid. The pond looked ten times better on the boat. It was absolutely beautiful. The one lady, Jean, was tickled pink to be with thru-hikers, "I just got a book at the library about the Appalachian Trail."

The other lady on the boat took longer to warm up, "I couldn't go without having a shower every day." Bill was Jeans friend and was operating the boat. They took us to Upper Goose Cabin, a place known for giving out pancakes. We thanked them and got our things. As *Scavenger* was getting off, they asked if we wanted to stay a night at Jean's house. *Scavenger* was on the verge of not going, since he was trying to be serious about finishing the trail before his visa ran out. I persuaded him; this was too good of an opportunity to pass up. I felt bad for leaving *Skippy* behind. I asked for a beer and a soda from Jean, and then ran up to the cabin to scribble down a letter for *Skippy*. I was explaining to the caretaker to give the drinks to *Skippy*, when *Skippy* walked down the steps.

"*Skippy*! Wow! Where did you come from?" He started talking, but I cut him off. "Never mind, *Skippy*, grab your stuff. There's a boat waiting for us. Hurry up." It was the most epic boat ride ever. Everyone was smiling and laughing.

They got pizza and took us to a bar. The whole bar scene wasn't exactly my cup of tea, but *Skippy* and *Scavenger* loved it. *Skippy* worked as a bartender so he was at home. Scavenger went to school for brewing. It got even better for them, when we were taken to Jean's home. I got a shower while the others were listening to their favorite music. Jean kept saying, "I'm probably dating myself, but..."

Then *Skippy* would say, "No way, I love them."

It made me slightly jealous that he could make her so happy in such a little amount of time.

Jean was fully stocked with all kinds of alcoholic beverages. *Skippy* and *Scavenger* happily indulged. They were hoping to stay up partying late into the night, but when Jean went to bed, Bill, Jean's friend, forced *Skippy* and *Scavenger* to call it a night.

Day 120

Jean had work. I could tell she was a bit stressed. She gave us each twenty dollars and invited us to stay if we wanted to. I told her I wanted to stay another night. *Scavenger* was determined to hit the trail. *Skippy* was still asleep. I tried out the hot tub and *Scavenger* called his girlfriend. When *Skippy* woke up I fried up some eggs and sausages for him.

Bill, who liked to hang around Jean's house, gave us a ride to town in Jean's 1924 Ford Model T. The motor reminded me of a lawn mower. It was super cool when Bill tooted the horn, and people in the streets all turned to wave simultaneously. I felt like royalty.

While we resupplied, we bumped into a hiker named *Blue.* I told him about our great luck. After *Skippy* and *Scavenger* got Subway, Bill came and picked us up. Soon after, we got back to the house, but the door was locked and Bill was gone. *Scavenger* tried calling Bill, but he would not answer. As we went around checking all the windows and doors, Jean's neighbor yelled, "Stop or I'll call the police!" I froze in fright. *This cannot be happening.* "Just kidding. I know a way in," he laughed and unlocked a door for us.

When Bill came back he chased *Skippy* and *Scavenger* out. It was awful to see. *Scavenger* had decided he wanted to stay and *Skippy* wanted to stay, too. It wasn't Bill's house. I guess he was super protective of Jean, but it wasn't his business. *Skippy* and *Scavenger* had no choice but to leave. I felt weird. I told Bill I had already told Jean I was staying, so he couldn't kick me out. I called Jean after they had left. Jean confided that she hated when Bill acted like that, but she was too preoccupied to worry long.

When Jean came home she was super stressed about work and her friends coming for a concert. Her work had called her last minute, while her friends were showing up. Finally when everything came together, the ladies left to watch their annual show of James Taylor. One of the ladies sons stayed behind with me. The son had his own drama going on. He had recently been fired from work, because a child accused him of sexually harassing him. Then later as this guy was in the midst of being fired the little kid ran up to him and jeered, "Isn't it funny? I got you fired!"

We picked up two movies, Diary of a Wimpy Kid, and Hall Pass. Halfway through, this guy went to pick up a pizza. He was gone for a long time and I started worrying if he drank too much to be out driving, since he was guzzling beer ever since he arrived. He came back with a Big Mac. He muttered he got lost, and ended up in Connecticut.

Day 121

I woke up to all sorts of people at Jean's house. They were drinking coffee and chatting. There seemed to be a bit of drama. One lady had lost her prescription sunglasses and Jean had momentarily misplaced her cell phone. The ladies teased Jean about Bill having a crush on for her.

"He's liked her for years. I always see him at her house whenever I come. He does whatever she tells him to. He mows her lawn and takes her on boat rides," teased Jean's friend.

"He was also close to my parents. He helped me take care of them before they died. It meant a lot to me," explained Jean.

I felt it was time to move along. The son gave me a ride to the trail. He was unsure what to talk about, but seemed sweet.

Once I was back on the trail, I booked it. This was the first part of Massachusetts, where I didn't like the terrain. Either I was walking through a bunch of long scratchy grass, or there was mud. When I didn't have to worry about getting my feet soaked, I hurried. I wanted to catch up to my pals. They claimed they would be in Dalton the same time I arrived, but I still felt uneasy.

Low and behold, after seven miles I found them at the shelter that they had stayed at the night before. I was exceedingly happy that *Skippy* and *Scavenger* had waited for me, until I found out that they were just being lazy. They were leaving just as I arrived. Their plan was to go to the Cookie Lady's house and ask for a ride to Dalton. In Dalton they were going to meet one of *Skippy's* acquaintances. *Skippy* and *Scavenger* were still licking their wounds from being kicked out of Jean's house, and wanted to make up for it. I joined them on the speedy walk to the Cookie Lady's house, but I didn't want to skip part of the trail and pay someone to drive me, which was what *Skippy* and *Scavenger* ended up doing; ten dollars each for a lift to Dalton. I thought that I could walk fast enough to make it to Dalton and still be able to catch a ride with them. I asked *Skippy* if he would take my pack so I could run the ten miles to town, but he didn't want to be responsible for my things.

I bid them good day, and headed out. It was flat and I went relatively fast. I told *Skippy* to text me when he got picked up in town, but he forgot. I missed the ride. I guess I should have expected it, but I still felt the blow. I didn't have a plan B.

I felt like an idiot. Only a couple weeks ago, I had killed myself to catch up to *Skippy* and Scavenger. *And now what? I lost them. I guess I should have skipped that section. I mean friends are more important, right?* I had an internal battle waging. I had to decide if I was going to keep true to the trail or stick with my friends. I chose friends, but it was little too late. All I could do was hope for a second chance.

I thought back if there was any way I could have changed the events from turning out the way they had. *Well if I hadn't taken the boat ride, they wouldn't have looked for another place to stay. And it's partly Scavengers fault, Skippy never skipped before. And he did say he didn't hike with Scavenger because he didn't want to fall into his habits. So we started hiking with Scavenger after Skippy got sick. So if Skippy hadn't drunk that bad water he wouldn't have invited Scavenger to his house, and we wouldn't have started hiking with Scavenger. And the reason we weren't paying attention to the water was because we were under the influence. It's all the Bacardi's fault.*

I knew it was a combination of different things, but all in all, there wasn't much I could do to remedy the situation.

There was a man named Tom, in Dalton who took hikers into his house. His place was called the Bird Cage. I stayed there. Tom was more than wonderful for opening his house to hikers. He was very clear about the rules of the house. I respected him for laying them down. Indeed, I was lucky that I even spotted the place. I split a pizza with *Blue*. He was a decent fellow, but I was too distracted. I was sad that I had lost my friends.

SEVENTEEN

Keeping it Pure

July 3rd – 8th

Day 122

I was woken up by Tom, early in the morning. He had to lock up the house because he was leaving to drop off some slack-packers.

As I made my way to the outskirts, it started to drizzle. Then the heaven opened and it began to downpour, which didn't help my slightly sour mood. On my way up the mountain, I found a PayDay candy bar. For a split second, I thought about finding the owner. That thought quickly vanished and I gobbled it down in a flash.

When the rain ceased, I wished that it hadn't, since the mosquitoes came out in full force, ready for a feeding frenzy.

In the forest, I came upon a lady with two dogs that aggressively ran towards me with loud, vicious barks. I panicked, thinking surely these dog were going to take pieces out of me. The owner simply whistled and the dogs obediently retreated. The lady didn't apologize – She didn't say a word! It was as if she blamed *me* for disturbing her dogs! I wanted to yell, "This is public property! If your dogs are going to pounce on pedestrians, you need to tie up your dogs!"

It was nine miles to Cheshire. As I approached town, the rain picked up again. I took cover under a pine tree in a front yard. I sat there as it poured. My guidebook mentioned a church hostel down the road. The rain showed no sign of slowing down, so I headed for the hostel. On my way there, a lady called from inside her car, "Need a ride?" I hopped in. They were astounded. "You're hiking the whole thing? Why, you're a girl hiking alone. And you're so young. Isn't it scary?"

At the church, the lady escorted me inside and before she left she handed me a twenty.

A man of the church showed me around and gave me a room. There were section hikers in the adjacent room. I thought it would be the perfect time to play a game, such as Scrabble or Monopoly. I asked the father and son if they wanted to play. Their only reaction was to stare stupidly at me. Finally, after asking them enthusiastically multiple times, I realized neither of them wanted to play. *Not cool.* So I curled up on the corner couch in my room and caught a few Z's.

When I woke up a few hours later, I looked out the window to see that the rain had ceased. I looked in my guide for a place to buy food. The only option I had was a gas station. I gave up looking for a better alternative and purchased an *expensive* loaf of bread and strawberry jam.

I went forward to climb Mount Greylock. It was somewhat famous, but at that moment all I saw was its steepness.

At the shelter, several miles shy of the summit, was a family. They were exceedingly friendly. They gave me some couscous and Jelly Belly's, and filled up my denatured alcohol supply. I didn't eat supper, since I had stuffed myself earlier by eating all the jam as well as most of the bread, so I wouldn't have to carry the glass jar.

Day 123

I was woken up by the family rustling, crunching, and whispering in loud voices. They claimed that they were trying to be quiet, but they must have been joking; in any case I didn't mind being woken up.

In time, I caught up to the parents who were insanely slow, but it was absolutely amusing to watch their flamboyant personalities interact.

At the summit of Greylock, I found Hannah their daughter. She told me about her exchange to Holland. We swapped exchange student stories. She was in grad school and was excited about joining the Peace Corps. She didn't know what country she would be assigned to, but she seemed confident that she would get what she wanted. I was a bit concerned for her, since she would live in her assigned country for the next twenty-seven months. I imagined her walking off a plane into a wasteland and a radio buzzing in her pocket announcing, "Welcome to your home for the next twenty-seven months."

Hannah apologized for her parents waking me up. She said, "They've always been loud and have no idea what the meaning of being quiet is."

I pondered relaxingly on the summit. With the overlook, I knew the fireworks would be superb. I imagined during the day that I would get some barbecue from picnickers. Sooner rather than later reality set in; I was bored. However, I did run into some folks who seemed intrigued about my hike. They asked the usual questions: "Are you alone? Is it scary? Have you seen bears?" They offered to drive me to the YMCA in North Adams. I couldn't allow myself to skip a part of the trail, even though I knew, in the back of my mind, that I might have been able to snag a free stay.

All morning was downhill. In North Adams I walked to the Price Chopper. My plan was to have someone notice that I was a stinky hiker in need of a place to stay. My backup plan was to stay at the YMCA. As I waited in line, I began to work my charms: number one, keep your arms down as much as possible to discourage odor leakage and number two, smile.

The lady ahead of me gestured to my watermelon on the conveyer belt, "Aren't those watermelons nice? I got one, too."

"I'm planning to eat the whole thing for lunch – in celebration of Independence Day," I replied enthusiastically. "By the way, do you know if I can stay at the YMCA?"

"Well actually, I don't think you can. I'm so sorry. You know you could stay at my house – except it is such a mess."

"Oh please, I don't mind. I would be happy to tent in your yard," I offered, smiling.

"No, no, no. You don't need to sleep outside. You are more than welcome to stay at my house."

"Thank you, thank you so much. I was... hoping to see fireworks tonight – it is, after all, the Fourth of July," I lured.

"Oh yes of course, we will be going to see the fireworks after the baseball game. I would love to take you."'

"Thank you. You are too kind." I couldn't be more satisfied.

We drove down the road and went to her house. She saw her neighbor and introduced me, "This girl is hiking the Appalachian Trail. Would it be okay if she joins us for the BBQ later this evening?"

"Yes of course, we would love to have her," the neighbor lady proclaimed happily.

We then unpacked the groceries. Marcia, the lady who had picked me up, declared, "I am so delighted to finally meet a thru-hiker! I've wanted to meet a thru-hiker for years. You are the first one I have ever met. Thank you so much for coming to stay at my house!"

I was stumped. *Okay, it's great she loves me staying at her house, but she's never met a thru-hiker before? Boloney. Hikers are as common as rats in this town.* As I thought it over, it dawned on me how fortunate I was for having mastered the art of meeting people. *Sure, hikers are everywhere, but that doesn't mean they are getting acquainted.*

Inside I was greeted by two yappy dogs, scratching at my ankles, and Marcia's husband, watching TV on the couch. I thought it odd that they weren't using their jumbo flat screen TV. When I asked about it, he spoke nonchalantly, "The bulb burn out in that TV. I just haven't gotten around to fixing it."

In the kitchen Marcia cut my watermelon in half. Marcia wasn't lying about the condition of her house. I learned quickly to keep my shoes on, because the dogs weren't potty trained. In her kitchen, I noticed the dishes were everywhere. "Sorry about all the dirty dishes. Our dishwasher is broken," apologized Marcia. There were clothes stretched out all about the house. "Our dryer is broken as well." She placed the other half of the watermelon in the fridge. I noticed all the shelves were taken out and Marcia had a stack of food on the bottom. "I was cleaning out my fridge one day, when I got distracted and never put the shelves back in place," Marcia explained.

For supper we went to the neighbors' and dined on ribs, pasta, and grilled corn. Then I had a swim in their pool and was accompanied by the little neighbor girl. She was really cute, but super bossy. I tried my best to humor her, but quickly got annoyed by her unrelenting bossiness.

After dark, we headed out to see the fireworks. It all was absolutely wonderful. There was a firework the shape of a heart and one was a smiley face. We sat on the hood of the car. These were quality people: they so loved and thanked me just for being there. I thanked them for having me. I fell asleep on their couch watching a movie that Marcia let me pick.

Day 124

In the morning, I had a long chat with my mother. She was home from Europe and I had missed sending her my daily texts.

I tried my best to finish the other half of my watermelon. Before I left, I gave my hosts both a hug and they mentioned if I ever needed help, I was just a phone call away.

It was great passing the border into Vermont. Ironically, even though I had just stepped foot in Vermont, I already couldn't wait to be out of Vermont. I was ready to be in New Hampshire and on my way to the Whites. I thought myself quite terrible for not giving Vermont a chance, but from all I heard, Vermont was mud and we called it Ver-mud.

When I passed the border not only was I in Vermont, but I was on the Long Trail. There was a mighty big sign in the middle of nowhere spelling out the significance and history of the Long Trail. The Long Trail was surprisingly older than the AT. The two trails shared the same path and the same white blazes for half of Vermont. The LT goes off another direction and ends on the other end at the border of Vermont and Canada. The only thing I was worried about was going the wrong way when the two trails split.

I ran into a girl named *Jupiter*. It was her first day out – she was hiking the Long Trail. I was glad for her; first days should always be enjoyed.

While we were taking a break at a dirt road, out came *Crumbs*. It was an unexpected surprise. "Oh, I got off the trail for a family reunion," explained *Crumbs*. "There were little Chinese kids running around screaming. It's great to be back on the trail again.

"You know *Three Bananas*? Well, he changed his name to *Machete Sandwich*. And from what I hear he has quit the following. Thru-hikers are finding him entertaining," said *Crumbs*.

Jupiter introduced herself as a thru-hiker.

"Thru-hiker? You mean you're hiking the Long Trail," I corrected. When I think of thru-hiking, I think: the Appalachian Trail, two thousand miles through fourteen states. The Long Trail was in one state and it was a measly two hundred eighty miles. It just didn't seem fair that she could claim that term for hiking only a handful of miles. *Crumbs* started at the Delaware Water Gap, three hundred miles away, and *he* didn't claim to be a thru-hiker.

When we got to the shelter, I made a fire to celebrate four months on the trail. A man came and handed out food and beer. He even popped some popcorn. As this man was cooking inside the shelter, he lit half the picnic table on fire. He seemed unfazed by it, as he kept chatting, "Oh, this is normal. You see I have to let a bit of the fuel out to get it started." The thing is, he had let out a puddle. The shelter may have burnt down, but luckily *Jupiter* had water on hand and tossed out the flames.

Day 125

Jupiter and I started out together, but it didn't take long before she fell behind. She was in her own dream world and she stopped to take pictures every five minutes.

I caught up with *Crumbs* at the shelter, on top of a mountain. We discussed his Chinese heritage, after he had called his dad and spoke Chinese.

At the next shelter there were three guys. Two of them, *Blue* and *Hand-Me-Down*, were planning to hike more. They had been enjoying the view from the shelter all day. *Crumbs* joined them as the thunder began to roar. I would have liked to hike with *Crumbs*, but I wasn't willing to get soaked in the imminent downpour.

I built a fire to keep the bugs at bay and John, the only guy left, was impressed at my fire making skills. Next he was astonished that I didn't treat my water. "Wow, you're taking a risk." He didn't expect me to have a video camera. He exclaimed, "Wow where did that come from? You have such a *small* backpack!" I was happy that I could impress him.

Skippy, who was behind me, sent me a text asking if I would like to join him and *Scavenger* to his house in Framingham for the weekend. Usually I can make a decision in seconds, but I mulled over the invitation. I didn't want to wait on them to catch up, but they were my friends, and I concluded that being with friends was more important.

Day 126

The morning was gray. The bugs that hovered over me made me feel like a walking trashcan. I passed the seventy-five percent mark. I didn't see any marker, so I ripped up some moss nearby and arranged it on the ground to read; 75%. I found out later other hikers snapped pictures of my handiwork. "I made that!" I got to point out.

The climb of the day was Stratton Mountain. On my way, I passed three day hikers. The last man gave me a granola bar and told me to tell his son that he was still alive. He boasted, "I'm thru-hiking the LT and next year I'm hiking the AT and then the next year I'm hiking the PCT." He was a large man with an enormous backpack. He mentioned something about snoring loudly. Later, I heard from *Crumbs* that he didn't just snore loud, he physically vibrated the shelter. The night before, this large man had cleared the hikers from the shelter. The poor sleepy hikers had to set up their tents in the rain.

Mount Stratton was taller than Greylock, but was a much easier climb. The only thing that bothered me was that I kept thinking that I was at the top. Somehow, the mountain persisted to grow. Unfortunately, there wasn't a view at the top, except for a lookout tower that had a 360 degree view over the tree tops.

Dozens of hikers were resting at the top. The man that gave me a granola bar on the climb confessed that he had too much food. I told him that I would be delighted to have whatever food he didn't need.

"We will be picking up a food drop tomorrow and I have no idea what we would have done with all this food," remarked the man. He and his son dug in their packs and gave me everything they didn't like: three rice sides and two packets of ramen noodles.

This handout ignited a chain-reaction of hikers giving food left and right. Tortilla chips from one guy and two cookies each from another.

Skippy sent me a text telling me to stop at Manchester Center, and that we would be picked up the following evening. Formerly I had decided to pass the town, since I had attained my resupply, so I was glad I hadn't already passed it.

At the shelter, two boys were trying to carve a wooden spoon. After watching them with amusement, I advised them to place a hot ember on the spoon and burn out the bowl by blowing on the ember. After that didn't work, we also tried burning denatured alcohol inside the bowl, which proved futile, but entertained the kids.

Day 127

I had the entire day to wait up for *Skippy* and *Scavenger*. I slept in until I heard someone outside. It was *Spot,* a man who was on his fourth thru-hike. He was concerned about hitchhiking. I volunteered to assist him. It was the least I could do. On our way to the road, he told me that he saw his eleventh bear that morning. I interviewed him since he seemed pretty interesting. At the road, it took perhaps six cars to pass before we got picked up. He admitted it usually took him half an hour to catch a ride.

After we got dropped off, I noticed that I had left my hat in the back of the pickup truck. That hat was special. I had picked it up along the trail, back in New Jersey. Many people had recognized it and asked, "Is *that* the hat I saw on the trail?"

"It sure is," I recalled with a smile. It was a proper business type of hat, with a feather on the side. I knew it wasn't a big loss, since some hikers forget hiking poles or even their whole packs in the backs of pickup trucks. I could imagine that their sinking feeling would be a million times worse when the truck pulled away. I was going to miss that hat. It went so well with my pea green tie, which I had also found along the trail more recently. I remember *Skippy* looking down at the tie around his neck, when he tied the tie for me. He reminisced the days when he used to dress up for work. "Dude, I haven't tied a tie in ages."

I was glad to see a Price Chopper in Manchester Center; it was my favorite supermarket chain on the trail. There was a picnic table outside where I spent the day catching rays. I noticed a sign that read, "No Loitering." I suspect it hinted at thru-hikers.

What pushed my buttons was that the locals assumed I was hiking the Long Trail. I wanted to say, "Yes Ma'am, I am hiking the *long* trail. It's so long – in fact it's longer then the Long Trail!"

Blue and *Hand-Me-Down* were there, too. They were a hilarious bunch. I teased them that they weren't *true* thru-hikers. The definition of thru-hiking was to hike the entire trail in a calendar year; they were doing it in two years. *Hand-Me-Down* had started the trail in the spring of 2010, but got Giardia halfway through. He returned with the intention of completing his second half. *Blue* was doing the northern half the trail and was planning to finish the following year. I asked if they felt bad for taking trail magic from coolers that said, "For thru-hikers." I later felt awful for being so harsh, especially after they kept bringing it up in following conversations. "...since I'm not a *real* thru-hiker."

It was nothing against them. I thought *Blue* and *Hand-me-down* were a fantastic bunch. It was just that the whole purist thing was bothering me. I kept wondering how strict the rules were to be considered a thru-hiker. *If people found out I skipped a few miles would they consider me unworthy of the title?*

Hand-Me-Down was such an amiable guy. He was roughly my age and had an afro of bright ginger hair, which I thought was lovely. He had an adorable southern accent and a smile to die for.

After I told *Blue* that I stayed at many folk's homes, he totally thought I was a beggar. He said, "Look, I'm well off. I worked in the army and made good money. I don't give others help and I don't ask help from others. If someone gives something to me, I feel entitled to give something back and I'm not willing to do that. I don't even take trail magic."

"What, because you feel you have to repay them?" I said.

Blue and *Hand-Me-Down* were having all sorts of drama. First, they had planned to share a hotel with *Crumbs*. Then, when they got to town they realized that *Crumbs* ditched the plan and went to stay at the hostel – which I heard great reviews about. I tried to give them my two cents that *Crumbs* was probably confused, since he was a nice kid, but they were convinced otherwise.

The drama continued. *Hand-Me-Down* had the buns and *Blue* had the hotdogs that they were planning to roast for dinner. However, *Hand-Me-Down* was invited by a trail friend to chill at his house, while *Blue* was not. *Hand-Me-Down* didn't want to hurt *Blue's* feelings, but decided to go to his friend's house anyway. It was hard to watch *Blue* being driven to the trail with a glum look in his eyes.

There was an outfitter next to the picnic table, and I window shopped. I was overwhelmed at the price of some of the gear. I would look at things, thinking, *Who would waste money on that?* Or, *no one ever uses those.* It made me angry. One of the employees asked if I needed help.

"Well, I have to admit, I could use a new pair of shoes," I mumbled hesitantly, looking down at my feet and wiggling my toes. My shoes were clearly falling apart, but I wasn't willing to buy a third pair. I told myself, *I don't need new shoes. I can make these last.*

Skippy called me when he and *Scavenger* arrived. It started to rain soon after I met up with them. It wasn't the most exciting reunion. *Scavenger* was still reading his thick book. We went inside Friendly's when it started to rain. I was feeling a bit impatient and when *Skippy's* mother finally showed up she wanted to order something to eat. The way back was a three hour car ride. It felt like forever. I was exhausted, but too uncomfortable to get any sleep.

At one point it was pouring so hard that we couldn't see *anything*. The car halted to a stop on the highway until the rain subsided. At that moment I was glad to be dry.

When we arrived, I was so relieved to have a shower. I got to see the surprising amount of bug bites I had, once all the dirt was washed off.

We watched a movie and went to bed at three. It was absolutely fabulous to be indoors.

EIGHTEEN

Sticking to the Schedule

July 9th – July 16th

Day 128

The following is some advice for wannabe thru-hikers. Pack light. Leave everything home except for the bare essentials. Simple is better and less is more. Try to have a pack that weighs less than thirty pounds from the get-go. Don't fall into the, "I might need this and I might need that," state of mind. It's okay to forget things because everything a hiker needs can be found in stores along the trail.

The three most important things to spend money and research on are a backpack, a tent, and a sleeping bag, the lighter in weight the better. You may be cheaper with everything else.

You don't need a water filter. They are heavy and are apt to break. In the start of the trail, all the hikers had water filters, but as the filters started to break everyone relied on Aqua Mira. If a hiker has a water filter in New England, they most likely aren't thru-hiking. Bleach is just as good as Aqua Mira. It is effective, cheaper, and probably equally as bad for health. I do not suggest using iodine.

If you want to be ultra outdoorsy try no purification. Drinking straight from waterfalls can be absolute bliss. Beware, you will feel sick a few times, but by the end you'll have a stomach of steel. I would suggest having some kind of purification on hand for states Pennsylvania through Vermont.

Resupply as often as possible and therefore carry the least amount of food possible. You will have more town visits. I don't know about you, but I would rather scanter across mountains and spend a little extra time in town, than heave hefty burdens up and down mountains. Choose your battles well.

For maildrops, be careful. If it's possible, only have a couple. Then have someone at home put together new ones if you insist on having more. Otherwise you will get sick of what you packed months before. Even better, don't have mail-drops, they are more expensive anyhow. You get exactly what you want when you buy it straight from the store. The places where it is clever to have mail drops are Nantahala Outdoor Center, Fontana Dam, and Harper's Ferry.

Good hiking lunches are tortillas or bagels filled with your pick of cheese, barbecue sauce, peanut butter, jelly, summer sausage, pepperoni – you name it. Hot chocolate is *amazing* especially when it's nippy. You find out quickly any food can be eaten on the trail. The question is how. Don't force yourself to eat rice and pop-tarts every day, or you will hate everything and everyone. I heard of a guy that survived on Hershey Chocolate Bars dipped in peanut butter and frosting. Bad idea. He had incredibly low mileage.

For silverware all you need is a simple metal spoon, plastic spoons will break. Please, oh please no sporks. I admit they look legit, but you'll be hating them too, after you can't scrape out the last of your peanut butter. If you like the pancake idea, get the equipment. It's possible to find a folding spatula and a small frying pan. The one item I wish I had was a pan gripper. I didn't have a pan gripper on the trail. I used a beanie hat, which is not recommended.

Trail runners are good shoes. The lighter the shoe you have, the better. There's a saying for every pound of shoe is ten pounds on your back. Remember, no five fingers in northern Pennsylvania – it isn't worth the pain. Anticipate going through three pairs of trail runners. Your feet will grow about half a size. If you have a heavy pack, you'll need boots, since the heavier the pack the more support you will need. You might not have to replace your heavy boots, but they will be shot by the end. As in, "Look! I can see my sock."

Gaiters aren't necessary, though if you want to get some, I would suggest Dirty Girl Gaiters. They are a fun accessory.

Have a good camera. Keep it simple. If you like music, get an mp3 with normal AAA batteries. Rechargeable batteries don't last as long and are a hassle. For any charger that you do have, make sure it plugs into an outlet and not just a computer, because computers are few and far between. Smart phones are very useful, even on the trail.

It's easy to make your own stove. Get a cat food can and punch out some holes. You may want to make some sort of stand to set your pot on and tinfoil works as a wind screen. Denatured alcohol can be used as the fuel, but HEET burns better and comes in a yellow bottle and is typically used for cars.

When it is cold out, the best way to keep feet warm is to keep your shoes on. Once your feet are cold there's not much you can do to warm them. Get a beanie. The head lets off eighty percent of the body's heat. This is where logic rules: keep your head covered.

If you start in early March or late April you won't be crammed in shelters. Try not to look like a beginner and don't bear bag. Leave the rope at home. The cans hanging from the ceiling of the shelters have a purpose. They save you a good half hour.

Give yourself enough time to finish and enjoy the trip. Remember to spare five to six months. Take your time in the beginning. Don't overdo it. Just be happy to hike double digits. Virginia is long, beautiful but long. Pace yourself. Don't be scared to take zeros. It isn't a race. Find ways to relax and you will enjoy your trip better. Go your own pace and then find people to hike with you. You don't want to go another person's pace, or make them go yours. This is easier said than done.

The best way to get trail magic is to be friendly and likeable. Let them know you hiked X number of miles and that you are starving. Talk to everyone. Don't think others have nothing to offer. If you're not a girl, hike with one. Girls get hitches faster and are invited to peoples' houses more often.

For those that want to do Trail Magic, take in account of what the weather is like. In the winter hot foods are amazing, for example hot chocolate, coffee, and piping hot baked goods. If it's hot, things like cold drinks and ice cream are appreciated. The fun thing about giving out Trail Magic is that hikers are so grateful. They can't repay you, and they have a hard time expressing how thankful they are.

By the way, men straight out of the woods crave hamburgers, pizza, beer, and soda – it's rather universal. The best time to get to town is in the morning. It is hard to hold off sometimes, but going in the evening means shelling out for an extra night.

Guys: expect to lose weight.

Girls: don't. Expect to gain muscle.

Lastly *everyone* prefers the AWOL guidebook. Don't be like me. Please do yourself a favor and start with a guidebook.

Day 130

The main reason *Skippy* wanted to visit home was because his niece Gabrielle was getting christened. I was dedicated as a baby so I suppose it was similar. The only thing that hindered my experience was that the entire service was spoken in Portuguese.

Skippy and *Scavenger* talked obsessively about finishing the trail ASAP. Every other conversation creeping up had something to do with hiking faster so that they could be finished sooner. In the back of my mind, there was a voice yelling, "If you want to be done as soon as possible, why are you taking so many days off?"

Skippy and *Scavenger* made it their goal to finish their hike the first week of August. They calculated that they had to average seventeen miles that meant hiking seventeen miles every day for the next month. I knew that *Scavenger* would be serious with this plan, because his visa would run out the second week in August.

I was nervous about putting myself on a schedule. It was not my idea of enjoying the trail. The whole reason I joined my friends again was because I enjoyed their company, but if we were sticking to a strict schedule, I feared no one would be enjoying anything.

They devised a plan to hike over seventeen miles in the beginning, so that we could create a pillow to buffer us when we hit the Whites.

218

"When we do extra miles we can put the miles in a bank. And when we get seventeen miles in the bank: we can take a zero day," observed *Scavenger*.

After being housebound for four days, I noticed to what extent *Skippy* and *Scavenger* enjoyed playing video games. I also noticed how much I couldn't wait to be back on the trail.

The ride back to the trail didn't seem as long as before. I had to show *Skippy* and *Scavenger* where the trail was, because they had skipped a section of the trail earlier to get to town faster.

Day 131

In the morning, *Scavenger* and I hiked up a ski slope and discussed faith. He grew up in a Catholic church. He disclosed that his Catholic teachers lied to him about the scriptures and lived lives full of hypocrisy. "You remember hearing about the priest who molested children? When I heard things like that I dropped my belief."

"But those are people. People will let you down," I said, most earnestly.

"I've heard that several books were taken out of the New Testaments and that people added the miracles in the New Testaments just to spice up the gospels."

I was flabbergasted. "No way, that is so not true."

We both agreed that we would do research about each other's perspectives. He assured me that he wasn't completely sure about anything and he promised that he would take time to do the research in the future.

We were walking on bog boards, when all of a sudden I sank deeper and deeper into the water. *Scavenger* was glad I went first. He was like a cat in the degree that he hated water. When his boots got wet they didn't dry out for days. I thought *Skippy* might like a warning, so I ran back across the floating bog board to warn him with a note.

At a break *Scavenger* began to talk on his cell phone, so I hiked ahead two miles to a shelter with a view of a lovely lake. I thought about staying there for the night, but unfortunately, the shelter was home to a caretaker who was charging everyone five dollars to stay.

In the nearby lake, I took a dip and then sun dried on the rocks. A section hiker came to talk to me and I learned he had hiked the same distance as me, but over the span of twelve years.

I joined *Skippy* when he arrived and I followed him, booking up the mountain. It was gorgeous. I loved the pine.

At the shelter, I cooked dinner and made too much couscous. *Skippy* wouldn't take it, so I saved it for *Scavenger*. I built a large fire just to ward off the bugs. We all took turns to bathe in the smoke. We went to bed sore and worn out, as the rain pitter pattered on the roof.

Day 132

I woke up to a deep throated snore. It was coming from the side *Skippy* was on, but last I knew *Skippy* didn't snore, at least not *that* resoundingly.

On the ground, near the shelter, was a man laying in a sleeping bag. When he awoke, I asked, "Why are you sleeping on the ground?"

"Well, my friend and I," he gestured to the snoring man next to me, "were relaxing at a beautiful waterfall yesterday, when it began to rain. We hurried to this shelter. But it looked like it was full and we didn't want to disturb anyone so we slept on the ground."

"In the rain?" I asked, in disbelief. "You know all you have to do is nudge us and we'll move. There's plenty of room in here. What are you going to do now? You're all wet!"

"We'll be going home today. We were just out for a couple days," he replied, unfazed.

I left and later ran into *Steady* and her friend. They were excitedly talking about staying at a friend's cabin in Maine. I joined them hiking and we met two southbounders. They told us about the Whites while I gawked at them in amazement, and asked all the questions on my mind. The Whites sounded extremely difficult yet magnificent. They mentioned that the huts were great and that we should hike miniscule days to prolong the raptures of the Whites.

"How were the bugs in Maine?" I asked.

"Terrible. You know those big gray flies that buzz around your head for miles?"

"Those are the worst," I agreed.

"Little devils. After killing one there would always be another to take its place. But they always land one of two places; the very top of your head or your right shoulder. All you have to do is; wait for them to land… and smack 'em dead. My record is fifteen in one day," he boasted.

At the five hundred miles-to-go-mark was a cooler full of soda. I opened two cans and drank them simultaneously as I took a seat on the provided lawn chair. I thought I heard an airplane, but when the same sound repeated louder a second time, I knew it was thunder – rain was inescapably on its way. My tranquil state of being changed to a hurried one and I guzzled down the sodas and rushed to the next shelter, burping as I went. The rain had come and gone by the time I arrived. A southbounder soon popped in. After settling down, he commented, "I'm getting sick of the terrain."

"Dude, I don't wanna hear it. You're not even a quarter finished!" I scolded.

There was silence. He went on to say that the Whites were spectacular. "Yeah, I ate at all the huts and actually gained weight." He pulled out a plastic cigarette. "Want some cannabis?" he asked

"What's cannabis?" I asked.

He was the tenth southbounder that I passed. Many northbounders feel like they get a snotty attitude from the Southbounders. *Scavenger* said, "It's like they're trying to prove that they're better by hiking the trail in a more difficult fashion."

Killington, the highest mountain in Vermont, had a four mile climb to the summit. With the tunnel of dense pine trees I had no idea how close I was to the top. When I came to a small break in the trees I stopped to peer out at the view. *Wow, I thought. I'm really high.*

The storm was coming for a second round. Thunder boomed and lightning flashed. The thought came to mind that my metal hiking poles might get me electrocuted, so I put my poles in my backpack and scuttled my last couple miles across the face of the mountain.

I was relieved when I finally made it to the rustic hunting cabin. Inside the stone structure were double sized bunk beds and two girls had already claimed the bunk closest to the door.

Exhausted and cold, I hunkered down in my sleeping bag and called home before falling asleep.

When I heard the voices of my friends, I awoke to see a soggy *Skippy* and *Scavenger*. They were sitting on the picnic table, boiling water, when they encouraged me in getting up to see the bright orange sunset through the small window.

Day 133

During the night, I woke up cold and uncomfortable. I must have been too tired before to notice that the boards on my bunk weren't level. I took a look around for somewhere else to sleep. *Skippy* was beside me and *Scavenger* was on the top bunk. Then I saw the picnic table and thought it would be flat enough. I bunny hopped in my sleeping bag, with my sleeping pad under my arm and soon fell fast asleep atop the table.

In the early morning *Scavenger* and I climbed up a side trail to the top of Killington, to see the sunrise. I had forgotten my glasses, but I brought my sleeping bag, in which I sat on a large rock and soaked up the majestic view. I wanted to have that picture in my mind forever. I couldn't see much behind me, but on all other sides I could see the mountains standing huge and mighty clothed in a carpet of trees. The mountain spine ahead that stretched northward had me wondering about what was to come. I felt like I was on a timeline. North was future and south was past. It was breathtaking.

I hiked mostly downhill for ten miles. Throughout the descent, a war persisted in my mind over pessimistic thoughts. I tried to make a tally of all the positive things, but I gave up and let pessimism win. I felt ill, my shoes were breaking, and we weren't going to get to Hanover in time to get my package before the post office closed. I was sick of walking. No kidding, right?

I came to a campground and sat down on a picnic table. During the hike, I had felt something piercing my nose to the point that it hurt. It was only until I was sitting down at the picnic table when I realized that one of my glasses' nose pads was missing. So in place of the nose pad I tried wrapping athletic tape around the part that was poking me.

A bit further along, I was thinking about the lake that I was walking by being a perfect spot for *Scavenger* to go fishing, since *Scavenger* was carrying several hooks and string. I took a seat against a tree as I waited for *Scavenger*. When he arrived, I suggested that he should go fishing. He blew it off, saying, "I would if we were done hiking for the day. Besides, I have plenty of food." He continued on to tell me about how wonderful his day was turning out to be. First, he and *Skippy* found food in the shelter. And then a stranger gave him an apple, and another stranger gave him some mountain houses. I tried to be happy for him and congratulate his success, but it was difficult. "Did you get any extra food for me?"

"No," he answered.

We stopped at a restaurant overlooking a lake and *Scavenger* ordered himself a meal. He enlightened me about how wonderful the food was, but I only started paying attention when he mentioned a hiker box inside.

The funny thing was that the entire day was relatively flat, which we should have been happy for, but no. *Scavenger* focused on the one little mountain. It was very steep and had no views. At the top, *Scavenger* vented his frustration by flailing his arm about. "Do you know why I came hiking? I came hiking to see views. Not to go hiking up mountains without views! Why did the idiotic trail maintainers even make a trail up this mountain? It's a total waste of time. I bet they made it just to infuriate us!" When we got to the shelter we waited for *Skippy*, who also vented his hatred for such an abominable mountain. The two of them explained their expectations of why they came out to hike and agreed that it wasn't to hike up mountains that didn't have views.

It was previously planned that we were going to camp a couple miles further along the trail. That way we would be closer to Hanover, so I could pick up my package before the post office closed for the weekend. But *Skippy* and *Scavenger* had grown lazy. *Skippy* suggested that I should call the post office to forward my package in order to make life easier. I had had that lovely parcel with its chocolates in mind for days, but at the same time, I agreed with *Skippy;* we shouldn't have to rush.

The athletic tape that I had on my glasses fell off. Somehow I got an ingenious idea and tried putting a raisin on the end where the nose pad would have been. It worked very well. All I had to do was replace the raisin every couple of days.

I sat down next to the fire and whittled two wooden dice. The guys came over to see my craftsmanship and were truly impressed, but they didn't seem excited to play a game with me. Only *Scavenger* played, but he had different rules to the game than me so I explained the game as we went along and *Skippy* accused, "She cheats. See? She's always changing the rules." *Scavenger* had the same expression the entire game, so figuring out when he lied was impossible and therefore led me to lose.

Day 134

Halfway through the day, I found *Skippy* and *Scavenger* sitting on a log. They couldn't decide if they wanted to exert the energy of hiking down the trail to get water. I joined them on the log and settled into their highly demoralized state. We threw rocks at trees and mumbled incoherently. When we finally began hiking again, they continued to wallow in their melancholic take on the viewless mountains.

In the late afternoon, we came to a road. Our minds were steeped in the thought that we still had another ten miles to go. *Scavenger* mentioned that he really wanted a beer. But they just sat there – not so much tired, but drained of spirit.

"Come on guys! Do you wanna keep hiking? Or should we go to town? You know you're lucky you have me, a girl? I bet I can get a ride in less than ten minutes. So do you wanna go to town?"

They gave no response.

Their pitiful state was wearing me down, and I knew we needed to do something. Because if something didn't happen quick I felt I would fall into their glum state and we would have all lulled in our depression until we'd be unmoveable. Time and time again I dug for an answer and became so frustrated that I shouted. Eventually they got up and I thumbed a ride to town. The man who picked us up explained he was a hitchhiker back in the day and that he picked up hitch hikers as homage for all the people that picked him up in the past.

We were dropped off at a pizza shop and our driver handed me his number to call him when we were ready for a ride back to the trail. The guys were happy with beers, sodas, and subs.

Later at the grocery store, I got salsa and lentil soup. The guys conspired to purchase five liters of red wine. They took the bag of wine out of the box and *Skippy* put it in his backpack.

We sat outside the grocery store like a bunch of hobos. *Skippy* and *Scavenger* went quiet; their faces were full of concern. "Uh, Amish? Do you mind if we skip ahead a few miles?" asked *Scavenger*.

I looked at the two of them – they had already thought this over. Why else would they be planning to carry five liters of wine? I didn't want *Skippy* to be tortured for the next ten miles carrying that kind of weight. When I gave my consent they breathed a sigh of relief. "We didn't think you'd want to skip, but we were sure hoping you would."

Scavenger told me he wanted to pay the driver. "You really don't have to," I assured.

"Yes, I do."

Skippy and *Scavenger* had asked me to chip in for the wine, but I thought technically I helped them with getting a ride so if anything I should be the one getting paid if *Scavenger* wanted to freely give money away.

When *Scavenger* offered the driver money, the driver declined. Our driver didn't mind dropping us further up the trail, "You'll be missing a very difficult section that goes straight up and straight down," he told us. I looked in my guide book. Sure enough the section looked daunting.

On the car ride to the trail, everything looked lush. We drove down tree-lined roads and peered out to see an abundance of green pastures. The sun was setting when we were dropped off. I stared at the orange and pink sky as long as I could. It felt like I hadn't ever seen anything so lovely, and I didn't want it to end. The woods seemed to be transformed and I felt like I was walking through a place with significance. It was as if a weight had been lifted.

After two miles, it became dark and we grew anxious over missing the shelter. But soon enough, we found it. We started a fire a distance from the shelter and divvied up the wine. The discussions began with quantum physics and ended with what it was like to have girlfriends.

Earlier that day, I had asked the guys, "Would you rather live in a world with no beer or in a world with no women?"

There was silence. "That would be awful. Neither is good. But I guess a world without beer," replied *Skippy,* in a defeated sort of way.

"What are your top three favorite things?" I asked.

"Uh, women, beer, and then I guess video games," answered *Skippy.*

"So, what qualities do you want in a girlfriend? I guess you want her to like beer?"

"Oh no, it's a bad thing when your girlfriend likes beer, because then she'll drink all your beer," stressed *Scavenger.* "One time I was on a plane and the flight attendant asked what my girlfriend and I wanted. I ordered a beer, but my girlfriend claimed she didn't want anything. After I got my beer she asked for a sip and drank most of it! I was infuriated! It still makes me angry thinking about it!"

Day 135

I was awakened by nature's detested alarm clock of mosquitoes buzzing in my ear. I grabbed my tarp and laid it over my face. But I could still hear the low awful buzzing. I slapped my ear, but the buzzing continued. I was instantly angry and turned over to fall back asleep. But sleep was not to be found since the buzzing continued to fill my ears and torture my mind. When I could take it no longer, I got up and left while the guys were still deep in slumber.

At the bottom of the mountain, I went by a yard sale, where baked goods were being sold. For a dollar, I got a loaf of chocolate chip zucchini bread, the size of a brick. Conveniently, there was a library nearby, where I used the internet.

After two tall mountains came a road. It was so steep downhill that I would be afraid to ride a bike down it – in fear I would die. I inched my way down in attempts not to gain momentum.

Part way down the road was a cooler of food for hikers. Inside were raspberries and cookies. I sat in the grass and enjoyed the fresh-tasting food. There were several more miles of road walking until I hit the town of Hanover. Usually hiker towns aren't as fantastic as I imagined, but Hanover lived up to its name.

I ran into an older man and his wife who were hiking. They had already taken showers and didn't carry packs. When we got to town, a redheaded guy came along. The couple greeted him like an old friend and introduced me. His name was *Owl*. "The fraternity I'm staying at has one spot left. Would you like to stay there? I'll show you where it is. I haven't much else to do anyways," he assured. I waved to the couple as we started walking.

"I heard there are a bunch of free things in this town," I said.

"Yeah, actually I just came back from getting a free slice of pizza."

"Can I join you in getting pizza after we go to the fraternity?" I asked.

"It would be my pleasure."

At the fraternity, I signed a paper before heading down in the basement. "Check out the soda dispenser," exclaimed *Owl* "I was told we're allowed to drink as much as we want." I filled up a cup before we left to scout out the town. "I already got a Snickers and Pizza, but I'll show you where they are. And then we can check out the other freebees in town." We waited for the walking light to cross the streets and weaved our way along the sidewalk. After picking up a Snickers and seeing nothing edible in the hiker box, we headed to the Pizzeria and both got a slice.

"Didn't you say that you already had a free slice?" I said accusing him.

"Yeah, but I guess they don't recognize me."

"I don't blame them, hikers all look the same; just dirty guys with beards, how could they?"

I returned back to the Frat, while *Owl* went to wait for his mom who was visiting him. I took a much needed shower, then sat on a sofa and listened to the students discuss household things such as moving the microwave.

One student had tiny hand-painted action figurines, which he laid out on the table; numbering around twenty. He was struggling with the idea of selling his precious figurines. They seemed silly and useless to me, but for this guy each little figurine had a piece of precious memory attached to it.

An older southbounder showed up at the frat and asked where he could get pizza. I got up, "I know where it is. I'll take you there."

On our way there, we ran into *Skippy* and *Scavenger*. They couldn't stay at the frat since there was a limit. The older fellow that was with me gave them a number of a place to stay, so I felt slightly less guilty for doing my own thing. And I knew they could take care of themselves. They mentioned going to the pub before I waved goodbye.

When we got to the pizza shop, the older fellow thought he could eat an entire pizza, but couldn't. I was happy when he welcomed me to join in the feast. I was plenty full, but I persuaded him into splitting a carton of ice-cream with me.

Back in the basement of the frat, I drifted asleep as I watched two guys play pool. The basement vibrated with music from the party above. Occasionally loud stomping occurred from people randomly breaking out into dance right above our heads.

Day 136

Owl and I went around town seeking out all the free stuff. We went to a pastry stand where we thought we could get a free pastry. The girl manning the stand apologized, "I'm not sure if I'm allowed. See, I'm in good terms with my boss and I want to keep it that way."

As she was saying this, a woman who was passing by stopped and insisted, "Go ahead, take what you want. It will be on me." The lady counted the bills, "My children are off to college and now I have no one to spoil." I was shocked by her instant generosity.

Next we went to the Bagel Basement and each got a free bagel with cream cheese as well as a bag of day-old bagels. *Owl* gave me his bag of bagels, so I had a dozen bagels.

As *Owl* and I sat outside a little shop eating our bagels, a car pulled up and *Skippy* and *Scavenger* walked into the shop with an older couple. A lady from the shop, who welcomed *Skippy* and *Scavenger* in her restaurant, also shooed *Owl* and I off her domain. "Can't you see the sign? It says for customers only."

Owl and I waited outside the Dartmouth Bookstore until it opened and we each got a free cup of coffee. I had no need to resupply after all the food I collected, including lots of cheese *Owl* gave me.

Many people told me that I needed a new pair of shoes. *Skippy* had advised me that I should at least have someone send an old pair of sneakers. It was finally when I called my mother that I was convinced to buy my third pair of shoes. I bought the same type I had before. When I put on my new shoes, it was wonderful. I felt like a new person.

Owl joined me on my day's walk. He was thirty and had a lot of history. It was a breath of fresh air to hike with him because he was super optimistic.

He told me how he dropped out of high school. He had a decent job until he got arrested for DUI. Since he couldn't drive any longer, he had to sell his house in the country and find a job in the city. "I started to deal drugs. It was the easiest thing to do to make money. The funny thing about dealing drugs is that I would have all my customers meet me at the same time. They would look at each other, guilty and nervous." Eventually, he went to prison, where he had to fight for his food.

"I can't stand the lady that is married to my mom," Owl went on. "She infuriates me. My mother works hard and pays the bills and this lady sits like a pig in my mother's house not doing her share. I went home for a little, but I couldn't stand her. She wanted to kick me out of my mom's house!"

"Sounds complicated. How long have the two been married?" I asked.

"Ever since I was little… I was so happy to move out, when I did. I never wanted to go back living with her, but I needed somewhere to stay after I got out of jail."

At the shelter we talked to southbounders and *Owl* fried up sausages on the fire to share.

Day 137

It came to my attention that there was a man who gave out ice cream up the trail. I was determined to get to his place before taking any breaks. I lost *Owl* on the uphill, when the rain was unrelenting. It was sad yet relieving to be away from *Owl*. I loved his energy and enthusiasm, but I felt that he would slow me down.

At the ice cream man's house was a sign that read: "Free water and ice cream." The last two southbounders mentioned that they didn't get to meet the Ice Cream Man, but I did. He had me come inside and the first thing he asked me was if I wanted to put my socks in the dryer.

I stayed for lunch. He wished he could hike, but couldn't with a machine hooked up to him. His sister was visiting since he had just had surgery. She seemed a bit skeptical about her brother giving freely to hikers, so I did my best to please her. Soon she was comfortable with me and when I asked for a trash bag she quickly assisted me.

The man told me the old trail used to go on the road; he advised if I went that way I wouldn't get soaked from the dewy grass. It was kind of weird taking the road. Once in a while, I would see fragments of the old trail with its faded blazes. The ATC made it their goal to get the AT off the road, but sometimes I would have rather road-walked, especially since road-walking was fathoms easier.

On top of one of the big mountains, I picked blueberries and gazed at the beautiful view. I grew sad, because I wanted someone to experience the beauty with me. I unhappily climbed a vertical trail up to the shelter. A man's stuff was hanging in the shelter. I looked around to see a hammock strung up, but the man never came out to greet me. It was strange being in a shelter alone.

Skippy called. He admitted that he and *Scavenger* had been hitchhiking up the trail all day. And at the moment were thumbing for a ride. In one day of hitchhiking they passed what I did in three. *Skippy* concluded the conversation by saying that he wanted to bike to Katahdin. He was insanely sick of hiking. It was hard not to feel influenced.

Day 138

I was so excited to finally pick up my resupply box. That was the one thing that motivated me. The hardest part was the start. There would have been a view for all the steep miles I climbed, but fog ruled the skies. I was plodding my way down a mountain, when two day hikers came along. They asked a few questions. When the one guy heard that I had started in Georgia and had been on the trail over four months, he was truly impressed. He even gave me an apple. It was delicious. It made all the difference because I had been eating nothing but stale bagels for breakfast, lunch, and dinner.

When I arrived at the first road, I just wanted to hitchhike to town and get out of the woods. I knew it would be a long hitch to town and that two more roads up would be closer. As I trudged on, I regretted not trying. Between the stinking mud and the buzzing of flies, I was swamped in misery.

Finally, I got to the next road. I knew the ideal place to hitch would be another five miles up the trail, but I was feeling so distraught that I decided to take a stab at hitching four miles to town. A car passed about every two minutes. Time went by and dozens of cars went by. My legs grew tired in the waves of heat, so I sat down for a couple of minutes between the breaks in cars.

Eventually I got picked up. On the way to town the man pointed out a mountain that stood tall like a large nose on a flat face. That was Mount Moosilauke, the first mountain in the White Mountain Range. The massiveness of the mountain was daunting, and I started to grow anxious about climbing it.

The man dropped me off at the post office, where I came to terms with the fact that my package hadn't arrived. It was a hard blow. I did nothing but have good thoughts about that resupply box ever since I had left Hanover. I stared blankly at the lady behind the counter. She asked, "Would you like me to forward it?"

"Huh?" I said, as if waking from a dream and gave a forced smile. "Uh, yes. Thank you."

"Where would you like it sent?" she asked. I felt rushed with a customer behind me.

"I don't know. I'll come back and tell you," I said, ducking out the door. I sat on the curb and leafed through my guide. I wanted *that* package as soon as possible, but I didn't want *this* to happen again. I decided to send it to Gorham; a town on the other side of the Whites.

Back inside, I asked where I could resupply. She pointed me in the direction of the only gas station. I walked over, feeling very crossed about having to resupply at a gas station – of all places. As I was picking out a half gallon of ice cream, I turned around and there was *Skippy* and *Scavenger* snickering. "We've been following you around the store and you haven't even noticed," they said, cracking up hysterically.

I looked at them, disturbed, and had nothing to say. I was having a bad day and getting laughed at wasn't helping my mood. All I wanted was a comforting hug. When I found out they came on a shuttle from a hostel, I asked the driver if I could join them. Just like that I was on my way to a hostel named, Hikers Welcome.

Legion was at the hostel. He gave me a comforting squeeze. I missed listening to his booming smoker's voice. I brought up the incident with *Nocello,* when he scrawled a three foot graffiti on a shelter, reading, "*Legion* was here." *Skippy* had heard of the drama, but thought the whole ordeal was lame. I think they got to see eye to eye – at least for a moment.

Legion said he was on his fourth day at the hostel, because he was ailed with shin splints and a cough in his chest.

"Where's *Steady?*" asked *Legion*.

"Last I heard, she was headed to a cabin in Maine to take a couple days off," I replied.

The common room had a wall of movies. We spent the day watching as many as we could. "When was the last time you could watch movies all day?" asked *Skippy* in a satisfied sort of way. We took turns picking out movies and watched them deep into the night.

NINETEEN

The Whites

July 17th – 26th

Day 139

I was a bit nervous about hiking Moosilauke. The hostel owner told me if I made it to Moosilauke from Georgia, I had no need to worry.

The climb up wasn't so bad, since I was expecting a rock wall. Near the top, I met some college kids, who hiked up Moosilauke every weekday to take measurements of trees for their class at Dartmouth College. They were really sweet and were interested in my trip. The guy said he attempted a thru-hike and got halfway.

Standing on the summit was absolute bliss. The wind was blowing and the view was magnificent. For all aspiring thru-hikers of the future: remember, the White Mountains of New Hampshire are worth it.

I called my mom and mentioned that I was cold.

"Cold?" she hollered. "It's nearly a hundred degrees here and I'm sitting underneath the air conditioner."

I was scared that the ascent would be a rock wall, but the descent actually was. It was the steepest descent on the AT. They had stairs and metal bars to assist. Inching down the steps wasn't hard; it just felt like the mountain would never end.

At the bottom, I hitchhiked. The driver was a nice man who was scouting out places to bike. "I'm looking for roads that have wide shoulders," he said.

I went to a Price Chopper and bought a bunch of junk food and tomato sauce. I found a seat and ate a box of ice cream, but couldn't finish it.

On the way back, I was amazed at how massive Moosilauke was and that I had climbed it only a couple hours ago. Back at Kinsman Notch was a section hiker waiting by the road. The hiker had a hurt knee and was going to take the day off in town.

I thought it was strange that he didn't even give hitchhiking a try. My driver offered to give him a ride, but he had already called a shuttle.

The next part of the trail, I didn't like. It was awful. There were boulders and mud. It was like playing leapfrog on the boulders since the mud was deep. It went up and down with no hint of an end, much like a heated argument.

I arrived at the shelter by nightfall. I sat in the shelter with some section hikers. We all watched some kid, *Zero*, practice a mixture between kung fu and sword fighting with a stick. I liked the section hikers immediately; however, I was pre-warned about *Zero*. He had been given an adequate description – in that he was said to be odd and asked people for food – since the next thing the two section hikers said was how honorable *Zero* was for taking their food, because like many beginners, they had over packed. I croaked, "Well, he's not exactly *that* special. I would have taken your food in a heartbeat."

Day 140

I had changed up my hiking pattern because my buddies didn't show up. I didn't see the point of hiking seventeen miles a day, if I wasn't hiking with *Skippy* and *Scavenger*.

I learned why thru-hikers either love or hate the huts. Hikers have to be lazy and do low mileages to stay at the huts and since some hikers have schedules, they don't want to stop hiking at five and only start at nine in the morning. I, on the other hand, desired to stay at the huts and hoped to enjoy them.

I got to Lonesome Lake Hut early, around noon. A tattooed guy with a black mullet named *Twig* sat with *Zero* on a deck facing the lake. I took a dip in the lake and then sun bathed. Everyone was talking about how much they hated *Zoro*. I felt bad for him, but that ended when he tried to yogi food from me! It all happened when I had been snacking. He demanded, "Give me some of your goldfish." In that split second, I disliked him. First off, yogi-ing was an art. You had to humor the person and be polite. There was none of that. All I saw was a greedy hiker, with a pack of food fuller than mine.

"No. Want to give me some of your food?" I said annoyed.

The guys hiked on and I met Erin. She worked on top of Mount Washington, at the observatory gift shop. She said people didn't realize how cold it was on Mount Washington so the store would sell many jackets. Erin enjoyed visiting the huts and hangout with the crew. She gave me her number and said she would love to house me in the future.

Around four, I asked to work for stay and the hut croo told me they'd have dishes for me to wash in half an hour. It was an odd feeling to have to keep an eye on the time.

Erin and I swam in the lake. It was breathtakingly pretty. The surroundings were by far the most picturesque of the entire trail. The majestic mountains surrounded the vast lake and cast their reflections in the clear water.

We dried off and went inside. I was looking through books when Erin joined me. "They have *The Lorax*!" she beamed. "It's my favorite childhood book! Would you like to hear me read it?"

"Sure," I replied.

"It is noisy in here. Let's go outside." We stood outside the door and she animatedly read through *The Lorax*. The story was about deforestation and the devastation it caused, depicted in Dr. Seuss rhyming kind of way.

After I did the dishes, I waited around. I was getting hungry. But thru-hikers have to wait until the others have eaten. Finally, when everyone was finished, I went into the kitchen to eat, but they had me sweep the floor first. I tried not to be grumpy while my unfed stomach gurgled. I got leftovers.

The sleeping arrangements weren't much better. I was told we thru-hikers got to sleep on the floor of the dining area. That was all fine with me, but the room was filled with noisy children. I sat at one of the tables until they kicked out the kids at nine thirty and turned out the lights. I laid out my sleeping bag under a table and fell asleep.

Day 141

Some odd instrument woke me up at the crack of dawn. I had to get packed up before breakfast was served. I was sick of waiting for these boy scouts and girl scouts to eat, so I asked for a bowl of soup and left.

I was sad Erin wasn't up in time to bid her farewell. I told the hut croo to tell her goodbye for me and hoped she would understand.

I started hiking and felt like I might be going the wrong way. Thankfully, I wasn't. It made me happy to find a cooler under a bridge marked as trail magic. I took a bag of chips and some peanut butter crackers. There was a rocky, steep climb up to Franconia Ridge. Part way I passed a stream. I was too lazy to stop for water, which came back to bite me. The ridge walk above treeline was wonderful. The view on both sides had visas of mountains turning bluer in the distance, as far as the eye can see. It was too beautiful. The weather was too perfect. Shivers ran down my spine. I felt so undeserving, yet adversely much more deserving than the tourists.

There were many people as lucky as I. Crowds surrounded the summits. The first summit of Franconia Ridge was called Little Haystack. There, people asked me to take their pictures. Further on was Lincoln. Last was the king of the ridge, Lafayette, standing proud and tall.

There was a whole group of us thru-hikers having lunch atop Lafayette. *Zero* was there, too. He ran about doing pushups on the boulders and frolicked about on the fragile alpine vegetation with no remorse. His behavior bothered the other hikers to no end. We even sent the ridgerunner after him.

In pleasant conversation, I asked a hiker where he was headed for the night. "Galehead Hut," he replied.

"How fun, I'm going there too," I said enthusiastically. Then a flash off fear crossed my face. I turned to the other hikers. "Where are you guys going?" It became apparent that we were all headed to the same hut. People started packing up lickety split. It was a game of tortoise against the hares. Even though I was one of the first ones off, I was getting passed up straightaway.

The whole way to the hut, I pushed myself, thinking, *Five minutes late could make all the difference: of having food in my tummy or more miles to mosey on. And I'm running out of food, so giddy on up.* I sang some songs to myself for stimulating support. At Galehead Hut, I spotted three glum hikers, all cooking up meals.

"What happened?" I asked.

"They only took one person to work-for-stay and *Hand-Me-Down* was here first." The news was grim.

"I gotta at least try, since I'm a girl," I said, striding off with a wink. I tried to work my woman powers inside the crowded hut, but my request quickly crashed and burned. Taking a seat with the lot, I cooked up some couscous and stretched, "This looks like a good place to camp."

"Yeah, but it's illegal," said *River Rat* with a sigh. "We're not allowed to camp in the quarter mile area around the hut. *And* the next stealth camping area is after *that* big climb." We followed his gesture. I gulped and my eyes shifted around the circle of hikers, hoping that one of the other hikers had another idea. But there was none.

Hand-Me-Down took pity on us and mentioned to the temporary hut croo with which he was working, that huts normally take in several hikers. They listened to him and the first four hikers to arrive were accepted as work-for-stay. We were overjoyed. The others were allowed to stay for dinner scraps.

Luckily there was plenty of leftover cheesy chicken and pasta with tomato sauce.

We could only set up for bed when they turned out the lights, so I looked through the books. I got excited when I saw there was a Dr. Seuss book. Then I looked closer and was let down when I saw it was *The Lorax*. I searched the bookshelves for another Dr. Seuss book, but there weren't any.

I started a Monopoly game with *Caveman* and *Hand-Me-Down*. We didn't get much father then handing out the Monopoly money, but it was nice to go through the motions. Finally when the lights went out, I took a spot on a wide bench.

Day 142

We all stayed to wait for breakfast. It was a regrettable notion. First we were woken up at the crack of dawn and were shooed outside. We sat on a long bench, while one after another, our stomachs started to rumble. We sat outside for hours. The wind chilled us and the rain came and went. It was torture to hear the cheerful chatter, the clinking of utensils, and the heavenly smell of bacon and syrup. It was all happening on the other side of the wall which we had our backs to. Some suggested we should just move on, but we had waited so long already, that none left. When it sounded like people were leaving, I declared, "I bet we can go get something now."

"Go ahead. I wouldn't, but you have a better chance," said Twig.

Inside the air was warm and I passed tables being cleared off. I entered the kitchen and meekly asked, "Is there any food for the hikers?" A man, who had not been there before, replied, "Yes of course," and handed me a container with fragments of egg casserole stuck to it.

Outside, some of the guys looked at it skeptically and others dug in. I went in to return it, and came back with burnt bacon. I was excited for the guys, I knew they would like bacon, but when I started eating it, I realized how burnt it was. It was like eating greasy charcoal.

I was feeling sick. I linked the cause to the high consumption of junk food I had been eating. I had no intention to hike a long day. The two options were seven miles or eleven miles. The seven was a hut, and the eleven was a campground, with an eight dollar fee. I went with the free stay with food, also known as Zealand Falls. The hut was named after a waterfall with pools of water, deep enough for a stinky hiker to take a chilly bath.

The other guys moved on. I was the only thru-hiker who stayed. The croo had me clean the fridge, by removing the food and scraping out the ice. Scraping out the ice wasn't easy. And organizing the food into categories wasn't sanitary. I had to ask: "Is this still good? What is this?" and "Guys, I'm pretty sure this is bad."

"Technically, on Saturdays we have to get both the freezers and the fridge cleaned out," stated the guy who I had asked for work-for-stay. "You know what? You've worked so hard on the two freezers. I'll let cleaning the fridge slide."

I was finishing up when other croo members were walking in. I felt like I wasn't wanted around. And when they asked me to sit outside I left with no complaint.

The wait outside for food was aggravating. I felt like I was being punished for something very naughty. When I thought it had to be time, I walked over to the croo and asked if I could eat.

"No, not yet. We still have to do dishes. Hey! Would you like to do a presentation?" asked a girl.

"I guess I could," I said uneasily.

"It could be questions and answers," she prodded.

"Okay," I said

The crew did a loud presentation and announced that after dinner there would be, "a reading of *The Lorax* and a question and answer session of a thru-hiker, whose name is *Amish*." Then they had people raise their hands. "Who wants to hear *The Lorax*?" half a dozen people raised their hands. "Who wants to ask a thru-hiker questions?" Two at most raised their hands. "Uh, okay, change of plans. If you want to know what it's like to thru-hike, then you can pull *Amish* aside and ask her yourself."

I joined the crew in the clean up. The way that the crew washed the dishes was almost violent. They threw the dishes into the tubs with loud bangs and water spewed about. I was petrified. "Just soak 'em for ten seconds and then move 'em to the next tub," shouted one of the girls. I was a bit shaken, but I did my best and tried to be less noisy. I wondered if it was their intention to make that much noise, to scare the guests away, since by the time we were done the guests were gone.

After hiking for so long that my own footsteps sounded loud, no wonder I was in shock when I was surrounded by such noise.

"Did *Amish* clean out the fridge and the two freezers?" the one girl asked skeptically.

I looked over at the guy. "Yes. She did," he lied.

"Top and bottom?" she asked, looking in the fridge.

"Yes," he repeated.

The food was satisfactory and the croo was friendly enough to join me around the table.

I sat in for *The Lorax* reading. At the end, the environmentalist of the croo explained how the Whites were clear cut. I looked around and notice all the young trees. The woods weren't much different than the rest of the AT, I thought about how the whole trail was probably clear cut at one time or another. It made me sad that there weren't any ancient trees and I felt slightly bad for getting annoyed that the huts only had one Dr. Seuss book.

The hut had some excitement when news of a man with a hurt tendon was found along the trail. A girl from the hut piggybacked the skinny man to the hut. Later, the two guys from the hut took turns piggybacking the man three miles back to his car.

A bit after lights out, one of the guests handed me a bottle of red wine. I asked, "Is this for me?"

"For you and the croo," he replied.

From the bottom of the ladder, I called the croo. Five minutes later, I was sitting with them up in their loft, where they lived co-ed. They were quoting the Princess Bride and the two guys both said that they intended to thru-hike in the future. They spoke of interesting thru-hikers, while giving the girls back massages.

"We had a bunch of southbounders a couple days ago," mentioned the one guy. "They were speaking about their experiences.

A large thru-hiker said, "You know how technically we are homeless? Well, some hikers actually *are* homeless."

And then one of the other hikers got angry and defended, "So what! It isn't that big of a deal."

But the big guy continued. "No, seriously, these people don't have a home to go back to."

"Mind you, this was all in front of the guests. I found out later the guy that was arguing really was homeless, but only because he stopped renting an apartment while he was hiking."

After that I spent my time deciphering their lingo. They kept on talking about Paco, which I later found out was their pet hamster. I went to bed after they decided to hit the falls.

Day 143

Early in the morning, I asked the guy cooking up breakfast if I could have yesterday's dessert for breakfast. When I got his permission, I poured in some milk (I got out of the fridge) before I ate up and left. I wanted to push to the Lake of the Clouds; a hut I knew I had to experience. It was going to be a long day and I was most likely going to show up late, but I figured from what I heard: The Lake of the Clouds was so massive that it accepted all thru-hikers.

I hiked along a flat section and then dipped down until I got to the foot of the mountains. I crossed a railroad and then climbed. I was worried about how steep it was. And there was no knowing when it would stop. I was encouraged when I passed a family with a little girl. I thought, *Come on, if a little girl is hiking, you certainly can.* I pushed on. Just being able to see the beautiful blue sky was an encouragement. When I came to a view, I was stunned. It was wonderful. I was nowhere near Mount Washington, but I could see the railroad I had passed and couldn't fathom that I had climbed *that* high.

I stopped in at Mizpah Hut and got my allotted bowl of soup. Then I soldiered on, since it was still early. I climbed through the Presidential Range, which was just as marvelous as Franconia Ridge. I felt like I was in a heavenly realm. The treeline was far below. In several places, I could see sheer drop offs.

Near the hut I questioned a southbounder. After telling me the Hut was close, he said, "I tried buying a spot, but there wasn't even room in the dungeon." He ended by saying that the hut had only accepted northbounders to do work-for-stay and that I might have a chance, since there was virtually no place to camp miles north of the hut.

I arrived to see a throng of eight northbounders, including *Twig, Hand-Me-Down, Caveman,* and *Blue.* When I arrived they greeted me, but a shadow of worry crossed their faces. They advised me to ask a certain individual about my work-for-stay.

I thanked them for the advice, but failed to take it seriously. *I'm a northbounder*, I thought. *I hiked twenty miles today. Surely it can't be that hard to get a spot.* I walked blearily into the dark hall of the hut which was brimming with people. I waited in line to ask a man at the desk if I could work for stay. He looked at me, frustrated. "We are at our full capacity. There are ninety guests here and the dungeon is full of southbounders. Huts normally take in two or three thru-hikers, we're at *eight*. We just don't have room! You can go to Mizpah, but you said your Northbound right?" he asked apprehensively. "There is also a shelter on a side trail two miles down the mountain."

Hiking down the mountain two miles sounded nightmarish. "Is it possible to stealth camp along the trail?" I ventured.

"*No!* It is illegal to camp above treeline. Violators will be fined a hundred dollars," he scolded. "You stand no chance hiding from the ridgerunners. On top of Mount Washington they can see hiker's lights on the ridge. Furthermore, there is no shelter away from the wind. Hypothermia is a killer up here." I could tell he was about to send me away just like all the southbounders before me. Then he furrowed his eyebrows in frustration, "But you're northbound. Let me check if we have *anything* available." He left and several minutes later came back. "The only option you have here is a floor space for twenty dollars."

I had no intention of paying. I had been depending on the huts for food, and with only a floor space I would go hungry. I suddenly thought of Erin. She had suggested picking me up on top of Mount Washington, in the case that I didn't want to stay at the Lake of the Clouds. At that time, Lake of the Clouds sounded like a fantasy. I wouldn't have missed it for the world, but now I needed rescued. We had arranged getting together another time, but calling her seemed to be my best option. Before leaving the man at the desk, I ask if he happened to have a phone. "There's no land line if that's what you mean, but you might have a chance of getting a signal on the left side of the building."

I dearly hoped there would be service, but it was doubtful, because I hadn't had service since Moosilauke. I hurried outside to where I got bombarded with questions from the northbounder. "Did you get a spot? Did you ask so and so? Oh no! What are you going to do?"

"I'm going to call a friend," I whimpered, before I sulked off to the side of the building, with tears flooding my eyes. I took a place by the tourists using the weak signal. I was astonished, when my text was sent. Moments later, Erin responds that she could pick me up, but she said I had to be at the top of Mount Washington in an hour since the road would close at six.

I was flooded with relief. I looked up at the barren rocky mile and a half that awaited me. It was daunting yet thrilling. There were unnatural looking buildings atop the summit of Mount Washington.

I shared the good news with the guys. "Well then, pronto. You gotta get going honey," encouraged *Twig*. I could see excitement in his eyes.

"No way, you're staying at someone's house again?" accused *Blue*, who was gulping down handfuls of trail mix. I instantly thought about my own hunger.

"*Blue*? Could I have a little something to eat? I have no snacks." I looked at him with puppy eyes, "This is me begging," I said, referring back to a conversation. *Twig* gave me something he was munching, while *Hand-Me-Down* bought a brownie for me. I looked at him surprised with nothing else to say other than, "Thank you." I hastily gave them a bow and smiled. "Farewell gents." Then I sped off. I could hear them cheering as I galloped along.

My stressed stomach formed into a knot. I bound along the trail, twisting and turning past the cairns. The weather atop was pleasant and warm. The view was spectacular. There wasn't a cloud in the sky. Instead of taking in the majestic view, I found a picnic table surrounded by buildings. I sat in pain, hugging my shipwrecked tummy. I made conversation with a lady. After I explained my hiking adventure, she remarked it was good her husband wasn't with her, since he wanted to thru-hike. She was trying her best to persuade him not to go. I thought to myself, had I not been able to get a ride; surely there was some chance of persuading a tourist to get me off the mountain.

Luckily, Erin came. She had to persuade the officials of the auto road to let her drive up. They had closed the road for the day, but they let her go up after she told them she wouldn't be dilly dallying, since she had a hiker to rescue. I kept saying "Thank you," as I imagined myself freezing to death on the side of the mountain.

On the way down, I saw a sign forbidding hitchhiking; said to create unsafe weight loads. The ride down was too slow for Erin. "These cars have *no* idea what they are doing. They should know not to ride their breaks down." As I watched the trees first become existent and then become larger and larger, the car in front of us smoked more and more. "Take the rest stop, come on. Take the rest stop!" Erin pleaded to the car ahead, but it continued on. The smell of rubber filled the car. It was all very exciting. At the bottom, through the gate, a lady greeted us and made a comment about getting rescued off the mountain. "Yes Ma'am," I said, vexed. *How could she know?* Erin explained as we pulled out, "That was the lady I had to persuade to let me come up and get you."

We went to Erin's lovely abode. I felt like a new person after my shower. We went to the grocery store, where she told me that whatever I got she would pay for. I tried to be modest, but it was wonderfully difficult and I got supplies to make a cheese cake. We then went to a lovely restaurant. She said I could order whatever I wanted. In short, it was a thousand times better than any other option I had. I even got to bake a chocolate cheese cake before going to bed. I was truly in debt to her.

One of the best things about staying at Erin's was being able to sleep in, something impossible in a shelter and most definitely at a hut. She took me back up the mountain. It cost twenty-five dollars to drive a car up the mountain. Erin got out of it, luckily, since she works up there. The strange thing was that she had to be willing to pay and "yogi", if you will, her way in for free. It was a long drive up, eight miles in fact. And people drive so slowly that it took a while. But it was better than the cog railway, which cost sixty bucks round trip or forty-five one way.

On our arrival to the top, I could see a cloud hovering over the summit of Mount Washington. The summit was filled with crowds and thick, looming fog suppressed any hope of a view. Inside the dining hall, I sat with six northbounders, all who did work-for-stay at the Lake of the Clouds. They were *Blue, Hand-Me-Down, Twig, River Rat, Moosehead,* and *Caveman.* I was bitter about how Lake of the Clouds treated me and welcomed any criticism they had to say about their stay. They started off by saying that they had to clean for hours.

"It was the most work any hut has *ever* made us do. We built stone walls and cleaned the entire kitchen," said one.

"They made me clean the space behind the stove. There was grease everywhere. I should have had gloves. It was freakin' nasty," exclaimed Twig. "It's possible I might have contracted a disease."

"Then we had to wait for supper out in the cold, *for hours.*"

I could imagine the wind chilling them to the bone, being that they were above treeline.

"And then, there wasn't much food left over. There was a bit of sauce, but no meat."

"What, you got sauce?" the one exclaimed. "All I got was some cold bow tie pasta."

"Worse yet," they went on, getting more and more frustrated. "We didn't get sleep. We were sleeping on the dining floor between the bunk rooms and the bathroom. So every time someone needed to use the bathroom, we could hear them getting out of bed, tiptoeing through their bunk room, and then they would stomp through the dining hall, where we were trying to sleep. Every time – without fail, they shined their lights in our direction! The bathroom door would creak open and slam shut. It would be quiet for a little, and then they would flush. I swear every person *slammed* the toilet seat." All the guys agreed *that* was excruciating. "Imagine ninety people getting up to use the bathroom. It was a never ending parade."

In retrospect, I knew Lake of the Clouds was way overcrowded. The huts were made to make money from tourists, not to cater to us hiker trash. From the perspective of the huts, thru-hikers were more or less a tiresome liability. With all of their other visitors why should they care how we felt? Although I understood all these things, I was still upset with Lake of the Clouds. Part of the reason was, all my way through the Whites and even weeks before, I had heard the same thing: "Lake of the Clouds is the best. It is the biggest hut and they never turn down thru-hikers. It's a hut you don't want to miss." It was pounded into my head. I found that with great expectations comes great resentment.

Then it was my turn. Adding insult to injury, I described the delightful stay with Erin. They cut me short, halfway through telling them what I had for dinner. I could see this was no way to make friends. I kicked myself for not bringing the other half of the cheese cake I had made. They would have each given me a hug and a kiss. I wanted to express how phenomenal it was to sleep in, but I refrained, knowing too well that they had all been woken up at the crack of dawn, to be hustled out, until all the guests had eaten. I had nothing else to say. I even feared mentioning how ridiculously clear the view was the night before on top of the summit.

There was a poster with the names of one hundred forty-five people who had died on top of Mount Washington. The majority were killed from hypothermia or slipping and falling on ice. Not quite the nicest thing to look at before descending the eerie fogged in mountain. The group of us all waited in line to get our pictures taken together at the summit sign. Then we got several tourists to take pictures of us, however, I felt like I deserved to be excommunicated from the group shot. I then hiked with *Blue*, until it rained, and then *Blue* scurried ahead.

I was accepted for a work-for-stay at Madison Springs Hut; seven of us stayed. The hikers were a different batch, who had hiked from Mizpah Hut. This time we had a little loft all to ourselves. Even though we were squeezed in, and had to step over each other, it was heaps better than waiting outside. We chatted happily. We even found a stash of alcoholic beverages with a note welcoming whoever found the stash to a drink. Plus we had the best supper in a hut to date. It was a full blown, straight off the burner meal. There was even enough for seconds.

Day 145

It was wonderfully nice not to be disturbed in the morning. I slept in, and we still had to wait for breakfast, but in the comforts of being indoors and inside a sleeping bag, it wasn't too bad. I went down to check if they were ready to have us. The other hikers told me, "The only reason you can get away with asking is because you're a girl. They would bite off our heads." I think they made extra food for us; there were tons of pancakes. Indeed, so many that us hikers couldn't finish them. My stay at Madison Springs was the best of all the huts. They were so helpful and cheery.

It was a shame though; I did such a petty job helping out with chores. No one told me to do *anything*. Since no one told me to do anything, I swept the dining hall. I now know I should have asked for more work. It was one of those things I was going to regret for a long time, because the other hikers caught up to me on the windy rocky ridge of Madison mountain and informed me that the croo had been looking for me. I felt like a naughty dog that shredded the family couch. Not only did I make the hut unhappy, my fellow hikers seemed disgusted with me. I felt like I had to make it up. I weighed the option of going back, but a voice inside warned me that I might be late in picking up my package at the post office.

Walking on the summit of Madison Mountain was rugged, but mystical. The trail was on a knife edge peak and the rocks were uneven. The wind didn't help and sometimes I would bend over to hold on the rocks in front of me as if I were on a balance beam. I took a step on a large rock on the edge that teetered as if it wanted to dump me down the steep side. My survival instincts kicked in and I stepped away with adrenaline pumping through my veins.

The climb down from the ridge was dangerously slippery. The one man started swearing. "Forgive my French but, those f-ing rocks don't move." He had slipped and hit his shin on a rock.

Once I got to the "flat part", I still had miles to go. I crossed the auto road that went up to Washington. *That's weird; I was just there a day ago.* It gave me a gnawing feeling of accomplishing very little. Finally, I could hear the road to town. The other hikers quickly passed me at their ultra-man hiking paces. Alongside the road to town was a gift shop and bathrooms – with toilet paper. *Hand-Me-Down* was there along with *Caveman* and *Twig.* "We're staying at someone's house," they called.

"What? May I come, too?" I pleaded, before realizing they were just teasing.

I sent a text to *Skippy*, about his whereabouts. He sent a text back saying, "Who is this?"

"*Amish?*" I texted back.

"Oh, my phone died so I lost all the numbers." He went on to say that he and *Scavenger* had gotten off the trail.

No way? It was a surprise, but it made sense: they had hated hiking for quite a while. *But why right before the Whites? And why didn't they tell me earlier?* I felt guilty for not being there to say farewell for the last time. I then thought, *Well, at least Skippy didn't have to deal with the huts. He would have hated waking up at the crack of dawn day after day.*

I met a lady who was totally out of food. Out of the generosity of my heart, I gave her some chewy bars and let her nibble on my fig newtons. She told me about her fascination with rocks. She had even gathered up a whole collection. I thought, *of all the hobbies a hiker could have, rock collecting must be the worst.* I invited her to hitch to town with me. She had never hitched before, but she said she would join me. She told me about a hotel she was planning to stay at and how she longed to steep in a hot tub.

She picked up all sorts of boxes at the gift shop – food, and gear. In all there were three boxes. It took a while for the people there to locate them. One of her boxes was damaged. Her boxes were huge and the shipping costs were catastrophic.

We stood by the road, thumbing. No one was coming, I felt like a liar since I told her it didn't take long. Still in good time, someone pulled out of the gift shop and gave us a lift. They asked about our hiking. The lady I was hitching with started in Pennsylvania and was heading north. She skipped a large portion since she was injured for a while. She had about twenty-five percent of the trail completed. She spoke a lot about her friend who had started out with her, but her friend had quit.

I was hoping the lady would invite me to share a room at the hotel with her, but she never did. I was dropped off at the post office and got out all alone, but was still waiting for the invite. When the car pulled away I felt deserted and stupid for not asking.

I plodded on to the Gorham post office, where they didn't have my package. I couldn't believe it. Although, I could understand after forwarding the package two times something could have gone wrong. The man there was extremely nice about it and called up all the possible places where the package could have been. He even called up a post office from another town with the same name.

Then a man came in and asked for a package. In seconds they brought it to him. He noticed I was having trouble and said that I could have his package. I was shocked. "Really?" Then he explained he was finished with his section hike early and didn't need his trail food. He then asked if I needed a ride anywhere. I told him I could go to the trail, but inside I actually wanted a place in town to stay. I was confused. There were a lot of emotions going through my head. I was sad that I hadn't found a place to stay; I was sad my package was lost; I was glad I was given a package; I wasn't sure if I should keep on searching for a place to stay. I felt like I had to make a hurried decision. I had asked for the trail and that was where I was heading.

We cruised past some white blazes; he explained it was just a road walk. At the trailhead, I felt a bit confused. He asked if there was anything else he could do. He noticed that I wasn't looking the best. I said, "No," and thanked him. After he was gone, I wondered if I was on the correct part of the trail. I looked at my guidebook, but I didn't know any landmarks nearby. On a steep slope, I realized that I must have been dropped off at a different place: in fact I was twenty miles ahead. I thought of walking back to the road, but instead decided to just hike from where I was.

I had no water and there was a long climb until I got to a miry stream. I called my mother and explained that I had skipped a section. I felt miserable. Four or five miles later, thunder began booming and then the rain came down in torrents. There were no shelters close, there wasn't even a campsite near, so I stopped and nestled my hammock in the thick pine trees. I fell asleep with a mind full of buzzing thoughts.

TWENTY
Bears & Swamp Donkeys
July 27th – 31st

Day 146

I woke up cold and wasn't able to fall back asleep. I was grossed out as I took down my hammock with sticky pine sap and slimy slugs on it.

When I was hiking, a gnawing feeling set in, *Have I taken a wrong turn?* I had to tell myself to take a deep breath. I hated backtracking. The landscape seemed too familiar. I racked my mind for a landmark that I had seen the day before. When I remembered the wall of stone I climbed while thunder had cracked above me, I told myself I wouldn't turn around until I arrived *there.* I went through a grassy section that seemed way too familiar. *It's just as scratchy as it was before,* I thought. Next, I came to a part where I could have sworn I had been before. I stood there awhile studying the landscape. I thought about turning back, but kept going. I had been hiking for over an hour. Just a bit further, finally there was a sign to the campsite. If my life were a movie, a beam of sunlight would have hit the sign and the chorus would have sung halleluiah. I was saved, and overjoyed to be able to place myself back on the map.

After a short water detour through the campground, the trail had hard climbs involving ladders and metal bars. Some of the descents involved hanging off rocky ledges and jumping down to the next boulder. There was more-or-less a half mile of inclined bog boards, with chunks of wood nailed to them – thus saving lives on rainy days. I passed three trail maintainers and thanked them one at a time for their hard work. I had a spectacular view on top. I could see distant lakes in the valleys.

This was the day I got to Maine. It was truly mind blowing and it was hard to grasp, *Okay, I've walked from Georgia, through North Carolina, Tennessee, Virginia, West Virginia, Maryland, Pennsylvania, New Jersey, New York, Connecticut, Massachusetts, Vermont, New Hampshire, and now lastly Maine. Wow! That took a while.*

I had Maine stuck in my head, so I started rhyming.

□■□

I've made it to Maine.

I'll never be the same.

Isn't that insane?

That I came to Maine?

I should take a picture and put it in a frame.

Oh what a shame,

I have no one to blame,

For I'm starting to wane,

Under the weight of the claim

Of finally being in Maine.

□■□

I was filled with all sorts of conflicting emotions. I knew I was supposed to be incredibly happy. I had waited for this moment, state after state. Now this was the very last state – truly the last. At the same time I felt lost. The sign was in the middle of nowhere. *Where are all my friends? Why did I lose them like I did?* I had no one to celebrate with, but no one was there to rush me through either. I wanted to call up friends and family, but I had no reception. Later, on top of Goose Eye Mountain, I called home. The phone was passed slowly from one family member to the next. I tried not to repeat stories, as I progressively grew cold on the foggy summit.

In Maine, the shelters were no longer called shelters, but lean-tos, even though they were one and the same. Southbound hikers were easy to point out, because they used different terms: like calling shelters lean-tos. Another way to recognize SOBO's was that their gear was brand spanking new. When I saw their Z-rests, which were in picture perfect condition, I was reminded of how clean and shiny my Z-rest used to be. By the time I was in Maine, it looked like a tractor trailer got it rolled around its wheel.

I realized as I got in Maine that the southbounders were much less experienced. Before the Whites, the southbounders kept us on our toes, almost scaring us about the unknown Whites; how hard and brutal they would be; how our mileage would plummet and we would only be able to hike fifteen mile days at tops. It was a different story on the other side of the Whites. The southbounders seemed fragile and now they were the ones asking us with puppy dog faces about their future.

I was so excited to stay the night at a lean-to. There were no fees, no work for stay, there was just pure and simple glee. What freedom! What bliss! I found it strange that the campground was absolutely packed for having seen only a handful of people all day. There was a whole troop of teen girls and some middle aged women. They were taken aback by my day's mileage.

I kept talking, unabashed, as I found space near an older fellow, resembling Father Christmas. He took a zero, since he didn't want to go through the Mahoosuc Notch on a wet day. I talked a lot and was more loud and rambunctious than my usual self; perhaps my behavior was due to the day's lack of human contact.

Day 147

I took my time and was the last one to leave the lean-to. I even happily swept out the lean-to before I left.

It hadn't really clicked that the Mahoosuc Notch was the next big thing. I knew of a big bolder field, but I hadn't connected the two being the same thing.

So there I was, at the big daddy: the Mahoosuc Notch. The notch was, frankly, a large bolder field, where the rocks were as big as baby elephants. I put my hiking poles in my backpack, and used my hands. I got a bit scratched climbing up and down boulders. And there weren't any clear paths marked. I remembered getting past the first section thinking, *what's the big deal?* Not much further, there was more to come. They weren't kidding when they said it was a whole mile. It was known as the hardest/funniest mile of the trail. It is said that there is ice on the ground of the boulders all year long, but I didn't take notice.

Near the end, I devised my own trail entirely; it seemed easier, but I had to find my way back.

After all that I was hoping for something gentle. Instead, I abruptly came to the Mahoosuc Arm, which was another famous part. It was a straight-up rock face, with only roots and rock ledges in which to grasp. I was glad I wasn't going down; I must say it would be a deadly endeavor in the rain. I had a heart-dropping experience at a part where there wasn't anything to hold on to, when I tried crawling my way up the smooth rock and then lost momentum and slid down a yard or so before catching myself.

On top, I dried out my belongings. I could see across the mountain's summit and would consider it thru-hiker flat. I could even see a lake. It was at the lake where I cooked up rice and used my Z-rest to block the wind. As I was cooking, a blast from the past came by; it was *Prescott*. Last time I saw him was in Maryland. We happily chatted for a bit.

Afterwards, I stopped at the lean-to to merely ask a man for some toilet paper. He dug his out, but there was too little of an amount left. Some hikers coined the phrase "white gold" for toilet paper, because when you run out, things get bad. That's when you start using books, or journal pages. I couldn't wait to have my own bundle of white gold and I told myself that I would never run out again.

On a long descent, I was out of water, but going downhill was better than going up when looking for water. All I could think about was apple juice. At the bottom, near a parking lot, was some soda set out for hikers. I was totally out of snacks and needed food. The hitch to town was seventeen miles. I stood by the road awhile, but no cars passed until a car full of three section hikers, who had just finished their hike, pulled in. The one couple let me ride with them. They were talking about going to the beach – that sounded like a splendid idea. I had a contact of someone who lived near the beach in southern Maine, so I tried calling them, but didn't get a hold of anyone.

I think I scared my drivers when I mentioned going to the beach with them. All they could think about were town pleasures: relaxing, having a hamburger, getting a shower, that sort of thing. They dumped me on their friend who was much more interested in hiking, which meant she was more interested in me. She drove me to the grocery store while talking my ear off. She was a prospective two-thousand miler and had gotten her friends to join her on a section. She asked me a ton of questions. I wish she would have stayed to drive me back to the trail, but this was not the case.

At the grocery store, I excitedly got a can of whipped cream along with blueberries and Nutella. New foods are always exciting.

I was confused on how to get back to the trail. I didn't even know what road to hitchhike from. I stood hitchhiking right outside the grocery store, but then decided there had to be a better idea. I asked a man for a ride. He didn't know where the trail was so he went inside to ask the ladies at the check-out. They said it was a twenty minute drive. After hearing that, the man was unwilling to drive me.

I decided to backtrack. It was quite a walk. Some joy riders kept passing me and honked each time while cheering. After I walked along a highway, I came to a gas station, where I fished for a ride and got progressively worried as the sky darkened. Finally, a man stopped in a big truck. He was a thru-hiker from years back. The way he described his hike sounded like he was alone for the entire trip. He said it was golden when his entire family came to see him on Mount Katahdin. He was lucky since his family lived in Maine. I doubted my family would come see me.

Back at the trailhead were two hikers hitching for a ride. I found it quite comical to see them from the other side. "Look! Hikers!" I exclaimed, smiling broadly as I recognized *Crumbs*. It was funny to see *Crumbs* become all surprised to see me. He asked me where I came from. I couldn't muster the courage to explain that I had missed a section. My driver offered to take the two of them back, but the more we chatted the more grumpy he became. The last thing I wanted to do was make *my* and more importantly *their* driver unhappy, so we parted ways with questions hanging. *Crumbs* said he was going whitewater rafting with his cousin. "Take me with you," I begged before he left. I wanted to do anything but hike.

There I was with a two mile climb to the lean-to. I tried to relax and not think about the miles. At the lean-to were a bunch of hikers that I hadn't seen before, save *Prescott*.

Toto was the friendliest of them all. He explained that Toto was the dog in the Wizard of Oz. It seemed odd that he was named after a little dog. It was not like he looked like a dog, although he did have a pleasant nose.

Day 148

I was so excited for breakfast; I had whipped cream with blueberries. I added the last of the cereal, which were remnants of my vegan phase. Unfortunately, the cereal was stale and tainted the would-be spectacular breakfast.

Several yards up the trail, I passed *Toto*. He was sewing up his broken backpack. The climb up the mountain was similar to climbing up vertical pavement. On the top was a 360 degree view of pinkish clouds nestled in valleys.

After four miles, I came to a lean-to where all the thru-hikers ironically met up. We were not alone, because there was an outdoors school with a bunch of youth, who were packing up. When I saw them, I thought, *I am definitely learning a lot more about surviving in the wild than these students are.* One of the hikers brought up the topic of a prestigious outdoor group called NOLS. Only days before, in Alaska, four teens were attacked by a mother grizzly, while crossing a stream. Two seventeen year old boys were in serious condition in the hospital.

After my break, I hiked with *Toto*, and later *Prescott* joined. I got the privilege of introducing the two to each other. I updated *Prescott* on everything between the time I last saw him and now: of falling behind my friends, hiking with my family, and then catching up with *Skippy* and *Scavenger*, who later got off the trail. I also shared about the wonderful homes in which I stayed, which was my way of showing off.

I learned that *Toto* was an engine mechanic for tugboats and ships. He said it got really hot and that it was hard work, but he only worked half a year at a time. He had a hobby of traveling. He traveled to Asia, Europe, Africa, and South America. It was his goal to go to every county in the world. When he went to other countries, he stayed at hostels and became good friends with other foreigners from other countries. This was possible because he lived a simple life. He told me about how he had Chinese and Japanese girlfriends. "Asian girls like American men, and they are polite and sweet, so they make great girlfriends. I have a Chinese girlfriend at the moment. We only see each other a couple times a year. She just told me recently that she's going to be in Bang-er."

"You mean Bangor? Right?" I asked.

"Yeah! Bang-er. She'll be there soon, so I'll have to do big miles to get there as soon as possible."

I was relieved when we finally got to the lean-to, since my knee was giving me pain. *Toto* would have done more miles, but decided to stay because it was going to rain.

Southern Maine had the hardest terrain of the entire Appalachian Trail. It was even more exhausting than the Whites. The Whites had longer climbs, but once I was on the ridges I was home free. In southern Maine it was a roller coaster of continual steep ups and downs. Out here, the hiking turned into rock climbing and you wonder what they did with the "easy" and "bad weather trails."

Day 149

We had an insane hike. When looking at the elevation it resembled a "W" quite well. I was out of food again and had to get to town. After the "W" there was a road, but no cars were passing. *Prescott* was there, just taking a break. I asked him if he would like to go to town.

"No. I avoid hitchhiking like the plague."

"Why don't you at least try?" I asked.

"It's not worth the aggravation. No one ever picks me up. Besides, I have enough food for another week," explained

Prescott. He was snacking on smashed up ramen noodles and was seasoning them with the packet provided. "Once I waited all day for a hitch. It was awful. In the end, I paid for a cab. Since then I only rely on hostels or motels to pick me up."

I felt bad for *Prescott*. It didn't seem fair that I could have such an easy time hitching. *Prescott* and *Toto* were still there when a car came to a halt, rolled down its windows, and asked if we needed help. I told him I wanted a ride to town. He then proceeded to tell me that he didn't have room. He told me there was a camper behind him that would pick me up. After he pulled away, I began wondering, *Was it because I stank? Don't people know that when you stick out your thumb it means you want a ride?* I was confused and still without a ride. I asked myself, *Why didn't you beg?* It was a while until other cars passed, but none stopped. Campers came and went.

After what felt like a half hour, a *huge* pickup truck stopped. I was dwarfed by the massive truck. The voices of people inside were muffled by the deafening hum of the engine. I couldn't make out what they said, until perhaps the third time. "Do you want a ride to the post office?"

I said, "Yes!"

"Hop in the truck bed," he said.

I pulled myself over the side and sat in the corner. As the truck bounced up road, I tried my best to remember the road for any worse case scenarios in which I would have to find my way back. The driver dropped off the man and told me I could take the front seat. He was a jolly sort of fellow. His name was Dave.

I took notice of the open windows and inquired, "Do I stink really bad?"

"I've had worse," Dave responded. "There was one so bad that after I invited him up front, I had to tell him that I couldn't stand his stench and made him sit in the back." Then he offered, "Would you like a shower?"

It was the most wonderful thing I had heard in days. "Yes! I would love a shower!" I replied.

So we went to his cabin a couple miles down the road. I got a shower and he made a breakfast sandwich for me, plus coffee. Then he asked if I would like another sandwich. That blew my socks off. It was wonderful.

He then asked if I would like to stay the night. It wasn't yet noon. He was a nice guy and there was nothing creepy about him. I wanted to take time off, but my mind was still on fire from being on the go-go mode. I thought about it for about a minute and promptly accepted the offer.

I went through my things and took out the items I could do without to send home; including cords and a grimy Camelback with remnants of V8. Dave took me to the post office, but it was closed. When I remembered something I had forgot, I felt terrible, but he had no problem stopping back at the cabin to pick it up. Then he took me to another post office.

He said there wasn't a decent resupply in town, so he drove me to a neighboring town. He gave me several choices in stores. I choose a dollar store. He asked me what I would like to drink. "Apple juice!" I exclaimed. He got a large jug of apple juice. I asked Dave why he was so nice and thanked him so much that I wore out the word thank you.

We stopped to pick up Dave's son at his friend's house. At the house was a gorgeous garden. I couldn't take in enough of its beauty. I seriously hadn't seen so many flowers all year. Back on the road, Dave's son asked if he could go gold panning. That confused me for a second. "Like, as in real gold?" I asked.

"Yeah," Dave replied. "We have found gold before."

That evening was just as fun. We watched TV, saw bison, and went mooseing – a term which means driving around in search of moose. He promised that I would see my first moose. Time and time again he was shocked that he couldn't find any, but for him it was a matter of time until we would spot one. Then he found one, my first moose! It was a large, slow moving, dark animal.

"It looks like its eating something in the water," I said.

"Yeah, they love eating algae. That's why people call them swamp donkeys," said Dave.

Afterward we had ice-cream. I was given a bed upstairs all to myself. In the room was a bear head at face level. Its face was frozen in an angry growl. I felt uneasy sleeping near it, so it got covered with a blanket.

Day 150

I slept in as much as I could that Sunday morning. Dave made breakfast sandwiches and coffee. I called my mom, who was on a bike ride. I got to talk with my younger brother who was going to Guatemala for a week. I teased him that I might get home before he did. That would mean I would have to finish incredibly fast.

We drove out to the trail where the mountain, Old Blue, was still standing to greet me. Dave and his son were on their way to check on their bear bates. Dave had been hunting bears for decades. He has a couple stuffed ones in his house, not to mention the rug with a growling bear face on it. Dave, however, didn't hunt bears anymore. He went out to watch the bears just because he found them fascinating.

In the past he let people hunt at his bear baits, which were barrels of food. One time he let his friend hunt. The man was told not to shoot any mother bears, but he did anyhow. This broke Dave's heart. When the mother bear was killed, her cubs were doomed to die as well. The man insisted he didn't see any cubs, but Dave looked at the bear, squeezed the tit and when milk came; he knew the cubs were still milking. Their friendship had been marred ever since.

Back on the trail, it reminded me of a maze the way that it weaved in and out. I ran into a group of three guys that all looked the same because their beards covered half their faces. One was British, another was Irish, and the other was American. I shared Sabbath Day Lean-to with them. They were very excited to head to town. The one said, "When I get to town, I want to buy three or four drinks and drink them simultaneously. I definitely want chocolate milk, then perhaps a juice and a soda."

TWENTY-ONE
Pickles, Crumbs, & Florida Girls
August 1st – August 8th

Day 151

At a campground, I stopped to get water and met a lady named *Pickles*. Soon after she left, I found a key near to where she was sitting. I determinately caught up to her and asked if she was missing a key. She said she had seen the key and that it didn't belong to her. We hiked together the rest of the day. I found out quickly that *Pickles* was a very compatible hiking partner. We were so compatible that it was mind boggling. For as long as I could remember, whenever I hiked with other people it was never my pace. Our timing was impeccable. We wanted breaks at the same time and for the same amount of time. She even preferred having me lead. It was perfect.

I wondered why *Pickles* and I hadn't ever met before this. We were both hiking from Georgia to Maine and had started the trail just days apart.

At our first break we watched the three identical-looking guys whom I had met the day before, help people dressed up as hippies with their car, which was producing a plume of thick smoke. I knew their sole purpose in assisting the hippies was to get a lift to town.

Above treeline, on top of Saddleback Mountain, we took a break and chatted with a southbounder as some thunderclouds bypassed us. The southbounder was extremely nice. He gave me the remainder of his food. I was shocked that he was thanking me for taking his food. I was running a bit low, so he saved me from a future rumbling tummy.

This man had thru-hiked the AT northbound before and had hiked the Pacific Crest Trail, too. On his third journey he was mixing it up by starting at the corner tip of the state of Washington and biking across the country to the corner tip of Maine. He then made his way to the northern terminus of the Appalachian Trail and was on his southbound trek to Springer. At the end of the AT, he planned to ride his bike to the tip of

Florida and then again across the country to the southern terminus of the PCT, where he would begin his northbound thru-hike – all in one continuous round trip. I was stunned by his endeavor, and wished him luck on his journey.

We passed many day hikers, who all smelled clean. I became conscious of my own smell after a darling little boy asked his mother, "Why are those people so smelly?"

When the people were a good bit passed us, I told Pickles what the little boy said. "I never think about it, but I guess we must smell really bad."

Pickles, who looked twenty, was actually forty. She was a lawyer, but wanted to change her career choice and decided a thru-hike would give her time to think about her future. "So is it working out?" I asked.

"No. Thru-hiking is not the best way to figure out the next step in life, but it's a great way to get away from the daily grind. If I had thru-hiked before, I would have known better not to undertake such a big commitment. I'm just glad I have a husband that can support me even though he is not the hiking type."

On the last section we both ran out of water and subsequently hiked slower. I felt like one of those people portrayed stumbling in the desert, hunched over as they take their last steps before they fall over, mumbling, "Water." I kept thinking, *When I get to water, I'm going to down a liter.* We did finally come across a stream, but I felt silly, because I wasn't able to drink all that much.

Crumbs was at the shelter. He had set his tent up inside the lean-to, because the bugs were bad. He was glad to see us, "Hey *Amish*! Hey *Pickles*! Long time no see."

Day 152

I needed to get to town, because I was low on food. *Crumbs* wanted to join the challenge. *Crumbs* noticed that I was low on food and kindly gave me some of his cliff bars.

For the past week, the haughty northern mountains of Maine had me hiking measly miles. It was a whopping twenty-one miles to town, but I was ready for a challenge.

We were both concerned about the number of mountains to get over and were in a bit of a rush, but I felt pretty good. Having no food was a big motivator.

After hiking with *Pickles* the other day, who was the perfect hiking companion, I wasn't sure what pace *Crumbs* wanted to hike and I didn't know when he wanted to take breaks either. We were both very poor at communicating.

We were determined to be as fast as possible. I ran down the mountainside with *Crumbs* following my tail. At the bottom we crossed a full throttle stream. It was straight uphill from there. *Crumbs* took the lead. I hated going fast uphill, but I followed him the best I could. We took our first break at a stream. Then we went higher and higher.

We got to a shelter just as it started to drizzle. It was a great feeling to be in the shelter, warm and dry, because in the next minute the rain picked up. The rain that first sounded like a pitter patter on the tin roof became a continual drumming above our heads. The ground turned into streams before our eyes. We watched less fortunate hikers running to the shelter with their backpacks held over their heads, but they were already drenched.

As the rain steadily came down, I boiled water for ramen noodles. The air turned cold, so I slid into my sleeping bag. The storm ended quickly, but there was some hail before it was all said and done. We marched out as dry as bones and couldn't be any more pleased with our circumstances.

On an unforgiving rocky downside of a mountain, a man came climbing up towards us with a goat following him. The goat was carrying a sizable load. We praised the fellow for his ingenious notion of having a pack animal carry all the weight. I was shocked that the goat had no problem climbing the steep, uneven rocks. *Why carry a heavy backpack, when you could have a goat carry it?* I took his picture and headed on.

We only had one more mountain to go when thunder began to rumble. "We're going to have to wait this one out," said *Crumbs*. "The next summit is above treeline and we can't be crossing it with all this lightning."

I didn't want to listen to him, but soon the rain was coming down upon us. This time, we ran to the nearby campground. It was my first time setting up camp in the pouring rain. *Crumbs* joined me under my tarp, until the rain subsided. It was pleasant to sit there with him.

Day 153

One good thing about getting down to the last of my food was that I finally ate the last of my old couscous. I was not sure I'd ever be excited for couscous again. My last existing food was a single cliff bar that *Crumbs* gave me.

There was a father and son team on their final section, camping with us. I had met the father and son group multiple times before. They were friendly, but I wasn't particularly friends with them. They didn't exactly make me feel at ease. They had informed me about how they had hiked the Appalachian Trail in sections for the last decade. They told me how it was a superior way to hike. "There have been so many different hikers throughout the ages that we've hike with. They all seem to be in their own groups, but we get to know all of them," proclaimed *Robin Hood*, the son.

Robin Hood tried to make a fire the night before. The only success he had was getting the birch bark to burn. After he gave up, I remarked, "It can't be that hard," taking it as a competition. I tried using the highly flammable birch bark to make a fire. The only problem was, between the pine needles and fallen birch trunks, there wasn't *anything* to burn. On top of all of this, everything was still damp. I burnt large amounts of birch bark, but the fire died out fast and all I got out of the whole thing was hands covered in soot.

I was about to head out while the others were eating, when *Robin Hood* offered me a packet of oatmeal, so I put all my things down and took his offer. They thought it was hilarious. "Wow, you must be hungry. We could really slow you down. Just think,

265

all we would have to do is offer you a packet of oatmeal every few miles," they laughed. I silently rolled my eyes at their comments, but was glad for the food.

I hiked fast enough that the others didn't catch up. They had all already reserved a stay at the hostel, but I wasn't sure where I was going to stay. Even though the hike was all downhill it was still very long. At the road, it was easy to get a ride to town.

I was dropped off near the hostel, which was right next to the grocery store. There were a bunch of hikers outside, chatting at a picnic table. They looked at me with excitement and I could see people pointing me out. Some hikers yelled my name, calling me over. I waved, confused, since I didn't recognize any of them. A hiker with a large grin walked up to me followed by some others. "Hi!" he said, sticking out his hand for me to shake. "I'm the guy that left the bottle of Bacardi in the shelter back in Connecticut. I heard you got to enjoy it."

"Oh, thanks," I said, giving him a strained smile. "Yeah, I got to enjoy it." I looked around at his comrades surrounding me. I didn't know what to say. I had never met any of them before, and I was left to wonder how they knew me.

I made myself two frozen pizzas using the oven at the hostel. Then I chatted with two girls from Florida. They were hiking south. And they had all sorts of problems. At the picnic table, I gorged on my pizzas while they educated me about their hiking horror stories. They had just graduated from high school. Three of them started, two girls and a guy, but they lost the guy, after he tripped and tore open his leg. At the time they only had a single liter of water between the three of them. One of the girls went to look for water. She was so dehydrated that she started hallucinating and spoke to trees, thinking they were her friends. Other hikers who passed later told her she spoke incoherently. She slurred, "Water, need, friends."

This girl who had been hallucinating was hurt badly and walked with a limp. They were taking days off, hoping that soon she would be able to walk again. It was already their third day at the hostel. The hurt girl told me how it was perfectly normal for her to get hurt, as if it was to be expected. Her friend nodded in agreement. The hurt girl continued, "I've been almost killed a couple times and about every bone has been broken in my body. This foot," she motioned to the one wrapped up, "has been broken several times before. I've also been thrown off a horse. And one time my mother was cutting my hair and she snipped my ear. Her mother ended up superglueing it back together. I can still feel the glue inside my ear."

The girls were extremely talkative. They told me about Florida, their home. They told me about the heat and how they had hurricane parties to put up shutters. They told me about their rundown school, with its normal gangs that had fights breaking out and recurring bomb threats. They told me about stupid tourists running on hot sand and wearing brightly colored bathing suits that attract barracudas.

After hours of listening to these girls, I suggested buying some ice cream. I later ate the whole thing and reimbursed them. We watched movies on the sofa and I eventually fell asleep.

Day 154

I stayed around the hostel chatting with the two girls until noon. Then I headed out to conqueror the Bigelows, the last big mountain before Katahdin. *All else will be pie*, I kept telling myself. Indeed there was a lot of climbing. I hiked the whole range alone and hiked deep into the night. At the shelter, I flashed my headlamp across a room of sleeping hikers and saw that it was full, so I set up camp outside.

Day 155

The next day, I thought I could hike slowly and steadily. That idea was smashed like a mallet coming down on a china set, when *Crumbs* whizzed by. He informed me about the Kennebec Ferry Service ending at four pm. I did my best to keep a good pace, but once I got to the shelter – not four miles before the Kennebec River, I decided to forget the rush. Besides, the lean-to was set right next to a scenic lake.

I went swimming in the peaceful cold water. It got deep quickly. I then found a beach chair sitting on a boulder out of view from the shelter. I soaked up the warm sunshine happily, until the guys decided to go swimming.

I tried making a fire, but it smoked miserably. *Peter Pan* and his dad thought I was silly, going about looking for firewood. I climbed up trees to pick off the dead branches and tried getting on top of the shelter, but *Peter Pan's* dad yelled at me. It was nearly impossible to find any medium sized wood, but I surprised them when I did get flames.

A section hiker was there. He was a stout fellow with a massive pack. He was in his twenties. It was astonishing that with all the things he carried, he lacked a shelter of any sort. He carried a massive first aid kit, that weighed close to five pounds and he carried a huge bag of trash, all the while complaining that there weren't more trashcans.

Day 156

The next day I got to the Kennebec River half an hour before the row boat was there. Many people arrived and waited for a ride. One guy was just out for a morning jaunt. He was really intriguing. He was not dressed for hiking and had taken a spill during his hike and ripped his pants. He praised us for our bravery and triumph for completing the trail. I thanked him, but admitted I didn't feel brave and said, "I certainly didn't finish the trail yet."

"Oh nonsense you'll be there before you know it. It ain't much further, compared to what you've done. How long have you been out?" he asked.

"Around five months."

"That indeed is something extraordinary." He then chatted on and on until the ferry came. The queue was still growing, but thankfully I didn't have to wait long. I was the second to arrive and the ferry takes two hikers at a time – if you don't have a goat.

I decided to do a longer day than planned and hike an extra four miles after already hiking eighteen. A large portion of my motive to hike further came from an annoying hiker who seemed to stay at every shelter since the beginning of Maine. I just had to rid myself of him. I doubt he was purposely following me, but every morning he would make such a racket that would wake everyone. It was as if he was deaf and had no idea how obnoxious it was, banging this and that about, plus his demeanor didn't help at all. He was an uncomfortable kind of man who laughed at his own jokes and made people squeamish.

On top of a large mountain, I sat gorging blueberries. It was dusk when I got to the lean-to. I headed over to join a man and woman reading out loud by a crackling fire. It was the most pleasant thing ever. I felt instantly at home.

I got up briefly to take a dip in the lake, which was only a couple yards away, and then joined them. I cooked my supper on the fire as I listened to the story. Afterwards, I chatted with the lady. They were southbounders who were taking their time, enjoying every minute of their time in nature. The lady gave me a soothing back massage before I retired.

Day 157

The day's goal was to get to town. It was a big undertaking, but I couldn't resist. There was a section of the trail roped off with a sign cautioning hikers about a nest of beavers and an alternative route was provided. The newly bushwhacked trail seemed to go around for what felt like miles. I kept imagining, the trail leading to some secret mission. Halfway through I thought, *Why didn't I go see the beavers? That would have been a memorable event.*

At the road, I hitchhiked to town; I sat in the leather backseat of a car, next to a little girl, whom I hope I didn't frighten.

The driver asked me, "Why didn't you take the side trail to town? It's a short walk and goes directly to the hostel."

"I just didn't." I replied.

It was more complicated than that. In reality I thought I could ultimately get out of doing the extra hike if I hitched at the road. That was probably one of the most uncomfortable hitches because we just didn't have anything to talk about after I felt accused.

In town, I found the Monson General Store. The closest legit grocery store was a good thirty miles away. So I had to deal with wickedly overpriced ramen Noodles, and other garbage food, like icing. I was bummed about the junky food and called home, but they were busy and told me to call later.

I decided I wasn't going to pay for a place to stay and thought I better just head back to the woods. I was about to cross the road to hitchhike, when a lady hollered a question. I turned around and we got talking. She invited me to set up camp in her backyard. Later she mentioned that I could stay inside, next followed a warm shower and a delightful dinner. I really wasn't expecting such wonderful hospitality to spring up out of nowhere, but it was exactly what I wanted.

The place was a ministry for the needy. The ministry wasn't necessarily to house people like me, it was used more to give out used clothing and shoes. "If you need any clothes, you are more than welcome to it," she urged, gesturing to the racks of clothes. She said I could grab some pajamas off the racks to wear for the night. So I did. I felt like a princess.

Day 158

I was invited to stay the day, so I took a zero. I lied on a couch and watched movies *all* day. She had cute kittens, but they had flees. She educated me about all the home remedies for flees, but the remedies clearly weren't working.

Her grandson showed up to hang out. He was a little younger than me. His parents were split. The lady of the house said she brought her children up in a worldly way. She blamed herself a bit for her children having divorces. She said she tried her best to teach them to be Christ-like, after they were grown up, but it was little to late.

My next adventure was the Hundred Mile Wilderness. Following the wilderness was Baxter State Park and lastly, Mount Katahdin. I was ready to finish.

TWENTY-TWO

Katahdin

August 9th – 18th

Day 159

I bid farewell to my lovely host, after I snapped a picture of her and her two grandchildren. Since she had no transportation, I had to hitchhike. The only problem was that there weren't any cars. I felt silly standing in the middle of Monson, with no cars in sight, so I decided to walk. Every so often I would stop and pull out my thumb, but no one took the bait. I got tired of turning around every time I heard a car coming and instead resorted in lazily sticking out my thumb as I kept walking. I was about a mile down the road when a car passed and then took a U-turn not far ahead. The car came back around to me, and a man leaned out the window and hollered, "Were you hitchhiking?"

"Yeah," I answered.

"Not to be mean, but you are the worst hitchhiker I've ever come upon. I couldn't even tell if you were hitching."

I felt a twinge of shame, but comforted myself by thinking, *Well, I can't be that bad. It worked, didn't it?* He told me how he used to hitchhike back in the day. After he got a car, he took pity on those without a means of wheels. To see the world pass by in a car was mind boggling. It made my jaunt seem measly. At the parking lot, I asked him what the weather was going to be like. He was overly optimistic. "Oh well, there is rain in the forecast, but it should clear up." Then he was gone.

I passed the sign; now I was truly in the 100-Miles Wilderness. The sign warned of the dangers of being in the wilderness and that I should have adequate supplies. I felt like I should be shuddering in fear of the momentous occasion.

At the first shelter, I found *Llama Legs*. I hadn't seen him for months. He was accompanied by another kid that looked like him. We didn't get all excited like I would have imagined the scene of meeting an old friend. I just smiled a nervous smile.

"Where have you been all this time?" he asked. "I heard you went to a bunch of peoples' homes and stuff."

"Yeah. I did. It was fun. I was hiking with *Skippy* and *Scavenger*. Well that was up until I got to the Whites. How about yourself, seems like you've been going just as slow as I."

"Yeah well, the other day this Asian kid wanted to go night hiking with us and he got us lost."

"You mean *Crumbs?* He got you lost?"

"Yeah, well, he felt bad for getting us lost and we haven't seen him since," said *Llama Legs*.

"What he feels that guilty? That he just ran away? Where did you stay in Monson?"

"Well, we chilled at Shaws, but we didn't stay the night or anything. We just watched movies all day and collected food from the hiker boxes. The lady there kept giving us looks. We left and camped in the woods."

"Wow, what a hiker trash move," I said.

Llama Legs asked, "Did you know *Mile High*, *Patches*, *BackFlip*, *Smurf*, and Harry have all finished together, like weeks ago?

"Yeah, I saw pictures on Facebook of them all on Katahdin," I replied.

"Did you hear that *Peach* is done?" he asked. When I nodded, he spoke harshly about her and said how he never liked her. I told him to not speak so ill of her. I didn't see the point; it had been such a long time since I last saw her.

Llama Legs sat cross legged with his back hunched over as he nibbled on different items of food. "We're going to finish on the twelfth," said *Llama Legs*. "When do you plan to summit?"

"I was thinking the twelfth too, but I don't know for sure," I answered.

All hikers asked each other when they're summiting and it definitely sounded like small talk, which was something I loathed. I noticed his friend and felt bad for not asking about him before, but I eventually broke the silence. "Who is this guy you're hiking with?"

"My brother, *Goat Legs*. He is out for the summer to hike with me," replied *Llama Legs*.

"I've always wanted to thru-hike, but this will have to do," added his brother.

I left before them. They seemed too lethargic to want to finish by the twelfth. Before long, they passed me at a brisk pace. I happened upon them several times; once at a waterfall and another time when they were skipping stones on a stream.

I liked *Llama Legs* and I doubted I'd see him again if I didn't keep up. But I was hurting and so I decided to be kind to myself by stopping at the second shelter, while the pack animals moved on.

The longer I stayed at the shelter the happier I was about my decision to stay. There was a clump of three hilarious hikers. These guys were all very new to the trail. There was one who was my age; it was his first time. His dad made fun of him for complaining about the strain of the five or six miles they hiked that day. "His trail name is *Bambi*," his father informed me. I was lucky to be the only thru-hiker to flaunt my knowledge, and mileage, for a perk of hot cappuccino.

But in reality it wasn't the food that made the stay so enjoyable. The best part was watching them interact – they had such life. I was used to hikers that retained every ounce of energy, but these guys acted like little kids. "Oh look, it's a gumbo sized toad!" They fiddled with their new stove, wanting to cook more and more, just to see it in action. They had a newspaper, which they let me read. I read about all sorts of new things going on: riots in England; stocks falling; gold rising.

When I started a fire, all three of the guys went berserk gathering wood and trying to break the large logs apart by seesawing them sideways against trees. We had a huge bonfire – one that I was proud of.

I talked to *Bambi*, who had just graduated high school. His father was a dentist. They had been traveling all summer. They even went to England and were soon headed to California for their annual trip in the next week.

While the dentist was out searching for more wood, *Bambi* told me about his job pulling out invasive plants in lakes, and how he wore a scuba suit. He told me about the college he was going to go to, but said he had no clue what he would have as a major. "Maybe marine biology," he said.

The three of them smoked cigars like rich men while passing around a bottle of whiskey. There was no doubt, they were living *the life*.

Day 160

It rained the entire day, making the hiking conditions horrible. I climbed over many mountains with no views. One of them was called Fourth Mountain. *Who would name a mountain, Fourth Mountain? How lame,* I thought as I trudged along. Finally, I got to the lean-to, but it was crowded. *Peter Pan* and his dad were there.

I had to ask them multiple times to allow room for me. Finally they made room and we were crammed in like sardines, sleeping pad against sleeping pad. In these situations I had to be careful not to hit anyone. There was no room for backpacks lying around. Everything was hung up. I was soaked, but luckily I had dry clothes to change into.

Brownie was there. He looked completely different, because he had lost over fifty pounds. I had to ask if he was the same *Brownie*. I hadn't seen him since Damascus, Virginia. He seemed vacant. Not only did his figure change, but his attitude changed. The *Brownie* I knew was fun and energetic. We had rolled down a hill together. This *Brownie* was solemn and he had no need to be friendly, maybe becuase he had a beautiful young lady accompanying him. She said they had been hiking together since mid-Virginia. I couldn't blame him for his lack of energy, none of us thru-hikers had any.

Not only was it cold, rainy, and miserable, but there was *no water* – other than the fine mist coming down from the sky. Some hikers had already laid out their pots to collect what water they could. I had no water to cook with, so I ate a bagel sandwich, made with chocolate icing and half an uncooked ramen in the middle.

Day 161

It was still misting in the morning, but nothing too wet. I found water after a steep straight down descent directly after the lean-to. I was a bit bitter about not knowing about its existence earlier.

After several miles of hiking downhill, it was fairly flat. I crossed several rivers. The one crossing looked crazily deep, the current was pushing hard. I searched around to see if I had mistaken the trail to cross the stream, but I couldn't find any trace. I decided I better keep my shoes on, since it would be better to have grip and balance on the slippery unseen stones than to have dry shoes that potentially could get wet from falling. I carefully placed one foot forward at a time, trying to find a foothold on the uneven rocks. The water rose higher and higher and the current became strong. I focused on maintaining my balance, but almost lost it a couple times. I breathed a sigh of relief when I got to the other side and took a seat on a log to wring out my socks, before plodding on with soppy steps.

At the lean-to were two people, one could easily mistake them as being married, but they were just enjoying each others' company immensely. They were very happy and I felt slightly like an impostor. They were even happier when it started down-pouring. I smiled as well. There was nothing better than lounging in a shelter when it was raining cats and dogs. The rain made my short day justified. I was happy to know that all the hikers that had gotten ahead of me were getting wet. The sun peaked out a bit before a thunderstorm took over the sky for the rest of the day and throughout the night.

These two hikers at the shelter were flip-floppers, now headed southbound. They gained the annoyance of having to explain to everyone, "We are *not* southbounders, we are flip-floppers!" The man flipped in Monson. The woman flipped in Pennsylvania. Both went to the northern terminus to head back to where they flipped from. The lady was glad she flipped, because she said Pennsylvania was hot, crowded, and had very little water. She continued on by praising the beauty of Maine. "I love the pine trees, the cool weather, and the lakes."

"But, have you noticed that there aren't any birds?" asked the man.

Something clicked in my brain when the man asked this. The forest always seemed so quiet, and I hadn't been able to put my finger on the reason, until now.

Day 162

As I climbed the mountains in the morning, I told myself these were the last mountains I had, that the rest of the way was going to be pancake flat. The biggest problem I had was that my back hurt terribly. I was getting thoroughly annoyed with my achy back, that when I saw a lady at a campsite, I called it quits. Lucky for me, I was yards from the shelter I was aiming for. The lady's name was *Catie-did*. I had seen her before, but hadn't talked to her. I recognized her from how the flip-flopper described her. He had said, "There was a lady with a big white backpack. What idiot would have a white backpack? It was dirty as you can imagine. It looked as if she rode it down the mountain."

I told her this. As she was setting up her tent she explained that the backpack was a test run made out of astronaut material, which unfortunately could not be dyed. She had hiked with it for decades and didn't want to replace it in a hurry. I commented, "If you've been hiking so much, why don't you have ultra light gear?"

"I don't want to spend mounds of cash on expensive gear, but as the existing gear falls apart, I will replace them with best of the best," she answered.

I was running out of food and, as all hikers, I was trying to figure out how many days I could last. She told me that I could resupply at The White House Landing, the only resupply in the Hundred Mile Wilderness.

I then went to the lean-to, where two guys were digging in the dirt. I inquired on what they were up to. The one replied giddily, "We're going to go fishing."

"But, why are you digging in the dirt?"

"We're looking for worms."

"Oh!" I said, astonish. "Have you had any luck finding any yet?"

"No, not yet."

"I bet you could find plenty of slugs. They love to climb into peoples' tents and stuff." I had never imagined slugs being of any use up to this moment. "You know what? Fish sounds delicious. I'm decent at making fires. How about I make the fire and you guys find the slugs?"

I went around collecting arm loads of sticks and twigs. I felt confident that I could make a real fire for the first time in Maine. I piled the wood near the shelter then took a seat. "We've found slugs!" the guys announced, gaily.

The one guy was carving a piece of wood, so I asked, "Whatcha doing?"

"I'm making a hook," he said, as if it was an everyday occurrence.

My heart sank. I had truly thought that I was going to have a sizzling fish for dinner. "What? You don't have a hook?" I noticed a grocery bag of food hanging up in the shelter. "What's that for?" I asked the second guy.

"Well, you see we brought too much food. So, uh, we are hanging it up for whoever wants it."

"I want it," I declared. "I'm running out of food." He took it down and handed it to me. "Wow, this is amazing! Thanks."

"I have some extra Snickers and energy bars, if you want some?" he offered.

"That would be amazing," I said most happily.

Everything was perfect; however, I noticed the one kid was still carving out a hook. It didn't look promising. "You know what? I bet there has to be a better way. Here, try a safety pin. Perhaps you could bend it some," I said, trying to help.

Catie-did passed by the shelter. She greeted us as she made her way to the stream. "This seems like a nice place to go swimming," she said, pleased.

The guys looked at each other and raised their brows judgmentally. In hushed voices they muttered, "I think she is a he."

"No. I've talked to her, she's perfectly fine." I tried to shush them.

"We would know. There are many crossdressers where we come from."

Before long, *Catie-did* made her way back from the stream and passed us, saying, "The water is nice, but there are some leeches."

"Thanks," I waved.

"Yeah, she is a he," one of the guys continued.

"Stop! She is not!" I said, annoyed.

The guys got a bit of fishing line and tied it to their hiking poles, then tied the safety pin on the end. "So how are we supposed to keep the slug from falling off?" asked the kid, holding up the slug.

"I don't know," I said, less inclined to help than before.

Twilight was coming on as the fishers went up and down the bank of the stream holding out their lines this way and that. Every five minutes they would come back for another slug. "They took my slug again," one of them said.

"At least they're biting."

"Hey," the one said, thinking of something. "We should cut the slugs in half so they last longer."

The guys were still avidly fishing when two other hikers arrived at the shelter. I could tell they were thru-hikers. They sloppily set up their things and sat zoning out. "What are those idiots doing?" the hikers scoffed, when they noticed the two guys fishing.

"They're *just* trying to fish," I said.

"Hey," said the one fisher, running up to me. "I found leeches! I bet they'll make good bait, since we ran out of slugs."

"Uh, no. Leeches do not make good bait." I could tell he wasn't listening, as he skipped away. I yelled, "I'm pretty sure fish don't eat leeches."

"That guy is seriously retarded," said the hiker

"No, he's not," I said in frustration.

"Oh, by the way I'm *Lemur*."

"I think I've see your Trail Journal," I said.

"Yeah, I'm kinda far behind, but I'm keeping a written journal, so that I can catch up when I finish. We're doing a fifty tomorrow."

"That's nuts! You're going to miss the beauty of Maine at that rate."

"Well, we thought we'd end the hike with a big bang," he retorted.

"Not like finishing the trail is a big deal or anything," I said.

"Well, anyway, we are getting up at 2:20 tomorrow morning–"

"To hike fifty miles," I said, ending his sentence. "Where are you camping?"

"We'll be stealth camping in Baxter State Park," he said, all pleased with himself.

"You know it's illegal to stealth camp in Baxter?"

"No? You're lying."

"Hey, calm down. I'm just saying what I heard. I think it says in the guide."

"Well, what are they gonna do, huh? Say, don't stealth camp, and walk away?"

"I heard about people getting jail sentences and being prohibited from ever entering Baxter again," I said.

The guys scowled, but dug out their guides all the same. After paging through their guides for a bit, they said, "We'll just hide well and if we get caught we'll say we didn't know." *Lemur* turned to me and asked, "Is the water any good?"

"Yeah," I said, shrugging.

I watched him go down to the brook, but he immediately said, "This water is brown and nasty looking! Anyone have a water filter?" One of the guys fishing said he did and got it for him. *Lemur* sat by the brook pumping and his friend joined him, washing his feet downstream. All of a sudden the friend freaked out, because several large leeches latched onto his leg. In his panic of pulling off the leeches he accidentally threw one at *Lemur,* which made *Lemur* jump up and scream like a girl. The leech was large and covered with things that looked like tiny legs and had a distinctly large sucker. "This is disgusting," he said, as he poked it with a stick.

Before he knew it, one of the guys that was fishing came over and speared the leech on his hook. "This one is a nice size. Thanks."

The hikers quickly finished what they were doing and got away from the water. They noticed the firewood that I had collected, "I should burn my old socks," said *Lemur.* "Do you think someone could make a fire?"

I wasn't going to make a fire for some lazy, judgmental hikers. "It was for the fish," I said nonchalantly.

They waited until the guys fishing came back to the shelter to ask them to make the fire. In a heartbeat they accepted the task. "Ah, my hands are covered in baby leeches," moaned the one guy that was fishing. I could see his hands were bloody. "Perhaps, using leeches for bait wasn't such a good idea."

I fell asleep to the sound of a crackling fire, while the thought of joining the guys on their fifty mile day danced in my mind.

Day 163

I heard the guys get up early, but I wasn't inclined to join them. I spent the day slowly hiking. I was tired and was trying to encourage myself on, when I met *Catie-did* getting water. She was done for the day, so I joined her. She was impressed with the fire I made.

Catie-did was welcoming. I learned *Catie-did* hiked the Appalachian Trail eight times: four were thru-hikes and the others were section hikes. She explained her name was short for Catherine did it.

"Are you excited to be almost done with your thru-hike?" asked *Catie-did*.

"Well, I keep thinking about how I skipped parts of the trail. And it bothers me."

"What parts were they?"

"The first, uh do you remember the really big shelter before the Smokies?"

"The Hilton?"

"Yes, well we just drove to it, so we missed a mile."

"That is nothing to worry about," said *Catie-did*.

"And then I didn't miss anything until Vermont. My friends wanted to skip. It was like eight miles maybe. It was stupid really. They put themselves on a schedule. It was by the town of Woodstock, I think that part of the trail is known for being really tough. In the guide book the elevation looks squiggly."

"I know exactly what you're talking about."

"The next part was right before Hikers Welcome. They didn't have my mail drop and I met my friend and rode to the hostel with them. That was four miles. I think. I hated hiking that day. I really don't think I missed much. The tall grass and bugs were making me go crazy, and I didn't see anyone the day before or on the trail that day."

"Okay."

"But, then I missed twenty miles. I was in Gorham, trying to locate my package, but they lost it. Some guy gave me his, which was so unexpected. He drove me to the trail, but I didn't notice that he had dropped me twenty miles up the trail. It took me a long time to figure out where I was, and then I decided to just keep going."

Catie-did looked at me. "Don't let it bother you. You are a thru-hiker. I've hiked it eight times, really let it rest. You've come all the way from Georgia; don't let this ruin your hike.

"The part where you missed twenty miles after the Whites, was the first place I went hiking. It was extremely hard. It still is. A lot of it is above treeline. The ridge it follows keeps going up and down. I remember thinking, when is it going to stop. Good thing it is one of the harder parts of the trail, because I was thinking, how in world do people thru-hike?"

Day 164

Catie-did hiked with me the whole day. It was quite wonderful. We chatted along the way, taking breaks by all the pretty views. "It's not often that I bump into a hiker that wants to take their time," said *Katie-did*. "I feel so fortunate to have you to finish my section with."

"It is sad. Isn't it? That thru-hikers come all this way to race to the end? It's strange really. All the past thru-hikers I've talked to said Maine was their favorite, and they said racing through it should be that last thing I do."

Since *Catie-did* hiked before, she knew of a sandy beach, where we planned to go swimming. We found out other people liked that spot, too. A couple was there handing out peanut butter and jelly sandwiches. I could tell the man was more excited about hikers than his wife. After we spread out our things to dry, she complained about our repulsive stench.

We just chilled on the beach as they packed their things and canoed across the lake to the road.

We had a little mountain to climb. It was one of those mountains where one wonders when it will end. *Catie-did* was more annoyed than I. In fact, I was enraptured by its exotic nature. The trail weaved through overhanging cliffs. Tree roots hung down off the cliffs, making the tree clumps almost seem like they were hanging in the air. I had never seen anything like it. As I waited for her to catch up, I stood on the top of the steps taking in the spectacular landscape.

At the top, we had a view of Katahdin. We sat on a boulder along with some other hikers. One man was calling home to schedule a pick up time. All of them where pushing themselves to be done. I no longer had to push to the end, because *Catie-did* invited me to ride down with her on a Greyhound bus and all the other fixings she had planned. With the last bit of service, I told my mother I found a ride home and that she didn't have to worry about my ride situation.

Catie-did knew a short cut, which was the actual trail back in the day. See, the old trail followed a road, but the ATC was so fickle about getting the trail off of roads that they engineered the trail to cross the road and proceed into an extra two mile loop and then cross the same road. We saw some of the hurried thru-hikers walking into the two mile loop, and we smiled at our ingeniousness.

"Last time I told someone about this short cut, they doubted me the whole way. And then never thanked me. They were so rude!"

"That's dumb. Well I'm glad you showed me. I love walking on roads. I don't have to look down constantly in fear of tripping and I love that there isn't any elevation. It's a great break. Plus I'm missing two miles of a silly loop."

After the trail crossed back, we came to a stream where some hikers were bathing.

"I bet those are SOBO's," said *Catie-did.*

"How could you know that?" I asked.

"Because northbounders are too focused on finishing, than to stop and take a swim."

"You never know, maybe they decided to take their time like us." I said.

But *Catie-did* was right, they turned out to be SOBO's.

There was a camp spot hidden away, out of sight, near the water. *Catie-did* was more excited about it than I was. "This is the best camping spot I've been to for this entire trip," she exclaimed. I didn't see the big deal, but I was just glad to have someone accompany me.

After we said goodnight, I was resting in my hammock when I heard my name being called. I regret that I didn't react because the next morning I was told a moose came down the trail near our camp.

Day 165

We had another wonderful day, except we both ran out of toilet paper, which can be a bit nerve-racking.

The trail wondered about. It was quite annoying when we were clearly not going directly towards Mount Katahdin. We arrived at the shelter right before it started raining. I took the one side of the shelter and *Catie-did* took the other. This was a mistake, because we were soon separated by a bunch of noisy hikers. The pounding rain and the hikers' voices blocked out any chance of us talking to one another.

Day 166

It was only a three mile hike to Abol Bridge. We were so happy for the camp store. After a week we were finally out of the 100-Mile Wilderness. We got a camping spot right next to a river in the shadow of Katahdin.

Catie-did was eying up the grill. When she heard they made breakfast burgers, she ordered two, one for both of us. She also ordered danishes.

Everything was turning out perfect. The weather was beautiful, and *Catie-did* was the most obliging friend. I kept looking up at the huge mountain looming in the near distance. *I'm gonna hike that.* It was a lot like Moosilauke in the way it appeared so large and it made me just as nervous. I still remembered the man at the hostel saying, "If you made it this far you'll have no problem."

There was another hiker staying at the campground. He was a southbounder and his name was *Dirty Dan.* He had an outrageous accent, yet his voice was creamy and deep. He said he once worked for a radio station, where he first used the name *Dirty Dan*. I could imagine him saying, "Hello folk. I'm dirty Dan. Welcome to classic rock."

"I got sick of the music. It was the same couple songs played over and over. So I started filling out my own song request. When I got caught, I got fired." *Dirty Dan* went on about how he worked at a printing press for magazines like Victoria Secret. "It sure was hard not looking at the girls in their underwear. I had to tell myself to focus on my work. I'd be like, Okay. Focus. Is that the correct flesh tone?" He continued on to say that he didn't like the huge company feel. So he quit and had been job hopping until he started hiking. "I've about worked at every printing press in Maryland. See, my last job was great. I had no intention of quitting early, but I mentioned that I wanted to go hiking, so they decided to fire me early. My boss didn't like me. I didn't do anything wrong, but he was always watching for me to make a mistake so that he could fire me."

We sat at the picnic table at *Dirty Dan's* camp spot drinking beer, and playing several games of hearts. *Catie-did* won every time, because she was a skilled card counter. *Dirty Dan,* on the other hand, got progressively worse the more we played.

We started talking about *Dirty Dan* after he left to get more beer.

"How far do you think he'll get?" asked *Katie-did.*

"I don't know, as far as he wants," I said.

"He has hiked up Katahdin and a tiny bit more and what did he say? He's waiting for his boots to dry? First off those boots aren't going to completely dry, and it's inevitable that they're going to get wet again. He's far behind the pack and winter is on its way. *Dirty Dan's* a nice kid, but it's going to be a long haul. He'll be lucky if he makes it to the Whites before they close."

Day 167

We got up bright and early to hustle our way to the sign-up sheet for the Birches. It was important we got there before it filled up or we would have to wait for the next day.

Baxter State Park was very strict. Some of the regulations for the Birches were: only stay one night, pay twenty bucks, and you must have hiked one hundred miles beforehand.

At the camp office, we signed in and paid our twenty dollars to stay the night. When I told them my name, they said, "Someone's been asking for an *Amish*."

I couldn't figure it out. It could either be my family or perhaps a stalker. Later at the Birches my brother ran up to me. He was so out of place. Then my family followed behind. They had decided to come join me on Katahdin and couldn't tell me, because I didn't have service. How wonderful.

It was strange to see them. I was glad they could come see the end, but I liked the idea of climbing the mountain mostly alone, but that was out the window.

"Do you have food?" was my first question. "Well then bring it out."

One of my brothers ran, and came back with a box. I gave *Catie-did* all sorts of goodies that I found in the box. Then I went around handing food to the other hikers.

I asked my dad to make a fire. There wasn't much wood, so he climbed some trees to break down the dead limbs. He had a hard time getting the wood to light, but won out in the end.

"We've been searching for you all day," said my mother.

"Yeah, we saw you're name at the sign-up sheet," said my brothers.

"The lady at the camp office told me someone was looking for an Amish, so I knew something was up," I said.

"They told us we weren't allowed to camp here, so we just kept checking in until they heard from you. We've been asking all the hikers we bumped into, if they had seen you," said my mom.

I was startled when my dad asked, "What's yellow blazing? One of the hikers we asked, said you where yellow blazing."

"Who? Who said I was yellow blazing? Was it Twig? He'd say something like that. But how would he know?"

"I don't know what his name was; we met him and his friend at the camp store."

After finding out it was *Twig*, I had to explain yellow blazing meant hitching hiking ahead. I wasn't too proud of it.

"What you skipped a section?" my brothers asked. "Does that mean you're not a thru-hiker."

I didn't want to deal with this, not from my family. "It was a mistake. I'm still a thru-hiker."

"We'll have to go hike it," they said.

Before I knew it my family had left. We had made arrangements to meet in the morning to hike Katahdin together.

Twig and *Hand-Me-Down* showed up at the Birches. *Hand-Me-Down* had tears running down his face when his parents came. It was so precious. They handed out beer, as we chatted around the fire.

As the night progressed, hikers and parents alike came in with boxes of beer to handout. It was a raging party all night from what I heard.

Day 168

We meet up with the family at the camp office. We traded in our packs for day packs. I felt like I was in a clan of boy scouts. There was Mom, Dad, Carby, Daniel, Isaac, a friend named David, *Catie-did*, and I.

Although my dad hated hiking and only came out for the first mile, he led the group and ran my mom into the ground on his mad dash. I had to take the lead for the sake of my mother.

My brothers were antsy. They would pass each other, racing back and forth. I had to keep a sensible pace for myself and my mother. I forced them not to pass me, so that I could insure a good pace. My brothers, who seemed to be more of a frustration than anything else, did come handy when it came to the steep rock climbs. They would push or pull us up the boulders one by one. We scampered up the spine of the mountain. The view upon the spine was gorgeous; I could see far. Lakes scattered the flat valley land. I could even point out the mountain where *Catie-did* and I had been several days ago. It felt surreal, as if we were looking back at ourselves peering at Katahdin, back when we had been hoping for good weather.

On top of the table lands we took a break. As my brothers chewed on Slim Jim's, I gazed upon the flat rocky ground. *Catie-did* pointed out the last climb to the summit. She asked if I was excited to be done. I didn't know what to say. "It doesn't feel like the end. Does it?" she said. "It'll take several days to sink in."

We rock hopped along the table lands of the mountain. We had a quick stop for spring water before we went on to climb to the top. I could see a cluster of people gathered not far away. *Twig* was making his way down, and gave me an exaggerated congratulation.

Once I got on top, there were more hikers there than I had seen on the climb up. I watched hikers snap pictures of one another. The group of three guys that looked all alike were there. The one handed me his champagne to have a swig. We all took turns taking pictures. This was it – I had hiked peak to peak.

The end of my trip felt anti-climatic. I was lucky to have such gorgeous weather. I'm not saying that Mount Katahdin is a cake walk or that it wasn't one of the most beautiful climbs, where there was a view for the majority of the climb. I just felt the best way to finish would be different. All my trail friends would be there; *Scavenger* with his champagne that he bought with all his coins. And *Skippy, Count, Smurf, Llama Leg, Data, Mile High, Patches, BackFlip, Legion, Steady, Ducky,* I'd miss them all. What was the trail without the camaraderie?

My brothers where fascinated with Knife Edge. "We should hike that," they all agreed, "while we're here. Why not do it now?"

I had loved how the trail had its way of letting you bump into old friends. I wondered if I would ever see my trail friends again. I could have stayed atop the mountain spacing out for hours, but *Catie-did* had other ideas.

"The longer we're up here the more dehydrated we'll become," she informed us all. "We still have a long descent. We should get going now. The weather can be quite fickle, too," she said gazing out at the few clouds.

I wanted to stay, but I also didn't mind leaving. It was like they say, "It's just a pile of rocks." To be truthful, I couldn't wait to sleep, to eat, to relax, to be with friends, and most of all, to not think of mileage day in and day out. Still, this was the end and I just couldn't wrap my brain around that concept. It seemed like an eternity that I had been telling myself, "Just a bit more." Even in Vermont, I had been telling myself that I was *almost* there. Now that I was finished hiking the Appalachian Trail, I had yet just a bit more to hike, before taking my seat in the van and driving off.

Katahdin, was beautiful, in fact it was perhaps the most beautiful mountain on the trail. But it didn't matter how beautiful the mountain was or how beautiful the weather was, I still felt like I expected to be surrounded by my thru-hiker friends. We had talked about how we would dress up for our summit pictures. We talked about what food we would bring to the top. We talked about many things, and it was only that, just talk.

We headed back the way we came, but this time we took the Abol Slide down. It indeed was a slide. The action was very much still present. We had to focus on footing or we were in danger of small rock slides. It was steep. The trail was like the aftermath of an avalanche. It was bare of trees and the sun beat hot. People made out their own trails and others would follow behind until they thought they found a better trail or the leader took a bad slip.

Once we got under the trees and the trail turned into flat dirt, the boys ran ahead. At the car, everyone passed out. We sat for a bit, passing bottles of Gatorade around.

My dad drove *Catie-did* to where she was camping for the night. I came along. I told her I was sorry for leaving her. She didn't hold it against me. "I'll make the spaghetti and sauce without you," she said. "Then I'll drink the bottle of white wine and sleep peacefully."

"Catherine, you know what?" I asked. "I started with a Katherine and I'm ending with a Catherine."

"Did the other Katherine have a C or a K?" She asked.

"She has a K," I said

"Oh, good." Catherine smiled.

I rode back with my dad, and then picked up the family. They couldn't stand my smell cooped up in the car. Nearly everyone was complaining. "Why do I have to sit next to stinky?" said my brother. They found me a shower at a campground before we traveled north to Canada to visit friends. The ironic thing was when we got to our Canadian friends' house, they apologized. "Sorry," they said in their Canadian accents. "Our power is out."

□■□

Miles, miles, I've walked many miles.
Everyday has its miles,
Every step leads towards Katahdin.
All those from the start dreamed of reaching its summit.
Many have fallen out,
Many have grown weary.
Many are gone.

Few remain who have held course.
We've soldiered on,
Enduring at all cost.
Every day, it was just a little more,
Just a little more to the end.
And now that I'm here my journey is done,
And there is no little more to continue.

For all these months I had a place I was headed,
A place to get to,
A place to go.
But now that I'm here,

My journey is over.
It feels like a death,
A death of an end.

All the sweat, all the blisters, and all the strain
I could endure,
but leaving my fellow travelers,
Is a loss I can't cure.
I've shared in the same dream.
We've had the same goal.
I was part of a movement
Part of a clan.
But they are gone forevermore,

Katahdin is the end,
We scatter, we blend.
I used to be a thru-hiker,
On my way to Katahdin,
but now I'm just a girl,
Just a girl surviving.

It was a beautiful thing,
Although it was painful to end,
I can only hope that I can do it again.

No matter how many times I walk the trails, they will still hurt and still leave blisters on my feet. After hiking the Appalachian Trail, I feel like I have a connection to not only the trail, but the people of the trail. I understand the simple desires of the hikers. I understand the pain of the miles.

My mother simply loved hiking Katahdin. She said she was scared. I could tell she was so proud of what I accomplished. For months, every other conversation she had was about my hike. I felt very special. I was just glad we could all get along. I could look back and say, "Persistence paid off."

Back home the most prevalent question was if I would hike the trail again. The longer time passes the more I wouldn't mind hiking. I've heard of guys who can't stop hiking, even though they hate the actual hiking part. It's the feeling they get when they're home. The feeling of luxury is absolutely extraordinary. Where running water makes your heart beat faster. Where fresh fruit and vegetables make you drool. Everything is heavenly. For those several days you are the most content that you have ever been and ever will be.

HIKER GLOSSERY

AT- Appalachian Trail - The most populated and most difficult terrain of the three longest trails in the USA

Aqua Blazing- Canoeing instead of hiking a section of the trail in the Shenandoahs.

Bear Cables- A system to easily hang up food bags.

Bear bagging- Hanging food up high in a tree.

Bivy Sack- A lightweight waterproof shelter that has bad condensation

Blow Down- A fallen tree or limb blocking the trail

Blue Blazer- A hiker that takes short cut trails or more scenic trails that lead back to the main trail

Bushwhack- To hike where there is no trail /to clear a trail with a machete.

CDT- The Continental Divide Trail - The most secluded and least populated of the three longest US trails.

Cowboy Camping- to sleep on the ground with no shelter

Cairn- Pile of rocks to depict where the trail is located when above treeline

Day Hiker- Usually a novice who is out for the day or several days.

DEET- A heavy duty bug spray.

Drop Box- Food or gear sent by mail.

Five Fingers - Shoes with toes.

Flip-Flopper- A thru-hiker who hikes one way, then skips ahead to hike the opposite direction

Gators- A piece of gear worn around the ankle to keep dirt from entering shoes

Giardia- Parasites that cause diarrhea from drinking unclean water.

Gorp- Good Old Raisins and Peanuts, aka trail mix.

HYOH- Hike Your Own Hike - A very common phrase that hikers tell each other.

Hiker Box- A box full of unwanted food and gear, free for hikers.

Hiker Midnight- When the sun goes down, usually the time hikers go to bed.

Nalgene Bottle- A virtually indestructible plastic bottle that holds a liter of water

Nero- Near Zero - A low mileage day

NOBO- North Bound aka headed north.

Northern terminus- Where the trail ends/starts in Maine, on the peak of Mount Katahdin

Pack Out- Items brought with hikers out on the trail.

PCT- Pacific Crest Trail is longest of the three trails, and grated for horses.

Pink Blazing- When a man hikes big miles to catch up to a woman

Privy- Outdoor toilet - Privy is short for private.

PUDS- Pointless Ups and Downs

Purist- A hiker who refuses to take any shortcuts or miss a single blaze of the trail

Outfitter- A store to buy hiking gear

Resupply- To get food and provisions for the next leg of the trip

Section Hiker- Hiking a portion of the trail

Shelter- A building where hikers can stay the night

Slack Packer- A hiker who has someone drive their gear down the trail so they can hike without a large pack

Southern Terminus- Where the trail start/ends in Georgia, on the peak of Springer Mountain.

SOBO- South Bound aka headed south

Stealth Camp- To set up camp at an unestablished area

Switch Back- A sharp turn going up or down a mountain.

Thru-Hiker- A hiker planning to hike the entire trail in one year

Trail Angel- A person that gives out food, rides, and/or shelter to hikers.

Trail Magic- Any form of kindness toward hikers; most often in the form of a cooler of soda

Triple Crowner- Anyone who has hiked USA's three largest trails; which are the AT, PCT, and CDT.

Trail Town- When the trail goes through a town.

Two-Thousand Miler- Usually refers to a section hiker that completed the trail.

Ultra Light- Hikers who carry a very light pack.

Vitamin I- Ibuprofen.

White Blazing- Following the white blazes on the trail.

Work For Stay- To work for meals and stay.

Yo-Yo- To thru-hike a trail then turn around and hike back.

Yogi- To persuade people into giving you food.

Yellow Blazing- To follow the yellow lines in the middle of the road to skip portions of the trail. Sometimes done by hitchhiking

Zero Day- A day off of hiking the trail, to do zero miles

Z-rest- A yellow foldable sleeping pad

16004777R00167

Made in the USA
Middletown, DE
02 December 2014